"Justice Louis Brandeis .... of the Union, and their constituent communities, as 'laboratories of democracy'. Arrington and Marlowe are skilled scientists in those laboratories. Their ethical passion, their evident faith in democracy and their keen powers of perception are on display in this work. . . . Their call to a new or rediscovered form of sustainable governance, balancing the economic, environmental and social interests of whole regions, is a realistic challenge to return to ancient civic virtues."
—**C. Allen Watts, Attorney, Former President, 1000 Friends of Florida**

"This book has changed the way I think about public policy."
—**Dr. Larry Martin, Professor of Public Administration, University of Central Florida.**

"This book describes Florida politics and governance in a timely and accurate way. The authors rightly portray the forces and trends affecting Florida as harbingers of things to come for America. It is well-researched and written with care, balance and compassion. Every responsible citizen should read it."
—**Sam Bell, former House Majority Leader, Florida House of Representatives, and Chair of the Local Government Study Commission**

"This book connects with the best of American governance and interprets present challenges facing leaders, using the theory of sustainability as a guide. The authors point the way to the quality of public leadership, policy and administration required to build sustainable communities. Every public manager and policy-maker will benefit from reading it. And every interested citizen will learn from it."
—**Dr. Thomas C. Kelly, former county manager, recipient of the Distinguished Service Award, International City Management Association**

"The timing for this book and the theories could not be timelier. It's spot on…"
—**Vivian Alarcon, Executive Director, Children's Services Councils of Florida**

"The book is a cogent explanation of how Florida got to where it is today. . . . For anyone who watched politics in the past decade and wondered what happened, it's a relief to have someone interpret the tea leaves. If you ever wondered why citizens seem so angry, politicians seem so nasty and the state of Florida seems to be sinking into the abyss, this book is for you..."
—**Pamela Hasterok,** *Daytona Beach News Journal*

"*Sustainable Governance: Renewing the Search* is a must read . . . Arrington and Marlowe clearly demonstrate how our economy, environment, and social institutions are fundamentally interconnected in an integrated system that we must protect by developing a sustainable system of governance."
—**Mike Abels, former city manager and Professor of Public Administration, University of Central Florida**

SUSTAINABLE GOVERNANCE: RENEWING THE SEARCH

by

Lawrence W. Arrington and
Herbert A. Marlowe, Jr.

Llumina
Press

© 2009 Lawrence W. Arrington and Herbert A. Marlowe, Jr.

All rights reserved. No part of this publication may be reproduced or transmitted in any form or by any means electronic or mechanical, including photocopy, recording, or any information storage and retrieval system, without permission in writing from both the copyright owner and the publisher.

Requests for permission to make copies of any part of this work should be mailed to Permissions Department, Llumina Press, PO Box 772246, Coral Springs, FL 33077-2246

ISBN: 978-1-60594-372-5 (PB)
 978-1-60594-373-2 (HC)
 978-1-60594-374-9 (Ebook)

Printed in the United States of America by Llumina Press

Library of Congress Control Number: 2009909749

TABLE OF CONTENTS

Acknowledgements   i

Chapter I
The Re-Thinking:
Governance and Sustainability   1

Chapter II
The Retrospective:
Florida's Vision in Transition   33

Chapter III
The Reflection:
Probing the Philosophical Currents   57

Chapter IV
The Reckoning:
Taxation and Budget Trends and Consequences   79

Chapter V
The Re-Investment:
Tax and Budget Reform and the Green New Deal   121

Chapter VI
The Re-Planning:
Growth Management, History and Future   151

Chapter VII

The Re-Structuring:

Governmental Reform: Necessity and History   184

Chapter VIII

The Re-shifting:

From Bureaucratic Government

To Sustainable Governance   214

Conclusion

A Time for Remembrance and Reconciliation   241

Endnotes   259

Bibliography   273

Dedication

TO THE MEMORY OF MARVIN FREDRIC ARRINGTON
(1958-2002)

Acknowledgements

This book would not have been possible without the support of many people. We are grateful to Dr. T. Wayne Bailey, Senior Professor of Political Science at Stetson University who read portions of the manuscript and gave us guidance and advice. He shared his students with us during his Seminar on Florida Politics, allowing us to test our ideas.

We appreciate the help of the many colleagues and friends who gave portions of our manuscript review. These include Samuel P. Bell, III, a former Majority Leader, Florida House of Representatives and Chairman of the Local Government Study Commission.

We thank Michael Abels, a former city manager who teaches public administration at the University of Central Florida. Mike shared his ideas and his students with us, and helped organize a research colloquium featuring our work.

We also appreciate the contribution of Sims Kline of Stetson's DuPont Ball Library. Stetson international student and recent summa cum laude graduate Alesia Sedziaka provided editorial, research, and administrative support. We share her remarkable story in the concluding chapter of the book. Friend Carol J. Kerrigan was helpful in proof reading the manuscript.

We accept full responsibility for what we have written, know that any wrong-thinking or misstatements of fact are ours alone, and that those who gave us feedback maintained their own views and opinions that were not always consistent with ours.

Sustainability refers to a very old and simple concept (The Golden Rule)...do onto future generations as you would have them do onto you.

—Robert Gillman, Washington State University

Chapter I

THE RE-THINKING: GOVERNANCE AND SUSTAINABILITY

Introduction and Background

C.S. Lewis, the famous 20th Century British author and philosopher of religion, provides rich insight into the question of human progress. Lewis believed history provides no evidence that linear and upward "progress" occurs through time as the inevitable result of ever-improving human capacities. His belief contradicts the view held by thoughtful people of many generations, especially since the Enlightenment, that the human condition advances as humanity's collective experience and knowledge increase. Rather, Lewis was convinced that civilizations move through history occasionally adapting well to the forces that shape them; but often failing to do so and falling back, sometimes irretrievably. Calling on the wisdom of theologian Martin Luther and respected philosophers and scholars, Lewis writes:

> Luther surely spoke very good sense when he compared humanity to a drunkard who, after falling off his horse on the right, falls off it next time on the left.
> It is, indeed, manifestly not the case...that there is any law of progress in ethical, cultural, and social history. No one looking at world history without some preconception in favor of progress could find in it a steady up gradient. There is often progress within a given field over a limited period...If this process could spread to all departments of life and continue indefinitely, there would be "Progress" of the sort our fathers believed in. But it

never seems to do so. Either it is interrupted... or else, more mysteriously, it decays.[1]

Lewis' view of history suggests that Americans will have to think clearly with an open mind and a passion for truth; and work very hard to rise from the difficulties of the present time. A successful outcome must not be taken for granted.

It is useful to keep Lewis' insight in mind as we begin this journey into the theory of sustainability and a renewed search by Americans for sustainable governance. Sustainability involves living mindfully of the future, embracing, honoring and respecting life in the present, and caring deeply for the well-being of generations to follow. The concept is broadly defined as meeting the needs of the present generation without compromising the ability of future generations to meet their needs.

Sustainable governance is about how collective decisions are made by a society that aspires to live in this way. Governance and leadership must have distinctive features to produce sustainability. These features are defined in this introductory chapter and explored throughout this book.

The search for a sustainable society has a long history. John Winthrop articulated a vision reflecting sustainability when he delivered his famous sermon aboard ship prior to landing on American soil in 1630. Winthrop pledged in a covenant with the Creator that the work of the colonists under his pastoral care would be dedicated to building a "City Upon a Hill" as a shining example for all humankind.

Quoting the Old Testament, (Deuteronomy 30), he established the first vision for what was then labeled "The New World."

> "Beloved, there is now set before us life and death, good and evil, in that we are commanded this day to love the Lord our God, and to love one another, to walk in his ways and to keep his Commandments and his ordinance and his laws, and the articles of our Covenant with Him, that we may live and be multiplied, and that the Lord our God may bless us in the land whither we go to possess it... Therefore let us choose life, that we and our seed may live. But if our hearts shall turn away, so that we will not obey, but shall be seduced, and worship other Gods, our pleasure and profits, and serve them; it is propounded unto us this day, we

shall surely perish out of the good land whither we pass over this vast sea to possess it."

Advancing society in ways that foster sustainability demands changing the way we think about the meaning and purpose of our individual and collective lives---how we live and what we live for. This call for soul-searching comes at a time when Americans are living through a day of reckoning with the consequences of straying from the course Winthrop's vision demands; or, put another way, of losing sight of his vision. Viewed with the power of Winthrop's language, a strong case can be made that Americans have been "seduced" by "our pleasure and profits" and have come to serve our appetite for making and consuming them. We are now coming face to face with the harsh realities of losing our way.

Sustainability is about reconnecting with the nation's vision and purpose, and rekindling the values that underpin them. Sustainable governance is about redefining what the nation needs to do through civil society, and the public institutions designed to serve it, to get back on track.

Sustainability is a means to an end: to serve and live the blessings of life in the present in ways that preserve them for the future. This involves a change of present direction, a turning away from the patterns of production and consumption we use to create wealth and the way we relate to the natural environment. Citizens of a sustainable society remember their duties to ease the suffering of the dispossessed, the sick and the needy; and to remove barriers that keep all citizens from becoming as healthy and prosperous as possible. Sustainability also means rediscovering what the nation's founders meant when they aspired to create a homeland where people would have the freedom to pursue opportunity equally.

Some see sustainability as a modern concept, but the foundation of Winthrop's vision, when studied closely, reveals a pedigree reaching into antiquity. Like the wisdom of the tribes of Judah Winthrop consulted, Native Americans had their vision of the Promised Land, and understood the importance of sustainability long before the Puritans made land fall. Native Americans embraced, respected, and sought to nurture life for themselves in ways mindful of their responsibility to create opportunity for future generations---their seed---to do the same. Sustainability is grounded in the wisdom of the ages, and is a core principle of the glory of life itself.

America has lived a contradiction with respect to Winthrop's covenant. The Puritanical society established by Winthrop reflected oppressive and intolerant practices against non-conforming members, leading to horrific punishment, banishment or death. Religion throughout history has justified much violation of human rights, contrary to the tenets of sustainability.

The land was seen as a material consumption good that the new Americans would "possess", as Winthrop's sermon implies. Moreover, the Puritans arguably out of ignorance and fear demonized the Native American Indians as manifestations of evil, and a threat to Puritanical righteousness. Conquest of Native Americans is justified on this basis throughout American history, exemplified two hundred years after Winthrop by the settlement of Florida, this book's case example. This genocidal tendency in human nature has shown itself often throughout world history extending into modernity. American history is not without its examples.

These social and governance practices and attitudes toward natural resources are inconsistent with modern understandings of sustainability, which value human rights and an ethos of stewardship of the natural environment. Winthrop's vision has dimmed at other times in our history as well: the advent and perpetuation of slavery; the disunity of the Civil War, the Great Depression, the assassinations of our leaders in the 1960's, the tragedy of Viet Nam, and the disasters of war and economy in our present time.

Yet, the promise implicit in Winthrop's sermon has been honored at high points in American history. The adoption of the Declaration of Independence and the Revolution that followed; the first Constitutional Convention; the commitment to unity and emancipation of slaves during the Civil War; the New Deal and American bravery in World War II; the Civil Rights Act; the nation's response to the terror of 9-11; and the election of the nation's first African-American President shine as examples of a promise honored.

In the midst of difficult times, Americans historically face challenges bravely, and find creative ways to renew the rich meanings of

Winthrop's covenant. Americans learn about themselves and gain strength from their dark experiences, which teach the nation the value of unity, and the meaning of the pledge that America is a land of equal opportunity for all people. The determination and resolve shown by Americans during the Great Depression and World War II prove what Americans can do in the face of crisis. America emerged from the Depression and World War II as the most powerful and admired nation on earth. This rising involved self-sacrifice and a deep concern for the well-being and prosperity of future generations of Americans. The courage to face serious contemporary problems poses a similar challenge to America's character and standing in the world.

How can we discern wise lessons during the present time of crisis, a time the likes of which have not been experienced by Americans since the Depression? One way is to develop a deep-seated understanding of the meaning of sustainability, and the capacity to begin building a sustainable society. This book will examine the modern understanding of sustainability as it applies to governance and leadership in theory and practice. These ideas have value to all people who seek the promise of freedom and democracy and a better life for themselves and their children. Since they are understood best by an in-depth examination in a limited arena, the state of Florida will provide a case study of lessons. Florida, with its incredible population growth rate (before the recent slow down) and mixture of people from many nations, is by many considered a "Bellwether State."

Florida: A Case Study

The state faces an uncertain period of hopeful transition from the traditional vision to increase its population base to a new vision calling for a "sustainable Florida". While the exact definition of the new vision remains unclear, thoughtful citizens across the political spectrum agree on its broad features. Several statewide associations of interests, academic centers, and business and civic leaders are calling for a "new leadership framework" designed to lead Florida toward the new vision. However, citizens lack consensus about the necessary and proper roles of state and local public institutions, the quality of governance and public leadership needed, and the public policies required to transform the new vision from concept to reality.

Realization of the new vision demands an understanding of the rich meanings of sustainability, and consensus in support of the precepts of "sustainable governance". Our purpose is to contribute to this understanding and consensus. Three key ideas shape this introductory chapter: sustainability; sustainable governance and public leadership; and quality citizenship. We explore the meanings of each of these, and present a model grounded in the principles and practices of democracy to demonstrate how the key ideas interrelate. We argue that democracy practiced with intelligence and commitment is essential to sustainable governance, and to the realization of Florida's new vision. We introduce the Florida case study in Chapter II, and trace the history of Florida's development under its "old vision" and the emergence of its "new vision." We examine in Chapter III the underlying philosophical challenges and difficulties the state faces as it transitions from the old to the new visions.

Next, we review in Chapters IV, V and VI two areas of public policy: taxation and budgeting, and growth management. We select these two policy areas because of their overriding importance to the challenges facing Florida, and because they are fraught with lessons about the character of public leadership at the state level. The review includes summaries of the histories of reforms of these policies, and reports "real time" events occurring during 2007-09. Reforms of budget and tax, and growth management were being debated in Florida government during this time.

This account of events gives an authentic discussion of the issues, and the quality of political dialogue and outcomes involved in reform discussions. We use the analytical model in our review of these policies. We examine these issues under the lens of sustainable governance to evaluate how existing tax and budget and growth management policies have performed, how attempted reform processes were conducted, and the results they achieved. We use the model to identify the course these policies and other principal policies must follow if they are to contribute to sustainability.

We examine the key policy implications of President Obama's "Green New Deal" as they were developing during 2009. We conduct a comparative analysis from a sustainable governance perspective of Florida's taxation and budget policy-making efforts with key features of the Green New Deal as leaders struggled to cope with an unprecedented crisis in the state budget.

Chapter VII summarizes Florida's governmental reform landscape during the past several decades, including traditional attempts to reform government structure and the influences of the reinvention of government movement of the 1990's. We analyze the leadership style and approach to governing of former Governor Jeb Bush as he sought to satisfy his self-described "passion for reform". Chapter VIII presents what is labeled as the "shift from bureaucratic government to sustainable governance." This is an analysis of current theory and practice of new ways of building sustainable governmental institutions and effective working relationships among public, private and non-profit sectors. We will show that the government to governance shift is an outgrowth of prior reform efforts, and is linked to the transition from the old vision to the new. Florida case examples will illustrate the successful use of governance and public leadership approaches that reflect the features of sustainable governance.

Part II of our work provides a toolkit for sustainable governance. It surveys theoretical understandings, presents core competencies, and includes tools and techniques to build a "new leadership framework". Part II, which is not included in this book, will be made available in digital and web-based formats and will help those who participate in governance develop and implement public initiatives in a sustainable manner. A concluding chapter follows at the end of Part I.

While the authors collaborated on both parts of this work, Arrington assumed primary responsibility for authoring the book; Marlowe for development of Part II.

About the Authors, Our Purposes and Perspectives

The authors view the major questions of this book from the "ground-up", consistent with our collective backgrounds in local government administration, academic research and teaching, and management and planning consulting. Lawrence Arrington is a former County Manager of Volusia County, Florida. He received his Bachelor and Master of Arts degrees in political science from Stetson University, where he has served as an adjunct professor teaching in the university's political science department. Herbert Marlowe is a former member of the research faculty at the University of Florida, where he received his undergraduate and doctorate degrees. Together they provide consulting services to public, non-profit, and private sector clients throughout Florida.

Arrington and Marlowe have completed visioning and strategic planning efforts during recent years for Pinellas County Government, the City of Orlando, Town of Longboat Key, and City of Naples, the City of Oviedo and for other clients throughout Florida.[2] This practical experience with community visioning and planning, coupled with our other consulting and professional experiences, has furnished a proving ground for development of ideas about sustainable governance and the need for a new leadership framework. This book examines case examples from our work.

We must proceed as citizens of Florida first and not political partisans, if we want our children and grandchildren to inherit a government worth having and a state worth living in. Our only strong philosophical position here is a belief in the power of democracy to elevate free people to aspirations beyond narrow self-interests. We also hold that democracy, practiced well, is capable of promoting the common good, and advancing society toward the goals of sustainability.

We recognize that our critique of Florida politics and governance is blunt and sometimes harsh. We mean no disrespect to individual leaders or citizens, past or present. Both of us have worked with and for Florida public institutions, and are multi-generation native sons of the state. We are living with both the successes and the failures of our professional careers, of those of others in our generation and of those who came before us.

The problems facing Florida and the nation are not attributable to any one generation, individual, political party or group. The challenges we face are systemic, deeply-rooted in our history and culture, and complex. This means that meeting these challenges will demand systemic and complex responses that understand our history and culture with all their contradictions---the good, the bad, and the ugly. Sustainable governance demands a grip on reality, even when it bites; and a turning away from the "blame game" in recognition that we are all in this together, and need the talents and energy of all people of good will.

We argue throughout this book that Americans and Floridians have placed too much emphasis on a limited understanding of the economic component of sustainability. We have failed to acknowledge that a strong economy is dependent on a healthy natural environment and a society that creates opportunity for all people to live a decent quality of life. The dominant contemporary belief in exclusive dependence on market-based solutions to challenges has failed, threatening both our prosperity and that of future generations. Understanding and acting on this insight has become the central challenge of the age.

Devising effective responses will demand that we confront with courage and acknowledge with candor the ways of thinking and patterns of behavior that have led us to the present crisis, and make the hard choice to renounce them precisely because they are unsustainable. Honest self-knowledge, which is the essence of the spirit of humility, must guide us. Old ways of comprehending the problems facing us and of understanding each other---especially our political views---no longer apply. Sustainability sets a higher moral and intellectual standard.

Decisions about how to respond best to our collective challenges do not fit the old categories, "conservative", "moderate", or "liberal". Bipartisanship must replace partisanship, and unity must prevail over disunity, recognizing that passionate disagreement followed by compromise and consensus is at the heart of the American political tradition. Most of all, democracy must replace ideology and hope must transcend fear if we are to renew the search for sustainable governance with the vigor and success that marks the best of the American experience.

Sustainability and Sustainable Governance

Sustainability for the purposes of this book is defined as the capacity of a human organization, guiding policy or law to help maintain indefinitely a state of being that meets the needs of the present generation without compromising the ability of future generations to meet their own needs.[3] Whole societies, specific human communities, individual organizations, and public policies, programs and projects can be studied to determine whether they exhibit the features of sustainability. Processes essential to society such as public leadership and governance can be analyzed from a sustainability perspective.

This broad definition has its advantages and disadvantages when governance and leadership are being studied. On the plus side, sustainability can be used as a way to study a wide range of human endeavors and activities. The challenge is to do so without losing touch with the basic principles, and broad goals and objectives of sustainability. In an effort to understand these, it is useful to start with the modern history of the concept, which, as we will see, has touched many fields of knowledge and has produced simultaneously intellectual excitement and confusion.

Sustainability: Roots in Complex Adaptive Systems Theory

The concept of sustainability has gained popularity in the general media as well as in academia. It has even found its way into political rhetoric. The idea is in danger of being overused and misunderstood. Understanding is clouded because sustainability is a rich idea that is open to a variety of interpretations. It originated in the 1970s in the fields of natural resource management, environmental engineering and biology, as specialists sought to understand the developmental patterns of various biological life-forms and the impacts of environmental change.[4] During this same time period the field of social ecology emerged,[5] and the field of architecture began to address sustainability with the concept of "designing with nature."[6] All of these developments represented efforts to apply systems theory.[7] As the environmental movement emerged, sustainability as a concept was further developed in the 1980s and early 1990s by economists,[8] political economists,[9] and business leaders.[10]

As with any powerful idea, particularly one driven by issues of increasing significance to the public, sustainability took on the features of a movement as disciplines of all types sought to understand and re-frame their work in the context of this idea. The 1990s, for example, saw the emergence of the fields of ecological design,[11] sustainable community planning,[12] sustainable urban planning,[13] perma culture,[14] and clinical ecology which examines health impacts from a sustainability perspective.[15] By 2009, sustainability theory has impacted many fields of knowledge outside of its original beginnings in the natural sciences.

The most powerful platform found in the social sciences for understanding sustainability is complex adaptive systems theory (CAS), which has the value of being comprehensive, integrated and of sufficient scale to be applicable to both physical and social systems. The public policies, governance organizations and arrangements, and processes examined throughout this book are *complex* because they are diverse and made up of multiple interconnected elements. They are *adaptive* because they have the capacity to change and learn from experience. CAS theory identifies the specific features of sustainability. These features are presented in this chapter and are interpreted in ways that are suited to the study of governance arrangements and processes, and public policies and initiatives.

Two key terms from complexity theory add to the understanding of sustainability and facilitate the implementation of the idea of sustainable governance. Sustainable solutions require *the design, enabling and execution* of "complex adaptive systems" to "complex problems". Sustainable governance, from this perspective, must have the capacity to formulate, energize, and administer ways and means (systems) to address highly complicated public issues and challenges (complex problems).

A key premise of complexity theory is that the nature of the problem to be solved drives the design of the decision-making systems used to solve it. This is an adaptation of the adage, "form follows function". When public problems were relatively straightforward and comparatively simple, society's governance arrangements and public decision-making systems could be correspondingly uncomplicated. As public problems increase in complexity, the ways and means of making laws and developing and implementing public initiatives (the forms of governance) must be redesigned to find workable solutions to the increasingly complex public problems at hand (the functions of governance). Many contemporary governance arrangements, including the patchwork architecture of state and local government agencies (and the initiatives they administer), were designed during simpler times to address the relatively uncomplicated problems of rural and, later, developing communities. As communities urbanize and society and its public problems become much more complex, design of new governance arrangements and public decision-making systems becomes an urgent priority.

In the Florida case example, for most of the state's modern history the primary purpose of governance arrangements was to provide the basic infrastructure and services needed to accommodate the demands of rapid population growth. The nature of public problems changed and became much more complex as the state urbanized; but the governance arrangements, decision-making systems and public policies used remained substantially unchanged. The resulting disconnection between function and form is unsustainable, according to the precepts of CAS. This is because the ways and means of solving complex public problems do not "fit" the nature of the problems themselves.

This helps explain why the design of new governance systems using decision-making systems appropriate to the problems of urbanized communities is at the heart of Florida's search for sustainability. The purpose of the new leadership framework is to aid in that search by offering new and creative designs for public decision-making systems and arrangements for governing and solving problems in a sustainable manner; i.e. to align form with function. The purpose of the framework is to translate "sustainability thinking" into "sustainable action". This requires new ways of understanding problems, devising solutions to them, and administering those solutions. The important point here is to recognize through the wise insight "form follows function" that building a sustainable society requires ways and means of governing that are capable of producing sustainability.

Sustainability: Understanding the Basics

Given the range of uses of the term "sustainability", it is worthwhile to undertake continuing efforts to clarify the concept, which is precisely what the University of Florida's Stephen Mulkey has done in a report prepared for the Century Commission for a Sustainable Florida. He observes: (T)he 2002 World Summit on Sustainable Development identified three objectives (of sustainability): (1) protecting natural resources, (2) eradicating poverty, and (3) changing unsustainable production and consumption patterns.[16] Three generally-accepted component parts of sustainability arising out of these objectives were identified by the 2002 World Summit: natural resource (environment); social; and economic.

These three component parts may be studied to determine whether sustainability is in evidence. These parts are interconnected and interdependent. For example, a strong economy depends on a healthy natural environment and strong "social systems" such as education, equal opportunity, and communities with a decent standard of living and quality of life. The reverse is also true. A strong economy helps produce the wealth needed to build healthy social systems. Moreover, a healthy natural environment is essential to both the economic and social well-being of a community. The key point is that the three traditional component parts of sustainability are interlinked and depend on each other. A sustainable community recognizes this interdependence and seeks to achieve a proper balance among all three the components.

One way to think about the "process of sustainable development" or the "dynamic of sustainability" is to picture it as involving a "living system" interacting with its environment. This "living system" may be thought of as a community of people or an organization or a social process, policy, program, or project. The living system has to contend with the challenges, including threats and opportunities, of the environment in which it exists and seeks to thrive and prosper. The living system must adapt to these challenges, taking advantage of opportunities and overcoming threats if it is to sustain itself through time.

Imagine that the living system has moral purpose it wants to achieve. At a global level this moral purpose for human communities has been defined broadly as: "meeting the needs of the present generation without compromising the ability of future generations to meet their needs." This is to be done by (1) protecting natural resources, (2) eradicating poverty, and (3) changing unsustainable production and consumption patterns.[17] The community reasons that as it produces and consumes during its lifetime it must protect the natural resources its members depend upon for health and well-being, develop a prosperous economy; and rid its human members of conditions and barriers that rob them of their capacity to be successful in pursuit of the good life.

Now imagine there are three categories of challenges the living system has to meet: natural resource, economic, and social. Under each category there are innumerable "sub-challenges." For example, under the natural resource challenge if we think of our living system as a city, the challenges involve protection of its natural resources. The city's air and water quality and other natural resources are vital to its prosperity and need to be protected through both voluntary measures taken by residents and businesses and collective regulatory action through adoption of public laws, policies, programs and projects.

The same holds true for its economic and quality of life "social" interests. All three of these categories of interests affect each other and must maintain balance. Leaders must address challenges to these interests---both opportunities to advance them and threats to destroy them. They must make adaptations if the city is going to achieve moral purpose. The city's desired vision of itself reflects its moral purpose. The city aspires to provide an excellent quality of life through a healthy natural environment and strong economy. Residents want to advance their interests without compromising the ability of future generations to do so. Residents need and value individual and collective initiatives that align with their aspirations and achieve their vision.

The community must have the capacity to develop and implement means of adapting well to the broad social, economic and natural environment in which it exists. The community must do this in ways that enable it to thrive and prosper, and achieve its vision and moral purpose. Sustainability is this capacity. Governance and leadership are essential to it. Governance is the means by which the system responds and adapts *collectively* to these challenges. Leadership is the way it goes about deciding how best to respond and adapt. Governance must be organized around the categories of the challenges the system faces: natural resource, economic, and social. Leadership must be conducted in ways that achieve alignment between the needs, aspirations, and values of those being led and the initiatives being pursued to respond and adapt to challenges.

Leaders organize, convene, facilitate generation of ideas and proposals, mediate conflict, develop consensus, and advocate sustainable directions and initiatives. Each policy established, every organized effort to administer policies and other decisions must itself reflect the features of sustainability if the overall end result---the community itself---is to achieve the goals and objectives of sustainability. This is why it is useful to examine each major element of the governance and leadership process from a sustainability perspective. A "leadership framework" consists of the assumptions, knowledge, tools, and core competencies required to lead in the ways sustainability demands. Taken together, the brand of governance and leadership described here provide the organizing principles for communities that seek sustainability capacity.

Governance and leadership must be of special character and quality if they are to perform their functions well and help produce what a human community needs, aspires to, and values, which is sustainability. The character and quality demanded are those of democracy for reasons that are illuminated throughout this book. Adapting to the challenges facing a human community in ways that achieve the moral purposes of sustainability is enormously complex and full of conflict. High levels of quality engagement in the processes of leadership and governance are demanded of the constituent members if the truth about the nature of the challenges, including the best way to rise to them, is to be found.

Effective ways of collecting and analyzing information, and choosing wise options among the many divergent points-of-view and interests are needed to find sustainable solutions to challenges. Of all the different ways human beings may organize themselves and make decisions, only democracy provides the requisite means to produce the wisdom sustainability demands. Neither ideology, whether grounded in religion or science, nor authoritarian leadership styles and arrangements possesses the means for cultivating sustainability.

This is the philosophical ground on which this book rests. The evidence from the Florida case example and many other sources supports this position. This explains why the search for sustainable governance and the effective practice of democracy are so closely related; and why we have organized our work with Part I, this book, dedicated to understanding sustainable governance and Part II to the practice of democracy.

The key questions to ask when making an assessment of sustainability are whether the goals and objectives of sustainability are being served; and whether the interdependencies and need for balance among the components of sustainability are evident. Sustainable phenomena exhibit certain features or characteristics, which we will present later in this chapter. These can be used to assess whether sustainable outcomes are likely to be achieved as sustainability is sought after.

Most scholars who study the theory of sustainability concentrate on natural, economic, and social systems with the roles of leadership and governance either absorbed by one or more of these categories, or ignored altogether.[18] Our emphasis is on "sustainable governance", and the quality of leadership required to advance society toward the generally-accepted goals and objectives of sustainability. We treat governance intellectually as the fourth component part of sustainability because of its importance to our purpose, which is about the "search for sustainable governance".

"Governance systems" are distinguishable from, yet interconnected with natural, social, and economic systems in powerful ways. Leaders across the United States are struggling to come to grips with how to develop governance processes and public policies that give real world meaning to the definition, goals and objectives of sustainability. The processes and policies of governing must be made to help meet "the needs of the present generation without compromising the ability of future generations to meet their needs." Governance systems and processes are means by which a sustainable society is sought through public policies and actions.

The term "governance" includes governmental institutions acting in law making, regulatory, and service delivery capacities or in collaboration with non-profit and private sectors to provide public services. The term extends to citizens who through civil society as individuals or in groups engage in the process of governance through participation in electoral politics; and in the development and implementation of public policy. We argue that the ultimate goal of public leadership through governance systems may be articulated in the language of sustainability.

A role of sustainable governance is to identify linkages among the components of sustainability to ensure that public initiatives are created and carried out mindful of the interdependencies among social, economic and natural resource systems; and that proposed solutions to public problems are integrated in service to the goals of sustainability. As noted, this requires balance among the components of sustainability; and the understanding that public actions that address one component likely will have effects on others.

The following graphic depicts these interdependencies among the three traditional components (spheres) of sustainability, as defined by the United Nations Agenda 21 Program world summit in 2002.[19]

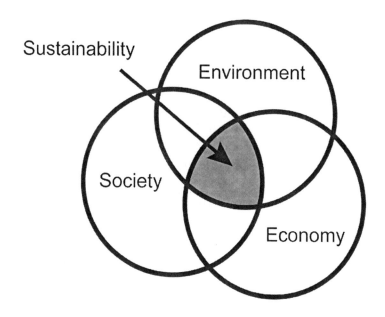

The City of Eugene, Oregon, for example, in a resolution adopted by its municipal governing body in 2000, recognized this interdependence, and articulated its sustainable governance role with a degree of clarity and a sense of relevance that merits quotation:

> The quality of the environment and the health of the economy are interdependent. A healthy environment is integral to the long-term economic interests of the City. The City is committed to protecting and restoring the natural environment as growth management and economic development decisions are made. The City is also committed to ecological decision-making where-in environmental criteria are integrated into municipal decision-

making processes. As we protect the health of the environment and provide for expansion of the economy, we must also ensure that inequitable burdens are not placed on any one geographic or socioeconomic sector of the population.[20]

We can obtain an excellent understanding of sustainability by close study of the work of the Thomas Jefferson Planning District Commission (TJPDC) headquartered in Charlottesville, Virginia. An affiliate organization, the Thomas Jefferson Sustainability Council, offers the following definition of sustainability and related information:

Sustainability may be described as our responsibility to proceed in a way that will sustain life that will allow our children, grandchildren and great-grandchildren to live comfortably in a friendly, clean, and healthy world that people:

- Take responsibility for life in all its forms as well as respect human work and aspirations;
- Respect individual rights and community responsibilities;
- Recognize social, environmental, economic, and political systems to be inter-dependent;
- Weigh costs and benefits of decisions fully, including long-term costs and benefits to future generations;
- Acknowledge that resources are finite and that there are limits to growth;
- Assume control of their destinies;
- Recognize that our ability to see the needs of the future is limited, and any attempt to define sustainability should remain as open and flexible as possible.[21]

There is no "one best way" to depict or describe the concept of sustainability or the way its components interrelate. Room for creativity exists. The key challenge is to learn how to master "sustainability thinking", and to apply it in a customized manner to the concrete circumstances under consideration. For example, there is no one best way to develop a sustainable community, a new mixed-use development, or any project or program. Achieving the best sustainable solutions requires lively experimentation with different approaches appropriate to the circumstances at hand.

The following graphic shows the components of sustainability with the governance component integrated:

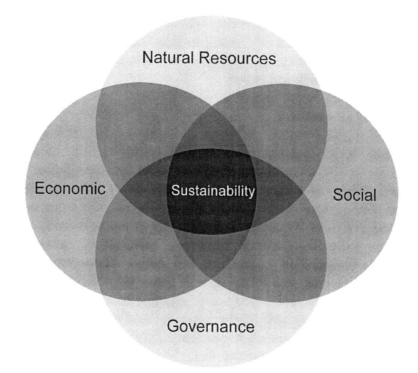

An in depth definition of sustainability, including an understanding of how "sustainability thinking" can be applied to practical governance settings, will be presented in Part II of our work in web-based and digital formats.

An appropriate analytical model is necessary to apply sustainability thinking to governance and leadership with proficiency. Such a model is a conceptual framework---a lens---through which to assess whether the goals and objectives of sustainability are being served by the phenomenon being studied (e.g. society, community, organization, functional process or policy, program or project). A model also provides the blueprint for designing sustainable governance systems and for exercising sustainable public leadership through a new framework.

We present later in this chapter such a model for analyzing the phenomenon of "sustainable governance" and the quality of leadership demanded of it. CAS theory is at the heart of this analytical model. First, it is necessary to understand how public leadership and the principles and practices of democracy fit into the picture. As noted, a distinctive species of leadership is required for development of sustainable outcomes. Well-grounded understandings of "first principles" and modern theories of democratic decision-making as practiced and comprehended in America are central to the analytical model.

Sustainable Leadership

Public sector leaders who establish sustainability goals and objectives have to take extraordinary care to understand whether public policies, actions and investments---the essence of governance--- are aligned with citizens' values, needs and aspirations. We argue that this alignment is critical for public leadership that fosters sustainability.

Since protecting natural resources, eradicating poverty and changing unsustainable production and consumption patterns have ethical implications and carry moral force they provide a moral compass for the leadership process of aligning needs, aspirations, and values of leader and led. The ethical implications of sustainability present a means of evaluating public (including non-profit) policies and actions, and private pursuits as well. The key question is whether policies and actions align with the goals and objectives of sustainability; whether they foster or hinder its achievement. This becomes the most important question for governance initiatives that seek sustainability. Leaders and communities that seek sustainability must ask this question of every policy, program, and project undertaken by public, non-profit, and private organizations.

Governance and leadership that get out of alignment with public needs, aspirations and values; or out of balance with the components of sustainability ultimately lose the trust and confidence of those whose support they require. The loss of alignment results in unsustainable conditions. Instability ensues; and, if the imbalance or misalignment grows in intensity and spreads, failure and collapse of unsustainable governance and leadership ultimately occurs.

This conception of leadership alignment and sustainability also involves the idea of political legitimacy of governmental institutions. Leadership alignment, sustainability balance and political legitimacy, while not identical concepts, bear a close resemblance. Political scientists use the concept of legitimacy to describe a government's acceptance and credibility among those governed. Political scientist Robert Dahl held that legitimacy is relative; and rises and falls through time. At a certain level, a lack of legitimacy, just as with a lack of alignment or balance, may lead a government to experience instability and, perhaps, collapse.[22]

The public sector faces particular challenges of alignment and balance. Unlike the private or non-profit sectors where customers or supporters can vote with their dollars, the public sector finds funding primarily on an involuntary basis and has grounding in constitutional and statutory authority and responsibilities. In the private marketplace, goods and services that do not meet the values, needs or aspirations of the buying public usually fail. In the non-profit marketplace, events or services that do not align with supporters' values, needs or aspirations fail to gain backing. Because of this free choice dynamic in the private sector, misalignment and imbalance among the components of sustainability can adjust readily. This is not true as often for the public sector. Payment of taxes and fees imposed by governments is not a free choice once in law. The point here is that misaligned and imbalanced public sector leadership is more difficult to correct than in the private and non-profit sectors.

Correction of significant governance system, public policy and leadership misalignment and imbalance may be made with sufficient public out cry, or by voters during elections or referenda. Even then, multiple variables may be the main drivers of political behavior, and mask leadership misaligned with public needs, aspirations and values or imbalance among sustainability components. Judgments about misalignment and imbalance are subtle and complex.

Public, non-profit or private sector policies and actions misaligned or imbalanced may incite another and more dramatic response: citizens may refrain from moving to---or choose to leave---the jurisdiction of the misaligned and incongruent place. Such a place in the extreme would be economically weakened, its natural resources over-stressed, its social systems in a deteriorating condition, and its governance systems and public policies generally out of alignment with the needs, aspirations and values of citizens. The Florida case example indicates that parts of the state may have reached this condition.

Lessons in Citizenship and Democracy: Towards a New Leadership Framework

Sustainable governance ideally does not derive from governmental institutions. It originates with private citizens acting individually, corporately, or in their various associations of interests petitioning their governments and influencing elected officials, rather than the other way around.

One of the frequent criticisms of contemporary governance is that many government officials forget that it is the citizenry who is in charge and ultimately responsible for the well-being of society. This happens when public institutions' founding values decay, and the primary purpose becomes institutional self-enhancement. Process triumphs over results, and form over spirit. The "turf syndrome" dominates institutional behavior.[23] Officials place too much emphasis on technical expertise, and treat citizens as consumers in a marketplace, rather than citizens in a democracy. These institutions become misaligned with public needs, aspirations and values because citizens are shut out from meaningful participation in the core processes of government. Citizens become spectators in civic life, constantly being urged to consume public services and policies crafted by those with special expertise and interests.

There is a corresponding problem. Citizens become disillusioned, confused, and civically-dispirited when unsustainable public leadership and governance systems are experienced. Exercise of civic duty, a sense of community identity, and civility disappears from the behavior of the citizenry. Politics becomes primarily a quest for advancement of individual interests, full of unhealthy conflict with little attention paid to the common good. Evidence suggests that the decay of founding values inside government institutions has spread to civil society itself when citizens act like angry consumers who can be mollified only by getting what they want when they want it.

Citizens cultivate virtues and learn behaviors by the way they experience civic life. The values and benefits of democracy, which must be nourished and learned through hard-won experience, cannot be sustained when consumerism trumps citizenship. Changing this particular "consumption pattern" consistent with the goals of sustainability (defined by the 2002 World Summit) may be the most significant of all such changes in the ways society consumes resources.

When citizens consume public resources as a matter of right with no sense of civic responsibility, this imperils a primary goal of sustainability: the development of public leadership and natural, economic, social and governance systems that meet "the needs of the present generation without compromising the ability of future generations to meet their needs."[24] To verify this perspective one only needs to ask any serious policy analyst about the consequences of the projected trend lines of Social Security, Medicaid and Medicare. As the Florida case study will demonstrate, taxation and budget, growth management, and other principal public policies on the state and local levels likewise are unsustainable.

A consumer mentality that threatens the future quality of life of our children and grandchildren has displaced the virtues of democratic citizenship. We argue that to reverse this pattern sustainable governance demands a renewal of democracy's founding values, and a rediscovery of civic responsibility.

The principles of democracy provide the best tools for navigating the troubled waters ahead as we work toward sustainability. The new leadership framework bases itself in these principles and is designed to put them into practice. The Florida public and its leaders must participate in quality civic engagement, a new understanding of citizenship and self-interests, and development of a sense of community identity, civic virtue, and civility. We agree with the following assessment of the importance of democracy to sustainability:

> Democracy is an inherent part of the sustainable development process. Sustainable development must be participatory development. Real visions for change rarely come from government or from the marketplace, but from civil society. For people to prosper anywhere they must participate as competent

citizens in decisions and processes that affect their lives. Sustainable development is thus about the quantity and quality of empowerment and participation of people. Sustainable development therefore requires community mobilization, i.e., mobilizing citizens and their governments toward sustainable communities.[25]

A set of understandings, core competencies, tools, techniques and approaches for providing public leadership in today's highly complex and contentious Florida political environment best describes the new leadership framework. We advocate the framework for customized use by public leaders at all levels of government, by the many non-profit providers of public services, and throughout the various associations of interests in civil society. We argue that use of the features of the new leadership framework will help produce sustainable governance; and, by definition, sustainable public policy through aligned leadership and balance among the components of sustainability.

Our research of the Florida case example indicates that many thoughtful analysts of the state's politics and governance have concluded Florida needs a new approach to public leadership. Within the Florida body politic fear exists about a declining quality of life driven by too much population growth. Many residents believe that the promise Florida held when they moved to the state has become an illusion. Long-time residents express frustration that the Florida they once knew and loved is being taken from them. This is the breeding ground of reactionary, authoritarian, and ideological approaches to public leadership and governance.

Public leaders receive criticism for developing public policies devised by special interests, and for imposing solutions from the "top, down" without meaningful public involvement. Some leaders are criticized for "telling people what they want to hear", preying upon public fears and hopes, and promising narrow-minded, ideologically based solutions to complex problems. The specter of religious fundamentalism, examined in subsequent chapters, also has entered Florida politics and governance.

These leadership styles and governance approaches may enjoy short term popularity; but over time they fail to serve democracy or to promote sustainability. These leaders fail to provide authentic leadership because their proposed directions and methods are misaligned with the genuine needs, aspirations and values of citizens. This increasingly frustrated citizenry feels largely cut off from meaningful civic engagement.

Cultivation of civic responsibility rooted in a sense of community identity and expressed through rediscovery and application of the principles of democracy is the antidote to the fear, lack of direction, polarization, consumerism, and apathy of the state's political culture. The word "rediscovery" is used because the authors believe that deeply embedded in the DNA of the body politic is memory of a version of democracy different from the present approach to electoral politics and governing. Many citizens, our experience indicates, yearn for the re-appropriation into contemporary times of the requirements for a meaningful and productive civic life. This desire is grounded in values of people weary of the political culture of the present age. These values, in turn, are rooted in the religious and republican traditions of America's experiment with democracy.

If effective leadership is to occur, leaders must acquaint themselves with the spirit of this tradition, and practice politics and governance consistent with the requirements of its proven wisdom. This is the common ground where the religious tradition so valued by conservatives meets the best of liberal democratic theory and experience. This is also the ground of hope for the thousands of people who migrate to Florida from nations with histories of repressive and authoritarian regimes, and who hunger for the promise of democracy.

If these are American democracy's decisive decades, as social critic and futurist Alvin Toffler has observed, Florida is a microcosm of the unfolding drama.[26] Sustainability and democracy are twin moral protagonists in this drama. Sustainability demands public decisions determined through rigorous employment of the principles and practices of democracy. Democracy requires the vision and moral compass provided by the goals and objectives of sustainability, which mobilize citizens to seek after its promise of the Good Society.

Sustainability like democracy is vitiated by ideology. Sustainability is about how to think and act to achieve desired ends. It is a way of being, not, like ideology, a prescription of fixed and rigid ideas devoid of creativity and the capacity to adapt to ever-changing challenges. When ideology dominates public life, sustainability turns into its opposite. Democracy---deprived of self-determined moral purpose---becomes the lost dream of a bygone era.

A happier ending to the drama would be a return to "first principles" underpinning the American experiment. This demands civic virtue, "...a political ideal whose realization require(s) not only the people's direct participation in civic affairs, but the subordination of their interests to the public good."[27] When citizens through time become cut off from this first principle, the capacity for practicing authentic citizenship is lost. "This inevitable process of corruption can be arrested only through the periodic revitalization that can be brought about by returning to original principles...and recapturing the concept of civic virtue."[28] Sustainability, as both a way of understanding the common good and a metric for its pursuit, depends on the renewal and intelligent application of this "first principle."

The Analytical Model

Our model for approaching this complex subject matter is depicted here. The model incorporates the concepts of leadership alignment and sustainability balance.

The model, like sustainability itself, is interdependent and synergistic in character. This means that when the component parts of the model interact systematically, the resulting whole is greater than the sum of its parts. Sustainable policy directions are dependent on sustainable governance and vice-versa. The model recognizes that public policy changes enacted through use of the leadership framework are interdependent: changes in one policy area can produce unexpected impacts in other areas of policy. Likewise, civic virtues and civility at once depend upon and result in sustainable governance, as does the cultivation of "self-interest, rightly understood". The model is grounded in what is termed in Complex Adaptive Systems theory, which is explored further in Part II of our work.

This model is built in part on a conception first introduced by Alexis de Tocqueville, author of the book *Democracy in America*, which was published in 1835. This classic work is based on his observations about the principles and practices of democracy in early America. Rightly understood, the interests of the individual and the community are interdependent because their respective fates are interlinked. Civic virtues are taught as citizens take on the responsibility of governance, not merely through politics and government, but through civil society and social relations generally. The principal locus for the practice of democracy in early America as Tocqueville found it was in initiatives pursued freely by individuals through various social associations of interest to them, including church, vocational and professional pursuits and civic organizations. Government's role was determined by citizens as public needs were identified that could be accomplished best through the auspices of official authority.

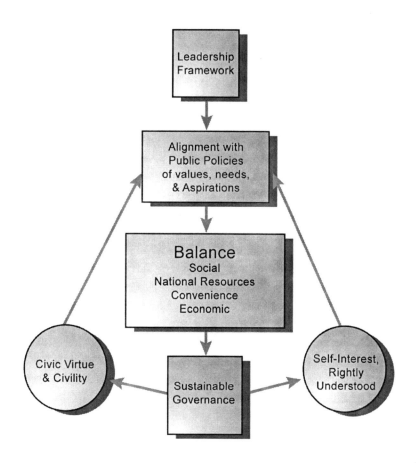

If democracy were to be practiced is this way today, government's role could go beyond merely providing services and infrastructure necessitated by commerce. Rather, government could be used to further the well-being of the whole community's various associations of interest, and to promote cooperation among them.[29] Sustainability demands attention to this whole of a community, integration and balance of its various components: social, economic, and natural resource. Government is in a position to "connect the dots", and help perform this facilitative and integrative function. But the citizenry, through the practice of democracy and the cultivation of civic virtue, must come to this understanding of the role of government as required by concrete circumstances of time and place. When such a role is necessitated, citizens must be willing and able to provide the support and engage in the hard work required. This is the meaning of the term "governance" as we define it. The "new leadership framework" is designed to help citizens govern in this way.

Tocqueville found that those who participated in governance were rewarded. They developed an understanding of public responsibility that enabled them to transcend narrow, self-interests. They became, "…orderly temperate, moderate, and self-controlled citizens."[30] Thus, virtuous behavior, called by Tocqueville "habits of the heart", resulted from the practice of democracy in social associations and throughout the institutions of society, including but certainly not limited to government. Democracy determined the role of government, not the other way around. Such a relationship between the two cannot develop without a high level of quality citizen engagement in civic affairs, broadly defined.

Tocqueville believed that as the "habits of the heart" are practiced in civic behavior, leaders and followers achieve higher levels of motivation and morality.[31] This perspective was developed further by James McGregor Burns in his Pulitzer Prize winning book *Leadership* published in 1978. Dr. Burns is Woodrow Wilson Professor of Government (emeritus) at Williams College and a former president of the American Political Science Association. Tocqueville's "habits of the heart" and "self-interests, rightly understood", are consistent with Burn's formulation that leaders "elevate followership as followers sustain leaders" when authentic leadership occurs.[32] Borrowing from the language of Abraham Lincoln, the resulting transformational leadership unleashes the "better angels of our nature", enabling a sustainable outcome.

The leadership framework is the engine that powers the model. As its principal features are put into practice, the energy needed to fuel sustainable governance is produced. The framework is grounded in Burns's conviction that leadership occurs when the needs, aspirations, and values of leader and led align with each other.

Use of the analytical model along with other research findings in the Florida case study produces evidence that Florida state and local government policies and arrangements are out of alignment with the requirements of the emerging new vision of a sustainable Florida. Existing public policies, means and ways of governing Florida are unsustainable precisely because they are misaligned with citizens' needs, aspirations and values and the tenets of sustainability. The leadership framework, grounded in the principles and practices of democracy, is designed to lead to alignment resulting in transformative leadership and balance among the components of sustainability.

This search for sustainable governance is through the same quality civic engagement observed by Tocqueville in the formative years of the American experiment with democracy. It is time to re-appropriate Tocqueville's lessons using technologies, models, principles, processes, tools, and case examples suitable to the 21st Century.

As this journey proceeds, it is imperative to stay in touch with the vision being sought, and to discover its profound meanings. Throughout history, broad visions defining the purposes of the American experiment have carried many labels including the "City upon a Hill"; "A More Perfect Union"; and, more recently, the "New Deal" and "Great Society". Today, a different definition of vision calling for a "Sustainable Society" has emerged. While consistent with the broad aspirations of prior visions, the contemporary vision is more modest than others Americans have articulated. Sustainability does not promise a benevolent society with boundless moral and material progress, although such a society may remain a hope. It certainly does not promise, as Florida traditionally has done, a Paradise on earth. Sustainability's demands are humble and realistic.

Sustainability envisions livable communities capable of surviving and flourishing in a dangerous world full of violence and terror and plagued by overpopulation's effects of ecological disaster, and crushing poverty and disease. Sustainability demands understanding self-interests in a brutally realistic way. Cultivation of civic virtue rising from the practice of democracy---Tocqueville's "habits of the heart"---is demanded not because it is an illusive ideal, but because without it, governance becomes a struggle for power between the weak and the strong, the rich and the poor. When this happens, both democracy and sustainability become impossible. America's founding principles and ideals in this context remain vital, and take on a new and urgent relevance, just as they did in the period leading up to and following the American Revolution. Sustainability demands Americans have a conscious awareness, a deep-seated commitment to founding principles, and a spirit of authentic patriotism.

The Features of Sustainable Governance and Leadership

It is useful to identify the characteristics of sustainable public leadership and governance and the pubic policy these produce. This analytical exercise helps sharpen understanding of sustainability, and lends relevance to the concept. The analytical model through use of the new leadership framework is designed to reflect these features of sustainability. Sustainable public leadership, governance, and public policy occur as those who participate in the development and implementation of public initiatives (laws, policies, programs and projects) are:

- **Visionary.** Leaders develop and implement public initiatives based on a shared vision for their community. Leaders use vision statements and strategic plans built on principles of sustainability.
- **Perceptive.** Leaders advance self-interests rightly. Leaders develop and implement sustainable public initiatives, understanding the interdependent relationship between individual interests and community interests. Engaged citizens identify their individual interests in the broader interests of the community and reconcile conflict through consensus building. Civic duty and the pursuit of the common good motivate citizens.

- **Aligned.** Leaders create sustainable public initiatives to fit the needs, aspirations, and values of the citizenry. Leaders develop and implement initiatives in a transparent and trust worthy manner. This requires public engagement in the decision-making process using tools appropriate to contemporary society.
- **Reality-based.** Leaders introduce sustainable initiatives recognizing the economic, environmental, political, and social realities faced by a community. Leader's base sustainable initiatives on current information. Leaders use the best technology and management expertise available.
- **Interconnected.** Leaders use sustainable initiatives to address multiple problems at once, understanding the interconnectedness and complexity of these problems. Energy and environmental policy; crime and human services; economic development and quality community venues and amenities; and quality, affordable health care and a productive work force are examples.
- **Creative.** Leaders promote sustainable initiatives that are imaginative, inventive, flexible, and adaptive to changing conditions and new information. Leaders undertake sustainable initiatives aware that complex problems carry risk and uncertainty.
- **Performance-Based.** Leaders create sustainable initiatives with measurable results.
- **Collaborative.** Leaders implement sustainable initiatives through collaboration among public, private, and non-profit sectors. Public and sometimes non-profit agencies serving the same community jointly pursue initiatives grounded in private sector management and technical expertise. The terms "public management networks" and "public-private partnerships" are used to describe these collaborative arrangements.

Forging new policy and governance arrangements reflecting the features of sustainability is a massive and daunting task. Many years of learning through experimentation will be required before substantial progress is made. Changes to political culture as well as formal, structural changes to the ways and means of governing are required. Positive change will be incremental, and much of it will be come as a result of citizen-driven efforts involving public, private, and non-profit providers of public services working together.[33]

Conclusion

Those who aspire to public leadership positions, whether in civil society or in a formal institutional office, will need to develop an understanding of sustainability and how this powerful concept relates to governance and leadership. Leaders also will need to grasp the importance of democracy to sustainability, and learn how to develop the art of "sustainability-thinking." They must be capable of helping to develop a broad social vision organized around the goals and objectives of sustainability; and become proficient at forging public initiatives that reflect its features.

Sustainable governance requires knowledge of the role of history and culture in shaping contemporary society, and the place of sustainability in developing a road map charting the future course. Next we overview the history of Florida's development, introduce its present challenges, and study the state's vision in transition.

Wandering between two worlds, one dead,
The other powerless to be born,

—Matthew Arnold

Chapter II

THE RETROSPECTIVE:
FLORIDA'S VISION IN TRANSITION

Overview

Florida provides fertile ground for this study of the way sustainability relates to leadership and governance. The state in recent decades has undergone explosive growth and change with more on the way. Between 1950 and 2000 the state's population skyrocketed from approximately 2.8 million residents to almost 16 million, an increase of more than 476 percent. This massive growth compares to a national increase of just 13 percent during the same period. The 2009 population of Florida tops 18 million.[34] In 2006 almost 85 million people visited Florida.[35] Florida's population is projected to increase by 72 percent to 27.5 million over the next twenty-five years, and double in fifty years.[36]

Florida's recent experience exemplifies the "mega-trends" facing the United States as a whole and much of the developed world. They promise to play out dramatically in the future: the challenges of immigration and cultural diversity; an aging population; effects of climate change; deteriorating natural systems; over-stressed basic public infrastructure and services as a result of massive population growth; skyrocketing energy costs; economic restructuring in response to the global economy; deteriorating social conditions including escalating crime rates and a rising gap between rich and poor; and lack of affordable health care. Forging public policies appropriate to the problems facing the state is a challenge for leadership and governance that will test the resolve, creativity, and character of the body politic.

We begin the Florida case study by arguing that for most of the 20th Century as the state developed, public policies and actions reflected a partial alignment between the citizen's values, needs and aspirations, and a degree of balance among economic, natural, and social systems. Florida's leadership and governance created the intended results as the state grew and prospered. However, both leadership alignment and sustainability balance dissolved over time. Over-development endangered Florida's natural systems; the emergence of the global economy demanded new ways of wealth creation, and social conditions deteriorated. An imbalance among the components of sustainability resulted. The state's natural environment and social conditions became secondary concerns to the perceived economic benefits of population increases. Governance arrangements and public policies were kept in place to maintain the state's rate of growth.

The Call for a New Vision

We will argue the traditional growth vision was unsustainable and the attributes that draw people to Florida have been undermined by the old vision's remarkable success. Alignment diminished between the needs, aspirations and values of citizens and their public leaders as the state experienced the consequences of this massive growth. State and local governments and non-profit providers of public services struggle to maintain legitimacy and relevance as a result of this misalignment and imbalance. In the midst of this turmoil, calls for the new vision for the state's future arise.

Florida offers a case study of how partial leadership alignment and balance among the components of sustainability achieves intended results. The state's example also illustrates the dynamism of alignment and balance, and their tendency to change over time. Partial alignment can evolve into misalignment, and balance can easily turn to imbalance as the issues and challenges reflected in Florida's experience indicate. Calls for a new vision for a sustainable Florida are best understood against this backdrop.

As leaders and citizens undertake the difficult task of crafting a new vision and direction for the state, we recognize that the problems resulting from Florida's incredible growth and change did not occur by chance. Contemporary problems stem from decades of a highly successful planned effort -- a vision and a set of strategies -- to attract visitors and new residents. State and local governments played a key role in devising and executing the growth vision, providing the infrastructure and services required by ever-increasing numbers of visitors and newcomers. Political leaders promised a development-friendly regulatory climate, low taxes complete with exemptions for homesteads and no inheritance or income taxes to lure permanent residents. The citizenry approved several of these incentives through Constitutional amendments. These public policies and actions aligned with private market forces and helped Florida realize its growth vision.

We argue here that consensus in support of this traditional vision has collapsed, and that a new vision is emerging. The new vision embraces a globally-competitive economy, high value on renewable energy and protection, preservation, and restoration of the natural environmental features that traditionally have attracted people to Florida, and development of livable, sustainable communities. The outlines of the new vision are evident in the thoughtful work of various academic centers, statewide associations of interests and others, including the Council for a Sustainable Florida, Florida Chamber Foundation, Florida Council of 100, and 1000 Friends of Florida. Aspects of the vision can be glimpsed in the work of Enterprise Florida, the state's principal economic development organization and the many regional and local organizations dedicated to the same purpose. The Century Commission for a Sustainable Florida was created by the Florida Legislature in 2005 to develop a 50-year vision for Florida. It works to develop a rich information base with ideas about how to define and achieve the new vision.

Multiple regional visioning initiatives are underway, most notably the Central Florida MyRegion process, which has made major progress toward articulation of a new vision, and has undertaken well-organized efforts to develop broad public and leadership consensus behind it. Several local government leaders have taken up the call, and have sponsored visioning and strategic planning efforts that reflect features of the emerging new vision, and offer plans to act locally to bring abstract vision to concrete reality. The Growth Management Act in

2005 was amended to require community visions as part of the comprehensive planning process.[37]

While a general consensus exists in support of the broad ideas of the new vision among some public, civic, and business leaders, no agreement has emerged about the role of government in developing and implementing the new vision. Serious questions remain about the governance arrangements and principal public policies needed to bring the new vision to fruition.

The best conceptions of this emerging vision are grounded in the idea of social, economic, and natural systems sustainability, to which we add sustainable governance. Directional change in budget and tax, growth management, health care for the medically indigent and other principal public policies must come from the state or federal governments. However, given the performance of state government in recent years, the state's diversity and the complexity of the problems it faces, we believe that advancement toward the new vision will have the best chances of success in Florida through sustainable governance arrangements and policies enacted at the regional and local levels. Leaders must grant home rule power and lawful authority for citizens to "think globally, and act locally."

We believe that Florida has arrived at a point at which the state's citizenry and public leaders must come to a consensus about governance and public policy arrangements needed to implement a new vision. Definition of the role of government is at the core of the challenge.

A Delicate Balance: Defining Government's Role

Questions about the appropriate role of government have been debated by Americans since the founding of the Republic. We will survey in this and the next chapter the philosophical positions involved in that debate as they paralleled the development of the two major political parties, and suggest that Americans at our best are a practical people who use common sense grounded in democracy, not ideology, to mold the role government should play in the context of time and place in history.

Florida politics during the past decade or so has turned to an arch-conservative, highly-limiting view of the role of government; and has produced powerful elected leaders who appear to view government as an enemy to be opposed at every opportunity. Calls for tax cuts, "no new taxes", spending caps, dismantling the bureaucracy, and other such approaches display a preference for marginalizing and restricting the role of government at a time when Florida's new vision demands proactive and vital leadership through pubic institutions.

We argue that it is inappropriate and misguided to treat Florida public agencies as if they were akin to the cumbersome and wasteful bureaucracies of the deficit-ridden federal government or of some socialist state. Florida governments by comparison are over-burdened with work, and face severe financial difficulties. The role they play is limited to providing infrastructure and services to fuel population growth and a modicum of declining support for the state's most vulnerable citizens. Florida public agencies are not arranged, directed or resourced to deal with the consequences of the massive population growth fueled by the old vision. The old growth vision continues to produce complex urban problems. State agencies (including institutions of higher learning), local governments and schools are woefully ill-prepared to help build a future based on the requirements of sustainability.

We hold that if such an approach to governance continues, Florida's existing urban problems will worsen, and the new emerging vision will be compromised and robbed of its vitality. The simple truth is that strategic investments in quality public services and infrastructure, a degree of smart regulation of the massive population growth of Florida and more humane treatment of the state's most disadvantaged citizens are integral to the realization of the new vision. State and local governments that are weak and cheap run counter to the requirements of sustainability, and simply won't get the job done.

We also argue that the practice of making serious budget reductions when short-term economic conditions (or property tax "reforms") drive revenues downward sets up long-term negative consequences for public service delivery systems and infrastructure provision. In Chapter IV, for example, we examine the consequences of cuts in higher education for the long-term quality of the state's university system, recognizing that the round of cuts during the 2007-09 legislative sessions prompted a "brain drain" of University professors seeking to leave Florida. This is but one illustrative indicator of the direction the state is heading. Its best minds are leaving.

Yet we argue in Chapter VII that state and local governments and schools, and the ways they relate to each other and the non-profit and private sectors must change to suit the requirements of the new vision if they are to garner the support necessary to play a meaningful role in the future. The path to reconciling the conflicts about the role of government demands sustainable public institutions and policies that merit public support. Public agencies must be restructured and redirected from the ground up.

The good news is that agreement about the visionary outlines of a sustainable Florida is widespread. The bad news is that the requisite governance system and leadership practices remain illusive. We argue that through the incremental practice of democracy in public policy-making government defines its role. Its role is not defined best through broad application of abstract philosophical principles. Ideologues at either extreme of the political spectrum do a disservice to democracy and to sustainability when they seek to manipulate public opinion or otherwise bully or buy their way through the political process to advance their philosophical positions. As examined in Chapter VII, the devices of sharing of powers within a system of checks and balances, respect for the rule of law, and the separation of church and state are designed to advance democracy, and not ideology, as the best pathways to defining the role of government in serving the public interest.

Florida's recent "era of ideology" must mature into a more reasoned, practical and commonsensical approach to governance guided by the tenets of sustainability and the wisdom of democracy. Forging the creative and innovative new approaches to sustainable governance will require the talent and energy of leaders from the public, private, and non-profit sectors working together. Leaders and citizens must work together to transcend ideological proscriptions and political polarization.

The Rise and Fall of the Old Vision

The essence of the old vision was straightforward: attract as many visitors and new residents as possible by offering them a paradise of fertile land, great weather, plenty of sun and surf, lakes and clear water springs, strikingly strange and unusual wildlife, cheap, but promising real estate investments, and pleasurable leisure activities.

This vision has a long and storied past, which arguably began when the Territory of Florida gained statehood in 1845. Then, some 70,000 people inhabited the entire state. The state's first Constitution called for: "a liberal system of internal improvements, being essential to the development of the country, shall be encouraged by the government". The Constitution mandated the Legislature "As soon as practicable, to ascertain by law, proper objects of improvement." The Legislature created in 1855 what came to be known as the Internal Improvement Fund, which offered generous land grants and state backed construction bonds. This fund and other similar approaches initiated by local governments were used to leverage internal improvements, including an emerging new "technology", railroad construction.[38] By 1880, some sixty percent of the state was owned by five railroad companies, one drainage company, and Hamilton Disston, who purchased approximately four million acres of Florida land for twenty-four cents an acre.[39]

Progress was slow up through the Civil War and Reconstruction eras. By the 1880's, however, new opportunities presented themselves as the more developed northern states began to bear the fruits of the Industrial Revolution. A then "new vision" was overlaid on the existing one: lay railroad tracks and bring people down for pleasure and profit. Tourism became the gateway to real estate sales, a strategy that remains in use. By 1880 there were 518 miles of track; by 1890, 2,489; and by the end of the 1920's some 6,000 track miles had been constructed.[40]

The state's population growth mirrored its internal infrastructure improvements. By 1900, the population exceeded 500,000, almost double that number by 1920. The rest is history. The state's population growth would skyrocket following the Great Depression and World War II:

Year	Population	Year	Population
1880	269,493	1970	6,791,418
1890	391,422	1980	9,746,961
1900	528,542	1990	12,937,926
1910	752,619	2000	15,982,378
1920	968,470	2010	19,251,691
1930	1,468,211		
1940	1,897,414		
1950	2,771,305		
1960	4,951,560		

Source: U.S. Bureau of the Census

The interdependencies among population growth, economic development, and infrastructure were recognized early. Leaders forged the principal role of government--- beyond keeping the peace and dispensing justice---as being the servant of the growth vision. Notions of the role of governance in addressing the needs of the young state's "social and natural ecologies" were not in evidence likely because these needs were not practically apparent as necessary priorities. The initial vision was to grow the population base to create markets and economic opportunities. Roads, rail and drainage infrastructure would be needed from government and little else.

Florida's Philosophical Heritage: Jefferson and Jackson

The prevailing philosophy of government evident in Florida during its formative years was reflected in the structure of public institutions and the role they would play in the development of the state. The philosophy is known as "Jacksonian Democracy", so-named for Florida's first territorial governor and later President of the United States, Andrew Jackson. Its beliefs included: government by the "common man"; reduction of the powers of elites; elected officials over appointed officials; a dispersal of power among elected government officials; the suspicion that too much government involvement in the economy would play into the hands of the elite class; and the use of the ballot as the principal means of oversight of government.

We can trace Jacksonian Democracy back to the philosophy of government espoused by Thomas Jefferson, whose understanding of democracy "…came out of the everyday experiences of the American frontiersman, and as such it was pragmatic rather than introspective, functional rather than universal, and it was applied to state, county…and city governments alike."[41]

Jefferson held that representative democracy should be the preferred model for governance, with each citizen carrying a duty to assist the state, resist corruption, and work against all forms of aristocracy.[42] He favored an agrarian society modeled after the laws of nature, and was suspicious of the agents of industrialization and capitalism.[43] He viewed the national government as a "necessary evil," and resisted centralization of political power.[44] Jefferson was a staunch believer in a wall of separation between church and state.[45] He held that the rights of individuals reflected in the Bill of Rights of the U.S. Constitution must be strictly constructed.[46] Jefferson believed that local government should be the most powerful and important level in the Federal system, but it would be state legislatures that would dominate during Florida's formative years. Home rule powers would increase as the state urbanized, but state dominance, especially over fiscal policy, remained.

The principal features of Jefferson-Jacksonian philosophies still influence Florida governments. The tension between state and local governments embedded early in Florida's governance history, continues today.[47]

A key lesson from this brief summary is that the role, structure and functions of government in the minds of Florida's original leaders were grounded in the principles and practices of democracy; and were adapted to perform practical functions as necessitated through time. Thus, the "ideology" of governance was rooted in practicality and necessity, with democracy as the means of making public decisions, much as Tocqueville had observed in early America.[48] Beyond this, no systematic ideas linked to economic theories, religious understandings or fixed principles of leadership had influence on the way Floridians chose to govern themselves. Government certainly was not the "enemy"; and as the state developed, the government's role was respected, not marginalized.

Florida's traditional governance philosophy, in part, is congenial to the requirements of sustainability, which demands adaptability; diffusion of power through collaborative means; a firm footing in empirical realities bearing down on society; recognition of self-interests, rightly understood; civic duty in service to the common good; and democracy.

But a vision that understands and seeks after sustainability must be present to claim moral high ground. The traditional vision reflected neither understanding nor aspiration to create a "sustainable Florida" as understood by contemporary definitions. The treatment of Native American Indians in Florida, as elsewhere, stains the development of the state with blood and shame. Indians resisted European and American settlement of Florida for more than three hundred years, with the Seminoles fighting the last of three wars of resistance ending in 1858. In similar fashion, exploitation of natural resources in the name of economic development shames Florida history, and must give way to an ethos of stewardship of the natural environment.

The old vision emphasized economic prosperity for the conquerors in the hope that all else required of the "Good Society" would follow in its wake. As we shall see, a vision with a history grounded in conquest and exploitation and centered on "pleasure and profit" would evoke the law of unintended consequences. As suggested in the opening chapter, Winthrop warned of the dire consequences to social development of bad choices. It sends chills down the spine to view Florida's development history and present circumstances in the light of Martin Luther's view of progress in human history as being analogous to a "drunk on a horse."

The new vision, like the old, requires governance arrangements and roles suited to the citizens' needs, aspirations and values, but this time grounded in sustainability. Yet, a sustainable Florida requires no radical change to the state's traditional governance *philosophy*, only a new and more encompassing vision and the will to dismiss competing ideologies that run counter to the requirements of sustainability. Certainly, the ideology of conquest and exploitation, which wrought so much havoc on Native American Indians and the natural environment, and any contemporary version of it, must be abandoned as Florida seeks its sustainability vision.

As the Florida case example shows, Americans, like all humans, are "creatures of contradiction", with good and bad tendencies present simultaneously. The nation's founders understood this view of human nature, and devised governance arrangements accordingly. The key idea in designing governance arrangements was then, and remains, to find ways and means to balance seemingly opposite human tendencies, and reconcile views and behaviors that will destroy each other if left unattended.

The necessary arrangements practically needed for the new vision will be examined in Chapter VIII. The analytical model we are using suggests that a renewal of the general governance precepts of America's and Florida's philosophical heritage and a re-appropriation of them in ways suited to the needs, aspirations and values of modern society are consistent with the requirements of "sustainable governance". Jefferson likely would have well understood the concept of sustainability, grounded as he was in Enlightenment theories of natural law, which suggest (as does sustainability) that human society—including the institutions of governance---should be in harmony with the laws of nature. We should be open to the possibility that Jefferson's views about the structure and role of government, which found their way into the arrangements of Florida's first governance arrangements, have remained and can be instructive to public leaders today.

The "Progressive Era" from the 1890's to the end of World War I prompted governance reforms that helped correct perversions of the Jeffersonian-Jacksonian approaches, especially in urban areas in the more industrialized states. But reforms also gave rise to governance practices which Americans continue to react against negatively.[49] These include rigid bureaucratic organizational forms, dependence on the expertise of appointed experts, and consolidation of power. While

Florida governance has had its fair share of corruption, the state did not experience the full force of the Industrial Revolution with its industrialized cities, early waves of immigration, and corrupt political machines. Consequently, the Progressive reforms of Jeffersonian-Jacksonian arrangements had less impact on Florida governance structures and functions.

Revisiting the philosophies of Jefferson as part of the search for sustainable governance is akin to going "back to the future". This will require divining and crafting governance arrangements representing the best of the past---including the state's formative years and its Progressive Era influences. We return in Chapters VII and VIII to the topic of Florida governmental reform and its roles in both the old and new visions.

Florida's leaders and citizens pursued the old vision independently and competitively for most of the twentieth century. As a result, governing was a relatively harmonious and stable undertaking. Florida's political culture for most of its history evinced no partisan bickering, (except for the Reconstruction period) because public leaders were governing from the same "play book". The old growth vision and its strategies succeeded in communities -- established and new -- throughout the state.

Growing Pains: The Old Vision's Success

Realization of the traditional growth vision achieved its most stunning successes in the half century following the end of World War II. An excellent summary of Florida growth during those five decades prepared for a documentary funded by the Florida Humanities Council includes the following:

> Florida's population grew exponentially over a half-century, with World War II sparking the first big wave of migration. Many servicemen, stationed in Florida for training during the war, were attracted by the balmy breezes, sugar-sand beaches, and lush tropical setting and pledged to return with their families after the war. Postwar developers saw opportunity and began promoting Florida as an affordable paradise, a place where even working-class families could buy houses under the swaying palm trees. Just as this idea took hold, the concept of retirement evolved in

America. Millions of people who had worked all their lives retired and traveled from the cold climates of the Northeast and Midwest to enjoy a life of leisure in the sun.

Beginning in 1959, the Castro revolution drove thousands of Cubans to seek refuge in South Florida. During the same period of time, the development of the U.S. space program caused a population boom on the east coast of Florida. Not long afterwards, Disney moved into central Florida, luring tourists, workers, entrepreneurs, and residents. The saga continues, with more and more development, migration, and immigration from all over the world. Since World War II, Florida has experienced a net average increase in population of 1,000 residents *per day*. A state that had a relatively homogenous population a half-century ago now is one of the most diverse in the nation.[50]

Looking back, we can see that consensus supporting the state's direction finally ran its course and collapsed in the latter part of the 20th Century. The reason is that the state's traditional economic growth strategy was based on a false promise, an illusion: low taxes, a role for government limited to producing infrastructure and services demanded by rapid growth, cheap land, and unlimited prosperity -- all with a paradise lifestyle. Paradoxically, the promise contained the seeds of its own destruction, and was broken by the harsh realities wrought by its success. The very attributes that attracted so many people to Florida, the quality of life, natural environment, the promise of paradise, were undermined by the magnitude of people who came to visit and live in the state, and the toll their presence has taken.

Construction, tourism, and, to a lesser extent, agriculture, drove the old vision's economic growth strategy. It proved unsustainable. Its principal failures included sprawling development patterns, destruction of the natural environment, over-stressed and under-funded public services and infrastructure, fragmented approaches to solving urban problems, and economic drivers that produce large numbers of low-wage jobs. The main lasting failure of the old vision is that it is misaligned with the needs, aspirations, and values held by the millions of people who inhabit the state; and produces imbalance among the traditional components of sustainability: economic, social, and natural resource.

An article about the findings of a Florida Chamber report states:

> Florida has moved from a low-cost state to a higher-cost state. Rising costs have brought many new challenges. Fewer people are moving to the state and more residents are moving out of Florida to other Southern states ... Last year, the state's schools lost students...[51]

According to an article published in the New York Times in December 2007, "Only 35,000 Americans moved to Florida from elsewhere in the United States, compared with nearly five times as many the year before."[52] Florida's overall growth has slowed. Florida dropped from the 9th fastest growing state in 2006 to 19th for 2007. The state increased its population by 1.1 percent to 18.3-million as of July 2007. The previous year the rate of increase was 1.8 percent.[53] According to the University of Florida's Bureau of Economic and Business Research, Florida's population declined during 2009 for the first time since 1946, largely the result of people leaving the state in search of jobs. Reports about residents moving out of Florida, or seriously thinking about it, are consistent with the interviews and focus groups conducted by authors Arrington and Marlowe in our work across Florida.

Continued population growth notwithstanding, many perceive that the "social contract" Florida promised through the old vision has been breached. The population growth itself exacerbates the problem. Survey data analyzed for the Century Commission for a Sustainable Florida indicate that:

> *Florida's citizens express major concerns about the pace and form of growth in the state*, with many of the issues associated with growth identified as major problems facing the state. There is some limited evidence that Floridians perceive their quality of life to be declining, in large part because of growth-related issues.[54]

A poll published in January 2008 by Leadership Florida found that 43% of Floridians feel that their quality of life is declining.

The results represent a 7% increase over last year's survey findings and an increase in the gap of those who say things are getting worse, now up to a margin of 3-1 from last year's ratio of 2-1. The trend looks to continue as 37% of Floridians imagine Florida becoming a worse place to live over the next year, with only 24% saying they think it will get better ... While 62% of Floridians would recommend that a friend or relative move to Florida, a third of Floridians say they would not encourage a move to the state. More alarmingly, the survey shows that 20% of Floridians are seriously considering leaving the state.[55]

The perceived breaking of the "promise of paradise" certainly is politically unsettling, and frustrates efforts to develop any economic, social, or political consensus.

The lack of community identity on the parts of millions of Floridians makes it more difficult to develop a consensus-based vision. It is as if a substantial percentage of Floridians live as vacationers rather than as citizens. Differing expectations and diverse views about the nature of community problems, ways to address them, and responsibility for doing so plague Florida public leaders. Sprawling urban development patterns have erased the physical singularity of communities in many areas of Florida. Traditional boundaries defining communities have become increasingly vague. This compounds the problem of community identity. So-called "new communities" have grown up, many in unincorporated places, where more than half of all Floridians now reside. According to a report prepared for the Century Commission,

> Of the total current population of Florida, only about one-third were born in Florida, while half were born in other parts of the United States (including territories and children born abroad to American parents), while 18 percent of the population were born overseas. Of the foreign-born population, 23 percent moved to Florida in 2000 or later.[56]

It is no wonder that Floridians have difficulty accepting ownership of the massive problems facing the communities they inhabit much less those of the region or state as a whole.

A sense of community identity and citizenship drive the nature of political participation. In much of Florida today, this sense is often established by an income-driven lifestyle. Floridians increasingly reside and establish community identity in what has been termed "lifestyle enclaves", whose membership consists of people with similar backgrounds, incomes, and careers. The presence of these enclaves together with the bewildering patchwork of fragmented governmental jurisdictions and agencies suppresses a sense of community belonging. New and long-time residents alike have no sense of the broader meanings of democratic community and citizenship. This declining sense of citizenship and community combined with the consequences of population approaching its limits has provoked calls for a new and more sustainable vision.

The Emerging New Vision: Key Features, Influences and Philosophical Challenges

The old growth vision was being called into question, and may have run its course by the dawn of the 21st Century. A new vision began to emerge; new ways of generating wealth and managing growth are at its core. This shift also demands changes in the ways of governing the state.

Dependence on tourism and construction driven by rapid population growth, and agriculture to a lessening extent certainly will remain intact for the foreseeable future. But it is the nature of this dependence that is changing. The dependence will no longer be exclusive; someday perhaps not primary.

According to the new vision, tourism, construction, and agriculture must be joined by knowledge and technology-based, high-wage generators of wealth. The new vision demands first-class public amenities, infrastructure and services, compact development patterns, and high-value placed on protection of the environmental assets that traditionally have attracted residents and visitors. The new vision also demands a healthy social ecology with support systems for the sick and the disadvantaged, job training, and high value on education. The concept of sustainability is at the core of the emerging vision.

This new vision expands and radically alters the traditional view of economic advancement, defined as accumulation and consumption of material wealth driven by population growth. This view has been embedded in Florida (and American) culture for many decades. This perspective carries the conviction that free market economics and the business arrangements and consumption practices that lead to profit-making are the principal means to social progress. Supply-side or trickle-down economics is the contemporary manifestation of this ideology.

Alvin Toffler in his groundbreaking work *Future Shock* labeled this conviction "econo-think". Econo-think carries the belief that the "worth" of products and services and the enterprises and individuals that produce them is determined by how well they sell to consumers in the marketplace. Econo-thinkers see this worth in terms of both monetary and moral value to society. A product that "sells" is considered good for society regardless of the environmental or social consequences of its production and use because the product creates wealth and jobs, the reasoning holds at its extreme. The economic dominates the components of sustainability and carries overriding importance.

An underlying premise of econo-think is that "even non-economic problems can be solved with economic remedies," Toffler observes. With insight that mirrors Florida's experience, he challenges this "root assumption of both Marxian and Keynesian managers" by offering a counter-idea:

> In its historical time and place, industrial society's single-minded pursuit of material progress served the human race well. As we hurdle towards super-industrialism, however, a new ethos emerges in which other goals begin to gain parity with, and even supplant, those of economic welfare. In personal terms, self-fulfillment, social responsibility, aesthetic achievement...and other goals vie with and often over-shadow the raw drive for material success.

Toffler observes that affluence serves as a basis for society to advance beyond this "old vision" of progress to a "new vision" he labels "social futurism." He notes that as society progresses and succeeds in economic pursuits, "economic variables---wages, balance of payments, productivity---grow increasingly sensitive to changes in the non-economic environment. Racism, the battle between the generations, crime, cultural autonomy, violence---all these have economic dimensions; yet none can be effectively treated by econocentric measures alone." He makes a strong case for what he terms "anticipatory democracy" as the means of establishing broad social goals and adapting society to challenges.

Toffler wrote these words with remarkable prescience almost forty years ago. Had he been writing them today, he likely would have added climate change, energy, heath care, immigration, terrorism, costs of health care and other contemporary challenges to his list; and, rather than labeling the competing perspective to econo-think "social futurism", he likely would have named it "sustainability."[57]

Contemporary public debate about the American obsession with sport utility vehicles and other "gas guzzlers" illustrates Toffler's point. Some view these vehicles as establishing an unnecessarily large, unsustainable and harmful "carbon footprint", contributing to green house gases in the atmosphere and worsening the nation's dependence on fossil fuel and foreign oil. U.S. auto makers and "econo-thinkers" defend the sale of these vehicles on the basis that consumers prefer them; and their success in the marketplace is good for the economy and therefore good for society.

The demise of the U.S. auto industry, caused in part because gas guzzlers became unaffordable, socially irresponsible, and unattractive to many consumers, vindicates Toffler's insight. The fate of U.S. automakers demonstrates that economic success causing environmental and social damage can be self-defeating precisely because such success proves unsustainable as its harmful consequences become clear to "consumers" as "citizens."

Toffler's "anticipatory democracy" in this context indicates the need for collective reasoning and corrective, preventive action using "sustainability thinking" *before* the tragic failure of a major industry results.

This perspective also illuminates what is meant by the term "sustainable governance and leadership." Had automakers been sustainability thinkers instead of econo-thinkers tens of thousands of Americans may have held their jobs, and untold damage to the environment could have been avoided. Advertising campaigns would have been geared around sustainability themes and benefits, and innovation in sustainable design of motor vehicles would have been a priority.

Instead, the most egregious consequences of econo-think multiplied over several decades to produce the day of reckoning for U.S. automakers. Failure of the U.S. auto industry was predicted by thoughtful analysts like David Haberstam who, like Toffler, foresaw many years in advance the direction events had taken and where they would lead.[58]

A similar post-mortem on the fate of the U.S. financial services industry could be written in the wake of the meltdown on Wall Street that became apparent in 2008. Nobel Prize winning economist Paul Krugman penned a column in the New York Times near that year's end which observed:

> At the crudest level, Wall Street's ill-gotten gains corrupted and continue to corrupt politics, in a nicely bipartisan way...How much has our nation's future been damaged by the magnetic pull of quick personal wealth, which for years has drawn many of our best and brightest young people into investment banking, at the expense of science, public service and just about everything else?
>
> Most of all, the vast riches being earned — or maybe that should be "earned" — in our bloated financial industry undermined our sense of reality and degraded our judgment. Think of the way almost everyone important missed the warning signs of an impending crisis.[59]

Former chief economist for the International Monetary Fund, Simon Johnson, wrote an article for *Atlantic* magazine in its May 2009 edition that offers the following insights about how the influence of econo-think on American politics was at the root of the nation's economic crisis:

> ...(T)he American financial industry gained political power by amassing a kind of cultural capital—a belief system. Once, perhaps, what was good for General Motors was good for the

country. Over the past decade, the attitude took hold that what was good for Wall Street was good for the country. The banking-and-securities industry has become one of the top contributors to political campaigns, but at the peak of its influence, it did not have to buy favors the way, for example, the tobacco companies or military contractors might have to. Instead, it benefited from the fact that Washington insiders already believed that large financial institutions and free-flowing capital markets were crucial to America's position in the world.

In a society that celebrates the idea of making money, it was easy to infer that the interests of the financial sector were the same as the interests of the country—and that the winners in the financial sector knew better what was good for America than did the career civil servants in Washington. From this confluence of campaign finance, personal connections, and ideology there flowed, in just the past decade, a river of deregulatory policies that is, in hindsight, astonishing."

Johnson points to the unregulated movement of capital across the globe; the repeal of banking regulations; and failure of Washington to regulate credit-default swaps and other financial practices.[60]

Conservative commentator David Brooks of the New York Times---in words that could well apply to Florida and its legislature as subsequent chapters will show---reflects on the necessity to transition the nation from a "bubble economy" to "an investment economy." He writes:

> The members of the Obama administration…are brimming with good ideas about how to move from a bubble economy to an investment economy. Finding a political strategy to accomplish this, however, is proving to be very difficult. And getting Congress to move in this direction might be impossible.
>
> Congressional leaders have been fixated on short-term conventional priorities…There is no evidence that the power brokers understand the fundamental transition ahead. They are practicing the same self-indulgence that got us into this mess. [61]

Had Toffler's "anticipatory democracy" and sustainability thinking been employed instead of short-sighted politics and econo-think, Americans may have averted these economic crises. The question becomes, "What will our grandchildren say about whether the present generation in the wake of the economic meltdown finally developed the political will to follow Toffler's advice?"

Florida and the Nation: Consequences of Consumption

Florida, the bellwether state, exemplifies the interconnected nature of these crises and points to their root causes and consequences. The state's population growth and tourist-based economy has taken a trajectory similar to the U.S. automobile and financial services industries, and could suffer the same fate unless a sense of democratic citizenship is renewed and sustainability trumps econo-think.

Little difference exists among the underlying dynamics and consequences of chopped-up and resold sub-prime mortgages, derivative swaps, gas-guzzlers, and construction of sprawling residential and commercial developments producing clogged highways, destroyed natural habitat, and places with no sense of community or citizenship spewing foreclosures across the landscape. The deeper crisis that has gripped the nation is in the demise of the housing market and reduction in property values, credit availability, consumer spending, and available jobs. Unsustainable production, credit and consumption practices are root causes. The United States has been described as "the most over-extended consumer in world history."[62]

The facts bear out this harsh statement about America's consumption patterns. In the same column referenced above, Brooks notes:

> This rise in debt fueled a consumption binge. Consumption as a share of G.D.P. stood at around 62 percent in the mid-1960s, and rose to about 73 percent by 2008. The baby boomers enjoyed an incredible spending binge. Meanwhile the Chinese, Japanese and European economies became reliant on the overextended U.S. consumer. It couldn't last.
>
> The leverage wave crashed (in the fall of 2008). Facing the possibility of systemic collapse, the government stepped in and

replaced private borrowing with public borrowing. The Federal Reserve printed money at incredible rates, and federal spending ballooned. In 2007, the federal deficit was 1.2 percent of G.D.P. Two years later, it's at 13 percent.

Florida's experience reflects the problem and its consequences with the state's dependence on borrowed capital from China for home building. China has been in a position to loan the money because U.S. consumers have been buying Chinese imports, often financing these purchases with credit cards and home equity loans. As the U.S. economy declines, American consumers can no longer afford purchases of Chinese products. China, in turn, can no longer afford to continue loaning money for homebuilding.

The "credit-consumption-more-credit-more consumption cycle" has been broken. As columnist Tom Friedman of the New York Times puts it: "The days of phony prosperity — I borrow cheap money from China to build a house and then borrow on that house to buy cheap paintings from China to decorate my walls and everybody is a winner — are over."[63]

These interconnected crises have direct impacts on Florida's struggle to shed its old vision and establish a new one. As Americans (and international tourists) have less money available to them to borrow or spend the state's tourism industry spirals downward. Thousands of people are losing jobs and thousands of businesses that depend on real estate and construction are in decline. Furthermore, as pensions, 401k's, and investment portfolios decline in value, the quality of life for the state's millions of retirees is in jeopardy; and retirement plans for millions of the state's aging baby boomers are put on hold. As noted, Florida's growth rate has flat-lined, as the nation's economic meltdown turns the dreams of millions of Americans into nightmares.

People who were blinded by econo-think, obsessed with ever-increasing levels of material consumption, and who failed to see that fidelity to the tenets of sustainability is a superior way to organize and advance society created these crises. Americans and Floridians have only us to blame.

President-elect Barack Obama expressed the character of the overall crisis in a speech January 9, 2009:

This crisis did not happen solely by some accident of history or normal turn of the business cycle, and we won't get out of it by simply waiting for a better day to come, or relying on the worn-out dogmas of the past. We arrived at this point due to an era of profound irresponsibility that stretched from corporate boardrooms to the halls of power in Washington, DC. For years, too many Wall Street executives made imprudent and dangerous decisions, seeking profits with too little regard for risk, too little regulatory scrutiny, and too little accountability. Banks made loans without concern for whether borrowers could repay them, and some borrowers took advantage of cheap credit to take on debt they couldn't afford. Politicians spent taxpayer money without wisdom or discipline, and too often focused on scoring political points instead of the problems they were sent here to solve. The result has been a devastating loss of trust and confidence in our economy, our financial markets, and our government.[64]

Understanding these crises helps explain the root causes of the global and national challenge and why the turning from econo-think to sustainability is at the heart of the transition from the state's old vision to its new vision for a sustainable Florida. The turning demands development of a broadened and more mature understanding of the economic component of sustainability. Those who lead at this turning point must find balance among economic, social and natural resource concerns and recognize their interdependencies.

Free enterprise and profits are as essential to sustainability as they are to econo-think. In reality, sustainability is the more conservative approach, geared to the long-term and concerned about the health of both the economy *and* the society that supports it. Econo-think at its worst is directed purely at fast-paced, short-term profit-maximization with little concern for social and environmental consequences. Econo-think is about materialistic consumption and markets; sustainability is about stewardship, citizenship and democracy. Floridians and Americans must decide which vision will dominate society's future direction, which will define society's needs, aspirations, and values; indeed which will shape the national character.

The choice should be an easy one for Florida and America, but it will not likely be so. Econo-think has prevailed as an ideology for advancing society for a very long time, as the brief survey of Florida's development indicates, and as any well prepared presentation of American history will teach. As Toffler observes, what may be termed a moderate version of econo-think served society well just as the Florida's old growth vision well-served the state. But the time came when population growth, urbanization, and the emergence of the global economy with its souped-up version of econo-think produced consequences harmful to society, the natural environment, and the economy.

It is as if Florida's and America's huge success, grounded in econo-think, has folded in on itself, morphing into new challenges at a time when the old ones were thought to be fading into history by virtue of "progress." C.S. Lewis, as suggested in the introduction, warned of the dangers of making the kind of history that causes us to lose our balance; and, as in Luther's metaphor, fall off the horse because over-consumption places us in a stupor.

The transition to a new vision organized around sustainability demands that citizens throw off their stupor, reach back into the past and re-appropriate the best of its governance tradition into the present and future in ways suited to contemporary needs, aspirations and values. We must develop a deeper understanding of the philosophical currents influencing the American experiment with democracy to do this. It is to that task that we now turn.

"Every nation is liable to be under whatever bubble, design, or delusion may puff up in moments when off their guard."
—Thomas Jefferson

Chapter III

THE REFLECTION:
PROBING THE PHILOSOPHICAL CURRENTS

The Role of Government: Jefferson and Lincoln

Perhaps the only widely-held American counterview to econo-think in the nation's history was Jefferson's dream of an agrarian society, which guided the development of the South, including parts of northern Florida. That vision competed with the early versions of econo-think during the nation's formative years and lost. While it is impossible to resurrect Jefferson's vision in urbanized modernity; as noted, its underlying philosophical positions may yet hold contemporary lessons for those who now seek a sustainable society. Thomas Jefferson was a brilliant man who was right about many things. He understood how sustainable governance helps a society discern wisdom and avoid social calamity.

We also should consult the views of Abraham Lincoln as Americans struggle to reposition the role of governance and the underlying philosophy of social advancement. Lincoln early in his political career as a member of the Whig and, later, Republican Party was a strong proponent of the power of government to advance society in a direction of economic prosperity, including urbanization and industrialization. His views were in contrast to Jefferson's and Jackson's, who were suspicious of centralized power and monied interests and urbanized, industrial society in general---suspicions that would lead to the creation of the Democratic Party.

Lincoln favored a strong national bank, a protective tariff, and a system for internal improvement. "These internal improvements to the infrastructure would enable thousands of farming families to emerge from the kind of poverty in which the Lincoln family had been trapped, and would permit new cities and towns to flourish," writes Doris Kerns

Goodwin in her national bestseller <u>Team of Rivals</u>. In language familiar to contemporary theories of sustainability, Goodwin makes the following observation using Lincoln's own words: "To Lincoln's mind, the fundamental test of democracy was its capacity to 'elevate the condition of men, to lift artificial weights from all shoulders, to clear the paths of laudable pursuit for all'. A real democracy would be a meritocracy where those born in the lower ranks would rise as far as their natural talents and discipline might take them."[65] A strong and practical role for government was implicit in Lincoln's philosophy, as were the roots of the strand of econo-think that sees a strong national economy as essential to social advancement for all people.

Could it be that Jefferson and Lincoln were both right; and that in the reconciliation of their visions lay the seeds of synthesis now required between econo-think and an activist role for government in building a sustainable society? The two men, who were born sixty-six years apart, had different visions for America and vastly different experiences of rural life. One rose from relative wealth and aristocracy; the other from the poverty of frontier life.

But what they shared is far more important to contemporary Americans than how they differed. Both believed in the equality of opportunity for all Americans, and while they differed on the role of the federal government in American life, each understood governance as a necessary and practical process grounded in the sovereignty of ordinary people.

It is ironic that Jefferson was the philosophical father of the Democratic Party, which in contemporary America stands for the stronger role for government; and that the Republican Party---the party of Lincoln---is where the modern version of econo-think with its intense animosity toward government finds its home. As Goodwin's book chronicles, the modern Republican Party was founded in 1854, primarily as an anti-slavery party. Most northern abolitionist Whigs became members of the new party. This new party chose the name "Republican" to demonstrate a philosophical linkage to Jeffersonian ideals of liberty and equality. Lincoln sought to revive Jeffersonian ideas and expand them in favor of an active government to modernize the economy, consistent with the views of Lincoln's political hero, Henry Clay.[66]

The era taught the criticality of reconciling differing philosophical points of view, especially when the nation's future direction and founding principles are involved. Lincoln comprehended from personal experience and exemplified the promise of the American Dream. The Civil War showed the importance of extending that promise to all Americans. As the war dragged on, he came to the understanding---in keeping with the deepest meaning of sustainability---of the importance to society and to the happiness of every person of unleashing the potential and respecting the dignity of each individual through equal opportunity and protection of natural rights.

Lincoln embodied a mature version of the American vision, molding and expanding Jefferson's hopes for liberty from oppressive governance with his own Hamiltonian belief in the power of government to be used as a means to human progress. Lincoln's vision of reconciliation faded for a season after his assassination. It seems to split off from itself through time. But it remerges with the brilliant force of its philosophical unity in times of national crisis and greatness.

As we shall see, Barack Obama aspires to lead during the present crisis in the fashion of the great presidents, guided by Lincoln's sense of the American vision. Only time will tell whether the American people have the character and will to turn away from paralyzing and dangerous differences, and unite behind him.

The Necessity of Shared Sacrifice

Americans, to achieve and sustain unity, will have to share the sacrifice demanded by the search for sustainable governance during times of great national challenge. Hopefully, through the legacies of Lincoln and Martin Luther King, Jr., unity will come in reliance on the lesson that appeals to conscience and not violence and hatred mark great civilizations.

These historical currents and lessons lead to the conclusion that differences of political philosophy about the role of government alone do not sufficiently explain the rancor and mean spiritedness of the nation's contemporary political culture, whether the venue is Congress or the Florida legislature. Some have asked whether the root cause of contemporary political disunity has to do with denial that sacrifice is demanded. More likely, and consistent with the national condition during the Civil War and the Great Depression, the modern divisiveness goes deeper into the dark side of the American experiment.

Contemporary disunity has to do with the perceived motivation to force required sacrifice onto others to protect the prerogatives and interests of one's own kind. This perceived tendency is opposed with strong resolve by those who believe they will be likely victims of unfair burdens and others who are repulsed by what they suspect is underneath the veil of opposing ideology. This dynamic applies to both sides of the philosophical divide about the role of government in society, and provokes divisiveness, mistrust, fear and anger.

This perspective helps explain Jefferson's aversion to both privileged aristocracy and to popular democracy inflamed by passion. His antidotes were representative democracy, protection of human rights, sharing of powers within a system of checks and balances, separation of church and state, and the wisdom found through intellectual pursuits grounded in scientific knowledge and truth. Lincoln likely understood Jefferson and other founders better than most people who have tried to stand on their shoulders, which explains his brilliance and his near universal veneration.

Arch-conservatives are mortified by the perception that the motivation of those who oppose them will bring personal and national ruination. Those standing in opposition to arch-conservatives perceive themselves, or those they care about, as likely victims of sacrifice unfairly shared. The danger is that each side will begin to demonize the other with an intensity that will set off a cycle of recrimination. This in turn will cause the catastrophic political, economic and social deterioration President Obama warned about during the early days of his administration in response to critics of his attempts to right the ship of state.

Obama also seems to understand that connecting with Lincoln's masterful understanding of the necessity of reconciliation and the path to unity has become the central challenge facing the nation. The struggle is not about winning a political or ideological battle. It is about preserving the nation's vitality, promise, security and respect as a leader in the world. These matters reach to the most profound meanings of sustainability. During such times of crisis, thoughtful people of conscience must hope that the spirit of democracy, well practiced, will make its presence known and its wisdom apparent to leaders and led alike.

In any event, the true needs, aspirations and values of the American people will be laid bare as the consequences of the present crisis are reckoned with. If Obama is aligned with these through his policies and actions, he, like Lincoln and FDR, may be able to produce the transformational leadership that marks greatness.

The good news is that Obama has American history on his side. The bad news, as Lincoln experienced and FDR well knew, is that the fear of having to endure hard times of sacrifice and anger at those perceived as responsible for it can become the most powerful enemy of all. We should be open to the possibility that fear and anger are at the heart of the nation's life, and are primary motivators of contemporary political, economic, and social behavior. All components of sustainability are infected by it. Because the crisis is global, the fear and anger extend beyond the borders of the nation. This moves people into warring camps where authoritarian, repressive and violent ideologies reside; and demagoguery and fundamentalisms with their false promise of security and certitude are found.

Respected author Fareed Zakaria observed before the nation's economic meltdown became apparent to Americans:

> (The United States) needs to stop cowering in fear. It is fear that has created a climate of paranoia and panic in the United States and fear that has enabled our strategic missteps...America has become a nation consumed by anxiety, worried about terrorists and rogue nations, Muslims and Mexicans, foreign companies and free trade, immigrants and international organizations. The strongest nation in the history of the world now sees itself as besieged by forces beyond its control... (This) is a phenomenon that goes beyond one president. Too many Americans have been taken by the rhetoric of fear.[67]

The failure of the American people to rise to the occasion as a nation united, to transcend fear, to put aside anger and to muster the courage to be a world leader by example could unleash forces that will de-stabilize economies and political systems worldwide, sparking much hardship and violence. If the fear turns into terror, the prime enemy of the nation and the world---those who advocate, sponsor and commit acts of terrorism out of hatred---will be victorious.

A Time for Soul-Searching

Americans must think deeply about what divides us, and, once again, find and follow the narrow and difficult path to reconciliation and peace in the knowledge of the biblical forewarning that to whom much has been given, much is expected. Lincoln expressed this spirit of unity when he said in his second Inaugural speech in March, 1865 near the end of the Civil War: "With malice toward none, with charity for all,…let us strive on to finish the work we are in,…to do all which may achieve and cherish a just and lasting peace among ourselves and with all nations."

The search for sustainable governance is about this striving. The soul-searching must take us deep into human nature to the same place that our founders visited intellectually when they devised the American governance arrangement with its sharing of powers within a system of checks and balances, and its wall of separation between church and state. It is a place where we recognize that human nature has a duality, a contradiction.

This contradiction makes us capable of great acts of creativity and insight into what it takes to live in a sustainable way. It also causes us to recognize that as humans we are capable of much self-centeredness, self-righteousness and judgmentalism against those forces and people we perceive as threats to our security and well-being. The best of modern psychology teaches that these perceptions often are wrong and the result of unjust transference of our own deficiencies onto others. Nevertheless, the dark side of our nature provokes much hostility and disunity which can easily escalate into dangerous conflict with those we misperceive as the enemy.

Americans who are enjoying the successes of the nation's economic pursuits are expressing this duality in our ambivalence about the direction of the contemporary political economy. On the one hand, we have enjoyed and want to maintain the fruits of modern American life with its emphasis on investor profit and consumption. On the other hand, we are uneasy about the consequences of our power and success. When we are honest with ourselves, we know that these have come at the price of undermining the common good of the present and of future generations. Our tendencies in favor of meaningful citizenship and stewardship stand in opposition to our ambition to gain power, avoid sacrifice and produce and consume more and more wealth for ourselves.

Those citizens who have not enjoyed the benefits of America's economic success look upon those who have with their own unfulfilled expectations and insecurity, and a rising sense of frustration.

As noted, the "haves" and the "have not" have a tendency to demonize each other. This is the breeding ground of much instability, runs counter to the promise of the American credo to provide equal opportunity for all people, and is unsustainable through time.

The reconciliation of the cauldron of conflicting needs, aspirations and values grounded in both sides of our contradictory nature is the central challenge to public leadership and to the nation's soul. This is what Lincoln likely was referring to during his first inaugural address on the eve of the Civil War. He expressed hope that unity would prevail over division through "the better angels of our nature" taking hold and protecting Americans of that day from themselves. The better angels come to us as we stop projecting the blame for our fears onto others, and recognize that we are all ridden with deficiencies and in need of the healing power of unity that only democracy practiced well normally can bring.

Lincoln was a humble, melancholy and deep-thinking man who understood the truth about human nature, and the hope of the national covenant to transcend its dark side through pursuit of the American Dream. Faith in the sanctity of this covenant formed the "bedrock principle" that guided his remarkable presidency. He laid down every power at his hand, sacrificed the blood and treasure of his fellow citizens, and personally paid the ultimate price in service to the preservation of the covenant.

Lincoln's example teaches that reconciliation of America's conflicts and contradictions requires transformative leadership. The appearance of such leadership is extraordinary, and requires a confluence of crisis with leaders of superior quality at the helm. This explains why the unity of consensus on complex and divisive issues is very difficult to attain; and why, tragically, the "better angels of our nature" come to guide our collective life only after much suffering brings the nation to its knees and forces the question: what do we truly value?

Republicans and Democrats: Modern Divisions

On a more practical level of understanding, it is important to come to grips with the modern ideological division between Republicans and Democrats. It originated in the wake of the Industrial Revolution and ripened during the Progressive Era. Econo-think became a dominant influence in American politics as the Republican Party became "the party of business." A respected reviewer of Lewis Gould's *Grand Old Party: A History of the Republican Party* (2003) notes:

> Gould, an emeritus University of Texas at Austin professor, has researched U.S. political parties throughout his career. He establishes the 1850s context in which the new party arose, examines Lincoln's wartime policies (including an activist federal government) that were pursued by the Republican administrations that dominated the rest of the century, and then analyzes the Progressive-era debate over regulating industrial society in which the GOP shifted to the small-government, low-tax, *laissez faire* approach it has now championed for nearly a century.[68]

Publishers Weekly observes that Gould:
> ....(P)ortrays the almost 180-degree shifts in GOP policy through the decades, making it possible to understand how the Republican platform of 2000 could so closely mirror the Democrats' platform of a century ago. Although the book gives serious weight to issues such as race, especially in shaping the party's antebellum origins...the account comes to life more effectively the closer it gets to the present, especially when considering Ronald Reagan, whom Gould considers so strong a

conservative influence that he obliterated any recollection of moderation in the party's past.[69]

One respected commentator, Nobel Prize winning economist Paul Krugman, suggests that the roots of contemporary arch-conservatism of the Republican Party can be traced to the so-called "Southern Strategy," which made the GOP "the party of racial backlash." Quoting a statement made in 1981 by well-known party consultant Lee Atwater, Krugman writes the party's hostility toward government, "...originally focused on opposition to the Voting Rights Act but eventually took a more coded form: 'You're getting so abstract now you're talking about cutting taxes, and all these things you're talking about are totally economic things and a byproduct of them is blacks get hurt worse than whites.' In other words, government is the problem because it takes your money and gives it to "Those People."

The Southern Strategy gained the southern votes and helped propel the GOP through the Reagan and both Bush presidencies. But, Krugman notes, "Today, Republicans have taken away almost all those Southern votes — and lost the rest of the country. It was a grand ride for a while, but in the end the Southern strategy led the G.O.P. into a cul-de-sac."[70]

Could it be an accurate read of history that the contemporary version of econo-think has its roots in a reaction to the role government assumed as a result of Franklin Roosevelt's New Deal, crafted in response to the Great Depression, and the need to mobilize the country for fighting in World War II; and in reaction to Lyndon Johnson's Great Society? Johnson expanded the role of government through enactment of Medicaid, Medicare, and legislation to address urban problems and transportation.[71] Many Republicans and Southern Democrats opposed the adoption of the Voting Rights Act of 1965 which outlawed discriminatory practices that had disenfranchised African Americans. It continues to draw opposition today, most recently by arch-conservative Republicans in 2006 when the Act was up for renewal.[72]

This reading of history suggests that treatment of "big government" and "the welfare state" as "the enemy" during the Reagan era became a reactionary ideology in the wake of New Deal and Great Society programs. Both Richard Nixon and Gerald Ford embraced and expanded the Voting Rights Act and other Great Society programs.[73] The departure clearly began with Reagan and his Vice-President George Herbert Walker Bush and was carried forward in both Bush presidencies, reaching its highest intensity as an ideology during administration of George W. Bush.

The Reagan and Bush reaction, while popular with many Americans, stands in contradiction to the role government has played in times of great national need. This ideology merges with supply-side economics to form what we have termed the contemporary version of econo-think.

Some Americans apply this version of econo-think to all times and circumstances as a matter of bedrock principle. Therefore, econo-think fails from the standpoint of sustainability to use governance as an agency of adaptation to diverse and ever-changing challenges, different needs of the regions of the nation and among the levels of government.

Would it not be wise now to fashion a pragmatic role for governance that marries Jefferson's belief in limiting government to Lincoln's thirst for using its powers to improve and unite the nation? Would we not benefit from a combination of FDR's and LBJ's belief in the capacity of governance to help ordinary Americans and Reagan's suspicions of too much governmental involvement in the lives of citizens?

What Gould's studied account teaches is that the philosophical origins of both major parties shared much in common, and that the contemporary econo-think ideology is out of sync with the heritage of them both. It is within the commonality of vision between Jefferson and Lincoln and the other great Presidents that the basis lay for synthesis between the passion to use governance to help build a sustainable society, and the caution about its potential over use and abuse. Both views hold true to the American spirit as Jefferson and Lincoln lived it. If Krugman's argument is right, it is certainly accurate to observe that the conservative wing of the contemporary Republican Party with its Southern Strategy would be a major disappointment to the man who signed the Emancipation Proclamation.

We should recognize that Reagan's version of econo-think ideology and the political strategies that flow from it did not materialize out of thin air. They are rooted in a well-intended strategic attempt to adapt to deep structural changes in the nature of the economy. These changes began in the 1970's and intensified through time.

The movement away from the economic stability enjoyed during the two and a half decades following World War II has to do with the way technology and globalization restructured production and consumption patterns. Technologies have empowered consumers and investors and changed the way goods and services are produced and consumed. The same trends forced hard choices that often run counter to the interests of large numbers of Americans who enjoyed relative prosperity and much more hope for a better life under the status quo ante.[74]

This reading of history suggests that the Reagan administration understood that the nation's extant economic arrangements could not compete in the emerging global, technology-driven economy. In the new global economy, mass production was giving way to customization; and consumers were demanding choice, value and low cost. Reagan gave voice to the necessity to get government regulation and the welfare state mentality out of the way so American business could compete. He set about to de-regulate, turn government into "the problem, not the solution", and otherwise to unleash the entrepreneurial spirit.

The problem is that the old social contract implicit in the prior arrangements of the "good old days" was unsustainable. The new social contract offered by the promises of Reagan's supply-side economics was breached as well, leaving large numbers of American citizens in jeopardy. When the bubble created by the seeming success of the new arrangements finally burst, the stark consequences of failing the needs of those left behind became apparent. The common good of citizens was trumped by the needs of investors and the satisfaction of consumers. Pleasure and profit ruled the day, especially for those at the upper income levels of society. There was little "trickle-down effect" for masses of people.

Reagan's road to prosperity, paved with the good intentions of econo-think and supply-side economics, ultimately lead to a dead end. Masses of Americans lost economic ground. Confidence in both government and big business plummeted.[75] The consequences of the damage done to the natural environment were ignored for too long.

Econo-think with its fierce drive to compete at all costs is now experiencing its day of reckoning. Social needs, aspirations and values changed, but those in political power remained strong defenders of the status quo. The question facing the nation is how long these apologists will prolong the agony of turning away from the present course and aligning with a new and more sustainable direction; and how much damage will be done during this process of national repentance and renewal.

Demanded now is a new political consensus in support of a new vision for a sustainable society. As we shall see in subsequent chapters, Florida is a microcosm of the broad forces and trends driving this necessity for sustainable governance and may provide hints useful to understanding the direction of the nation as a whole.

Some commentators believe this contemporary version of econo-think may have finally run its course with the election of Barack Obama and the economic meltdown that became apparent in 2008. Respected conservative writer David Frum quoted Republican leader Newt Gingrich in an article published by Newsweek magazine near the end of the first quarter of 2009. Gingrich, who developed the so-called "Contract with America" as Speaker of the House of Representatives in the mid-1990's, said in January 2009: "We are at the end of the Reagan era. We are at a point in time when we're about to start redefining…the nature of the Republican Party, in response to the country's needs." Frum writes:

> The conservatism we know evolved in the 1970s to meet a very specific set of dangers and challenges: inflation, slow growth, energy shortages, unemployment, rising welfare dependency. In every one of those problems, big government was the direct and immediate culprit. Roll back government, and you solved the problem.
>
> Government is implicated in many of today's top domestic concerns as well … But the connection between big government and today's most pressing problems is not as close or as pressing as it was 27 years ago. So, unsurprisingly, the anti-big-government message does not mobilize the public the way it once did.

Frum cites the following political data and information about the performance of the Republican Party in recent years:

- Seven years into the presidencies of George W. Bush, the average American worker was earning barely more after inflation than the typical worker had earned in 2000. "Political parties that do not deliver economic improvement for the typical person do not get reelected."
- Republicans not only lost the presidency in 2008, but in Congressional losses combined with those of 2006, the party lost 51 seats in the House and 14 in the Senate.
- Republicans are losing appeal to voters groups they normally have done well with, including college graduates, and voters in key Sunbelt states. Obama won Florida and California. Florida voted Republican in every presidential election between 1972 and 2008 with the exceptions of 1976 and 1996. California voted Republican in every election from 1952 through 1988 (except 1964). The Republicans in the 2008 Presidential election also lost the traditional strongholds of North Carolina and Virginia. Frum concludes: "Look at America's public policy problems, look at voting trends, and it's inescapably obvious that the Republican Party needs to evolve."[76]

Conservative New York Times columnist David Brooks suggests Republicans ask themselves:

What threatens Americans' efforts to build orderly places to raise their kids? The answers would produce an agenda: the disruption caused by a boom and bust economy; the fragility of the American family; the explosion of public and private debt; the wild swings in energy costs; the fraying of the health care system; the segmentation of society and the way the ladders of social mobility seem to be dissolving…Republicans are so much the party of individualism and freedom these days that they are no longer the party of community and order. This puts them out of touch with the young, who are exceptionally community-oriented. It gives them nothing to say to the lower middle class, who fear that capitalism has gone haywire. It gives them little to say to the upper middle class, who are interested in the environment and other common concerns.[77]

In words that capture the essential weakness of adherence to rigid econo-think ideology, Brooks writes: "The Republicans talk more about the market than about society, more about income than quality of life. They celebrate capitalism, which is a means, and are inarticulate about the good life, which is the end. *They take things like tax cuts, which are tactics that are good in some circumstances, and elevate them to holy principle, to be pursued in all circumstances."* (Emphasis added)[78]

Viewed in the context of the "sustainable governance" framework, the Republican Party with its emphasis on "econo-think" has not adapted to changes in the political environment. As a governing party, it did not help society adapt to economic, social or environmental challenges sufficiently to maintain support. Its ideological position, grounded in the Reagan era, may be considered "unsustainable" precisely because of this failure to adapt pragmatically to the necessities of the times. Frum argues in his Newsweek article that the party must "modulate" its social conservatism---especially on gay rights---develop an environmental message, and "take governing seriously once again." He writes, "Our party seems to be running to govern a country that no longer exists."

Whether consciously intended by Frum and Brooks or not, their perspectives view the problems of the Republicans through the lens of sustainability, citing the party's failures in all components: economic, environmental, social, and governance. As we shall see in subsequent chapters, the Democratic Party under the leadership of President Obama, appears to be steeped in "sustainability thinking", which has the power to accommodate seemingly opposite philosophical positions. Brooks agrees when he writes:

> If the Republicans are going to rebound…they will have to explain that there are two theories of civic order. There is the liberal theory, in which teams of experts draw up plans to engineer order wherever problems arise. And there is the more

conservative vision in which government sets certain rules, but mostly empowers the complex web of institutions in which the market is embedded. Both of these visions are now contained within the Democratic Party. The Republicans know they need to change but seem almost imprisoned by old themes that no longer resonate. The answer is to be found in devotion to community and order, and in the bonds that built the nation.

Because Frum and Brooks are respected conservative analysts who appear to be assessing politics and governance from a sustainability perspective, there may be room for the two parties to begin communicating with each other in a productive manner. At the very least, if both sides begin to use a sustainability framework, they may be able to narrow their differences, better articulate their respective positions, and even find some common ground. This is the reason why we argue---admittedly with more hope than hard evidence---that sustainability possesses the power to help reconcile unhealthy conflict and move the nation's governance in a direction acceptable to large numbers of Americans of different political persuasions.

Politics of Hate: Personal and Visceral

Krugman offers an important insight into the behavior of the arch-conservative wing of the GOP, which may be at the root of its contemporary problems: the Party's tendency to divide the nation in its fight against all those who stand for a more activist role for government. He writes, "...after the 2000 election the Heritage Foundation specifically urged the new team to "make appointments based on loyalty first and expertise second. Contempt for expertise, in turn, rested on contempt for government in general. 'Government is not the solution to our problem,' declared Ronald Reagan. 'Government is the problem.' So why worry about governing well?"

These statements are reminders of the well-known campaign tactics orchestrated by people like Karl Rove, who spent years inside the White House as George W. Bush's political advisor. The 2002 campaign against incumbent U.S. Senator Max Cleland of Georgia stands as one example of many divisive onslaughts. Cleland, a triple amputee whose limbs were blown off by a hand grenade in Viet Nam, was accused of being "unpatriotic." A Washington Post columnist wrote in the months leading up to the 2002 elections:

> If the mugging of Sen. Max Cleland of Georgia is a fair indicator of what is to come, the fall elections will be ugly. Cleland, a decorated veteran and triple amputee, was attacked by his Republican opponent, Rep. Saxby Chambliss, "for breaking his oath to protect and defend the Constitution."
>
> This statement has shades of Lee Atwater, the fabled Republican cutthroat politico who helped pilot the first President Bush to victory. But even Atwater might have hesitated before going after a man who lost both legs and an arm in the service of his country. Chambliss did not participate in Vietnam. He had a bad knee, he told columnist Mark Shields, who was the first to call national attention to Cleland's bizarre situation -- veterans whose war wounds confine them to wheelchairs are often given a pass on patriotism, especially by those who never wore the uniform.[79]

Cleland, a graduate of Florida's Stetson University and member of its Board of Trustees, lost his re-election bid, a victim of the GOP's much-heralded Southern Strategy.

If bigotry, hatred of government, divisiveness and character assassination stand side by side with supply side economics at the root of contemporary econo-think, should we not ask whether it is time to close this chapter of history and start anew in a renewed spirit of unity befitting the nation's true political heritage?

A new vision based on the tenets of sustainability requires a sense of civility and civic responsibility that is difficult to achieve in a rancid political culture. Sustainability certainly does not require that everyone agree on every issue, but, like democracy practiced well, it demands a measure of civic virtue that mean-spiritedness, hatred, and orchestrated divisiveness make impossible.

The intense nastiness of politics in recent times has kept many good people from entering the political arena, which plays into a strategy to ensure weak government. People who exhibit counter-productive political behavior out of hatred for government should question whether politics is their true calling. Hatred does not serve and sustain great civilizations.

These questions point to the quality of "soul searching" now required of Americans and Floridians who seek a sustainable society. It will be helpful to think deeply about Jefferson's iron-clad commitment to individual rights and liberty, faith in local government, and his belief in the necessity for developing a human society in harmony with the laws of nature. Understanding Lincoln's desire for the well-being of all people and their equal opportunity for the pursuit of happiness and prosperity should motivate contemporary leaders who aspire to shape a sustainable society.

In the combined visions of these two great men lay the same clarity of purpose that caused the nation's founders to covenant among them in the Declaration of Independence: "…we mutually pledge to each other our Lives, our Fortunes, and our Sacred Honor." It clearly is time for Americans to re-appropriate that pledge into the contemporary life of the nation in the same spirit of patriotic sacrifice, the spirit that continues to animate great Americans like Max Cleland, a man who both Jefferson and Lincoln rightly would be proud for his sacrifice and continuing service to the nation.

Florida's Era of Ideology

We will argue in subsequent chapters that the contemporary version of econo-think ideology during the past decade has had great influence on Florida public leaders, especially at the state level. A decided "anti-government", "starve the beast with no new taxes" approach to governing grounded in supply-side economics has dominated the governorship and state legislature, especially the Florida House of Representatives. Political actors like former Governor Jeb Bush and former House Speakers Johnnie Byrd and Marco Rubio were strong proponents of econo-think ideological fervor. Governor Crist and several prominent members of the Florida legislature joined conservative elected officials nationwide when they signed a "Taxpayer Protection Pledge" organized by former Reagan advisor, Grover Norquist of Americans for Tax Reform. The pledge states: "I will oppose and vote against any and all efforts to increase taxes." A news paper article reports:

A campaign gimmick, perhaps, but the Taxpayer Protection Pledge is sacred among those who take it and is a link to the legacy of Ronald Reagan, who encouraged Norquist to form Americans for Tax Reform.

In Florida, the Norquist pledge has been a nonissue until now because Republicans have ruled in mostly robust economic times. The boom has become a bust and now the pledge looms in the background, a tiger in hiding.[80]

A public opinion survey taken in April 2009 found that a vast majority of Floridians believe state officials should abandon their "no new taxes" position in the face of the state's budget crisis, as illustrated by the following tabulation of results:

QUESTION: Some legislators pledged not to raise taxes under any circumstances. The current fiscal crisis has prompted significant cuts in education and health care if Florida doesn't raise additional revenues. Which of the following two positions best describes your viewpoint?

- Legislators who pledged not to raise taxes should not consider any new taxes even if it means significant cuts to education and health care.
- Legislators have a greater responsibility to adequately fund schools and health care than to stick with a pledge of no new taxes.

	State	Men	Women	Dem	Rep	Ind
Keep Tax Pledge	28%	32%	24%	14%	46%	25%
Greater Responsibility	63%	57%	69%	80%	43%	64%
Not Sure	9%	11%	7%	6%	11%	11%

Source: Mason-Dixon Poll sponsored by Florida Alliance for Concerned Taxpayers[81]

We do not agree that Krugman's charge of racial bigotry applies to Florida elected leaders who have persisted in their no new taxes stance. They certainly do not deserve that charge. But their fascination with other aspects of post-Reagan econo-think is clear; and, as the best available opinion research data indicates, their views are out of alignment with those held by the Florida public.

It is also clear that during the past decade or so, Florida political campaigns have taken on a nasty edge, that both parties are responsible for it, and that the public is weary of this approach to politics. This brand of politicking distracts voters from the issues, encourages a spirit of deception, breeds incivility, and generally destroys citizens' confidence in governance. Sustainability demands engaged and interested citizens, a high degree of trust and transparency, civil behavior, and trust in politics and governance. While sustainable governance welcomes spirited debate and strong disagreement, the contributions of people who think and act in the fashion of Atwater and Rove and their counter-parts associated with the Democratic Party are unproductive and injurious.

Some politicians justify negative and nasty political campaigning on the basis that "it works." This conclusion itself is an out-growth of the egregious econo-think notion that whatever sells to the public is morally justified. Sustainability demands a higher moral standard that elicits and values the best in people, not the worst. Divisive behavior during campaigns spills over into governance, poisons relationships, and sets up a continuation of the cultural practice of manipulating the prejudices of people. This is the politics of fear FDR warned about. It is unworthy of the best of the nation's political heritage, and has no place in American politics or governance.

The lessons of history teach that it is unwise to continue this political and governance approach during the present time of economic crisis. As America and Florida seek new vision, they demand a more pragmatic and activist role for government and a stronger reliance on the principles and practices of democracy. This wiser course is consistent with the best of the American experience. Americans and Floridians in accord with the lessons of sustainability must craft political practices and a role for governance adapted to the complex challenges at hand.

Incumbent Florida Governor Charlie Crist has shown signs of choosing a more moderate course. Only time will reveal whether he is able to move his party toward a more sensible and moderate position.[82]

But as the next chapter's account of Florida's attempt to reform its tax and budget policies will show, the legacy of Jeb Bush, who is primarily responsible for introducing extreme econo-think ideology into Florida politics, remains strong.

Bush also is responsible for alloying econo-think with hard core social conservative positions grounded in religious fundamentalism, a topic that will be explored further in Chapter VII. There we will argue that mixing religion and politics is as toxic today as it was when Jefferson devised the principle of separation between church and state, and when Theodore Roosevelt, a major contributor to the philosophical heritage of the Republican Party, spoke these words: "I hold that in this country there must be complete severance of church and state; that public moneys shall not be used for the purpose of advancing any particular creed; and therefore that the public schools shall be non-sectarian and no public moneys appropriated for sectarian schools."[83] Mixing politics and religion is likely more dangerous to sustainability and democracy than any other single variable.

As the examination of political motives, convictions and attitudes begins in renewal of the search for sustainable governance, we should ask ourselves some serious questions. Is it not possible that facets of the ideology of all three Bushes, who were without question well-meaning and patriotic leaders, reach no further back in history than the popular rhetoric and celebrity appeal of Ronald Reagan, "the Great Communicator"? In reality are these leaders cut off from the wisdom and moral compass of history?

Is it not true that elements of their strategic approach to governance has contributed substantially to leading America and Florida down the perilous path of the present day? Could it be that these gifted men and the many elected leaders who based their political careers on Reagan's ideology, tragically failed to see the possibility that their understanding and application of certain of the "principles" they so proudly governed by often proved to be grounded in shifting sand and not rock?

It is possible that they were right to protect the long-standing bi-partisan tradition in American political thought in favor of preserving the integrity of the free enterprise system. It is also possible that at the same time they mistakenly helped to shape a weak role for governance that enabled the very forces and trends which fostered the contemporary political culture and led to the present economic crises at both the national and state levels.

Tragedy often results when well-intended leaders misunderstand or misapply bedrock principles. For verification of this insight, consult Luther's understanding of history, Jefferson's writings or Lincoln's life. Give close study of the meaning of Lincoln's death by assassination and that of some 600,000 of his fellow citizens at civil war. Misunderstanding and misapplication of bedrock principles has a tragic historical legacy, and has left much carnage in its wake. Is it not possible that democracy and the tenets of sustainability provide bedrock principles in abundance?

History teaches that Americans do much better using adaptable pragmatism grounded in democracy than principles based on fixed ideology. The former is in the spirit of the philosophical tradition of both major parties and is congenial to sustainability; the latter is a relative newcomer to American politics, and has proven that it leads to disastrous consequences. Sustainability as an organizing guide possesses the capacity to help reconcile these two divergent approaches to politics and governance; and for that compelling reason is an exceptional lodestar as Americans seek a renewal of the search for sustainable governance and the nation's vision.

Conclusions: A Slow Turning?

Today's society demonstrates unsustainable production and consumption patterns, a rising gap between rich and poor, and ecological disaster that could destroy the quality of life our fore-bearers fought and died for. Without a major change of direction---a new vision---those now living will fail to create a state of being that meets the needs of the present generation without compromising the ability of future generations to meet their own needs. Those who have come to these stark conclusions are making a clarion call in favor of building a sustainable society. The first step in doing so is to acknowledge and understand the nature of the economic, social, environmental, and governance problems, and accept responsibility for them.

The contemporary reality is that many Americans and Floridians appear to be suffering from Toffler's "future shock", and many are in denial. But a slow turning toward more concern about sustainability is taking place. The question is whether the new emphasis will be of sufficient quality and pace to avert more disasters for the political economy, the natural environment and society in general.

The choice is not between econo-think or sustainability, but the best of the former blended with the latter. Sustainability will require a role for governments that runs counter to purest eco-think ideology. But sustainability also will demand from econo-think profitability and an emphasis on productivity and efficiency. We should not abandon business arrangements and approaches that have served society well. We should transform them and utilize them in building a sustainable society.

The public and non-profit sectors have much to learn from these private sector arrangements and approaches. For example, in the case of Florida, the talent for building livable communities and redeveloping existing ones using sustainability as an organizing guide resides primarily in the private sector. A sole reliance on increased government regulation would result in disaster, as Florida's experiment in growth management analyzed later will show. The public sector nevertheless has an essential role to play, as we shall see. With the reconciliation and synthesis of sustainability and econo-think, we also must come to understand how to create a workable blend of the talents, energies, roles and relationships of the sectors themselves.

We will present a more thorough explanation of these ideas in subsequent chapters and will examine the history of governmental reforms and the required shift from "bureaucratic government" to "sustainable governance". This shift involves the transition from the old to the new vision for Florida, from econo-think to sustainability; and from a decayed and corrupted political culture to citizenship and democracy practiced well. Narrow-minded and sanctimonious ideological prescriptions, political polarization and divisiveness or partisan bickering have no room in this shift. A full-blown crisis is upon us. It is time once again for Americans and Floridians to unite behind a common vision in the search for sustainable governance, as Winthrop promised, Jefferson hoped for when he penned the Declaration of Independence and as Lincoln accomplished through his leadership during the nation's darkest hour---to date.

California's system of taxation and spending is almost entirely hardwired into the Constitution. It produces wildly fluctuating revenue booms and busts that put state services on a cruel feast-or-famine roller coaster that drags the poor, the elderly, children and even the business community along for the painful ride. Similarly, local funding is hogtied to the state's, forcing our cities and counties to suffer as well from outdated laws in the Constitution.
—Jim Wunderman, president and CEO,
the Bay Area Council, San Francisco

Chapter IV

THE RECKONING:
TAXATION AND BUDGET TRENDS AND CONSEQUENCES

Overview

Florida state and local governments must take a strong leadership role in efforts to meet the requirements of the new vision, just as they did in realizing the old vision. The traditional role of government--- provision of infrastructure and services demanded by population growth---changes to a much broader set of organizing principles grounded in sustainability. A new emphasis is demanded on development of research and technology, social equity and justice, development of intellectual capital and the capacity for innovation, renewable energy, inter-modal transportation systems, and environmental restoration.

Some progress toward realization of features of the new vision has been made. According to the Chamber Foundation's New Cornerstone Report, Florida in recent years has attracted a few high-profile bioscience employers, including the Scripps Research Institute and the Burnham Institute for Medical Research.[84] Technology sector employment has increased, placing Florida fourth in the nation. There are many examples of more modest successes by local economic development organizations. The case examples presented in subsequent chapters reflect sustainability themes, and give glimpses of sustainable governance, the new leadership framework, and point to the new vision. But other signs are not so encouraging.

Leadership that transforms ideas about social advancement and charts a new course is unlikely to be simple or easy. For example, strategies that seek to overlay the economic component of the new vision onto the old one often run into both intellectual and political difficulties. Work force development questions plague many areas of the state where the labor pool is geared to real estate development and construction, agriculture, and the low end service jobs of a tourist-based economy.

Those invested in the status quo are often reluctant to embrace strategies that will retool the economy by diverting available labor to the higher paying and better jobs the new vision portends. When local business and civic leaders are spending their time and money trying to advance the enterprises of the old vision, it is difficult to muster political support to broaden to a new one. People who have built their livelihoods on the foundation of the old vision for Florida possess neither the knowledge nor the incentive to steer the economy away from familiar waters.

Public leaders often reflect these parochial and narrow-minded perspectives, refusing to cooperate with neighboring jurisdictions and protecting turf, as if they were in economic competition. Cities are fighting counties, both fighting the state government. This behavior does not advance Florida's new vision.

Florida's image as a vacation destination and retirement haven with an exploding population growth rate is not attractive to the global technology-driven, information-based enterprises the state covets. Relatively low rates of investment in public education and research also undermine realization of the new vision. The 2007 New Cornerstone Report found:

> Florida is spending much less than other states on research and development, patents issued to Florida businesses have remained flat and the state ranks 46th nationally in high school

graduation rates. Recruiting young graduates from other states has gotten tougher, and the production of college degrees has stagnated.[85] Over-crowded schools, congested highways, and high crime rates also pose significant barriers to achieving a meaningful transition to Florida's new vision.

Former Governor and U.S. Senator Bob Graham has spent much of his professional life supporting Florida higher education and economic development. He had this to say in a Time Magazine article published in 2008: "The decisions about relocating high-paying businesses are made by people who value education and Florida isn't ready for the modern economy."[86]

By 2009, with major cuts in higher education being planned by the Florida legislature, Florida International University President Modesto Maidique, told a journalist: "It takes generations to build universities, but they can be destroyed in a very short period of time."[87] The President of Florida State University, T. K. Wetherell, a former Speaker of the Florida House of Representatives, tendered his resignation in June 2009. Wetherell likely resigned because of his frustration with state spending cuts. He was widely quoted as having said, "I'm a builder, not an undertaker."

With an overwhelming emphasis on economic development, there is little attention to Florida's social and community development. The conviction that economic development will take care of the "social ecology" has emerged as the principal strategy. But the increasing income disparity among Florida's rich and poor in the face of the state's growing social problems demonstrates that the promise of the "trickle down" strategy has yet to reach Florida. Moreover, this "econo-think" strategy evinces an affinity for cheap and weak government that is likely to do more to maintain the old economy than to usher in a new one.

Florida has made strides in protection, acquisition and restoration of environmentally-sensitive lands through its Florida Forever and its fledgling partnership with the federal government on Everglades' restoration. The state's growth management and environmental regulatory programs also have made contributions, although many problems with these approaches remain as the next chapter will show.

Local governments also have much increasing progress during the past quarter century in placing high value on environmental issues.

While some recent progress has been made in moving to a state energy policy, the Florida legislature in its 2009 session failed to adopt renewable energy portfolio standards that require utilities providing electricity to achieve a percentage of energy produced from renewable sources. The ultimate outcome of this debate will teach much about Florida's commitment to the problems of climate change and to addressing dependence on fossil fuels, which has national security as well as environmental implications.

Many significant problems remain with the environmental component of Florida's sustainability vision. Among these problems are "...declining water tables, groundwater and surface water contamination, storm water and agricultural runoff, coastal problems such as sea level rise, salt water intrusion of water table, sea grass and fishery declines, dead zones and reef declines, growing congestion, air emissions, global warming, widespread mercury contamination of freshwater and saltwater fish, and other toxics in the food chain."[88] If trends continue, Florida could lose more than 7 million acres of natural land over the next 50 years.[89]

All three traditional components of sustainability---economic, social, and natural resource---are imperiled in contemporary Florida with only glimpses of progress toward a new vision. Meanwhile, as data in the next chapter will demonstrate, there is much evidence that Floridians are highly concerned about the negative impacts of rapid population growth, and blame growth for most of the problems facing the state.

As the collapse of consensus behind the old vision began to take hold at the end of the 20th Century, reforms of tax and budget policies, growth management, government structure, intergovernmental relationships, and other principal public policies were urged for placement on the Florida public policy agenda by many serious analysts. But the old consensus has died hard. Nearing the end of the first decade of the 21st Century, there was no substantive reform of the state's antiquated tax structure, and its budget was a study in chaos. On the eve of Florida's 2008 legislative session the St. Petersburg Times wrote, "The fourth-largest state's antiquated tax structure is ill-equipped for a service-based, global economy, yet there is no urgency in Tallahassee to fix it. A frank public discussion is needed about the widening gap between the state's aspirations and its cash flow. Yet Gov. Charlie Crist is in denial." [90]

There was widespread agreement that Florida's "growth management" experiment failed to live up to its promise, as examined in Chapter VI. Governmental reforms were largely sporadic and unsuccessful, as shown in Chapter VII. The looming national crisis in health care, especially for the medically indigent and working poor, continues to drain scarce state and local public resources; and, coupled with the health insurance crisis, poses significant humanitarian problems that threaten the quality of life for thousands of citizens. This is among a growing number of public policy challenges that threaten the viability of the new vision for a sustainable Florida. The grip of the old growth vision, and the principal public policies and governmental arrangements designed to support it, remains strong.

In recent years the fissures in the state's tax and budget, growth management policies and ways of governing have cracked wide open. They revealed public disaffection, intergovernmental conflict and uncertainty about the state's future direction. Collapse of the real estate market, soaring property insurance rates driven largely by the state's experience with hurricanes and tornadoes, and the inadequacies and inequities of tax and budget policies have combined with the national economic crisis to produce much political uncertainty and unhealthy conflict.

These could be signs that the old vision has finally run its course, and the birth pangs of the new vision are well underway. Or, these could open a dark chapter in Florida history heralded by a Wall Street Journal article, *Is Florida Over?*[91] An article in Time Magazine, published in July 2008, contributed these foreboding perspectives in "letter from Florida":

> ...{T}here's trouble in paradise. We're facing our worst real estate meltdown since the Depression. We've got a water crisis, insurance crisis, environmental crisis and budget crisis to go with our housing crisis. We're first in the nation in mortgage fraud, second in foreclosures, last in high school graduation

rates…We do wish you were here, because attracting outsiders has always been our primary economic engine, and our engine is sputtering… 'This may be our tipping point,' says former Senator Bob Graham.[92]

One thing appears certain: if the new vision is to be successful bold, innovative, and transformative public leadership will be demanded. Success will depend on crafting sustainable public policies; and new ways of governing. A major aspect of the challenge involves retooling tax and budget policies. These must be linked to the new economy so public revenues can be raised from it, and infrastructure and services can be put in place to support it. Quality attention must be given to all three main components of sustainability; and their interrelationships and impacts on each other must be understood. Because all of this must be accomplished first in a condition of transition from the old to the new vision, high levels of ambiguity, confusion, complexity, and conflict can be expected. On that score, Florida is off to a good start.

The Roots of Crisis and its Impacts

The description of California's tax and budget system referenced in the epigraph of this chapter applies to Florida as well. Florida's tax structure was designed purposely to support the old growth vision by attracting newcomers with promises of low taxes. There has never been a state income tax or inheritance tax. Per capita state and local taxes paid by Floridians rank the state 39th; and 47th in taxes paid as a percentage of personal income.[93] The state's dependence on transaction taxes is widely considered regressive. The poorest 20 percent of Floridians are taxed at nearly five times the rate of the richest 1 percent.

The tax structure also is overly sensitive to downturns in the economy. State revenue growth has fluctuated drastically from a high of 27 percent to a low of -3.5 percent in the last four decades.[94] Florida's sales tax is full of exemptions for politically powerful special interests.[95]

The property tax is guaranteed in the Constitution as a principal source of revenue for pubic schools and local governments. Property valuation exemptions for homesteads, senior citizens, agriculture, and businesses; millage limitations, assessment caps, and limitations on local government tax levies have combined to control the amount of property taxes schools and local governments may collect. Portability of the savings derived from existing residential assessment caps when homeowners move to a new homesteaded property produces widespread perceived inequities that have prompted serious litigation.

Property tax reform proposals dominated Florida's political landscape during 2008, promising consideration of more state-directed constraints on local taxation and budget practices. On the eve of the 2008 legislative session, tensions between state and local governments were high as state officials promised consideration of measures for more control over local tax and budget policy. Local governments claim erosion of home rule powers and the principle of representative democracy. Opinion research demonstrates that the Florida public was highly concerned about property taxes.[96] But it was unclear whether these concerns were grounded in perceptions of inequities, amounts of taxes being levied, economic uncertainty, local government spending practices, a desire to stimulate the economy through tax cuts, or a combination of these factors.

Meanwhile, during 2007-08, the Florida Taxation and Budget Reform Commission (TBRC), which is constituted each 20 years, was deliberating. Consensus in favor of substantive reform appeared unlikely, with the outcome of the Commission's work unclear. This much appeared certain: budget and tax reform policy was being established in isolation from the work of the TBRC in a fragmented and reactionary manner. There appeared to be an abundance of ignorance about the root causes of citizen concerns about tax and budget policies at the state and local levels of government; and about how reforms will impact public aspirations, needs, and values.

While the general picture remained much the same a year later, the intervening economic meltdown intensified the crisis and the conflict. There were few signs of strong public leadership on taxation and budget policy at the state level. The TBRC concluded its work in 2008 and was a dismal failure, as the account in the next chapter shows. The state budget was in a chaotic mess. Local governments and school districts were reeling from massive budget cuts, exhausting reserves and struggling to maintain legitimacy and relevance.

Florida voted for the winning candidate for President, Democrat Barack Obama in the 2008 national elections, who impressed many serious analysts and citizens alike with his plans to build a more bipartisan and sustainable approach to social advancement. But as the New Year dawned, the Governor and leaders of Florida's Republican controlled legislature continued their anti-tax and anti-government rhetoric grounded in the pure econo-think of supply-side economics. The new vision for a sustainable Florida seemed like a mirage.

The financial outlook for state government, the property tax reform debate, and Florida state and local tax and budget policies in general provide examples of misaligned leadership and unsustainable governance.

Tax and Budget Policies: Consequences of Imbalance

The Tallahassee Democrat newspaper made the following observation about the tax structure of the State of Florida:

> We are a big, growing, diverse state with strait-jacket revenue system based on a regressive, Swiss-cheese tax code. The sales tax, mainstay of our budget, is riddled with exemptions that were enacted not because they produce jobs or spur the economy, but because somebody hired the right lobbyists.[97]

Florida is behind most states' investments in public infrastructure and services. Moreover, Florida's tax structure does not produce revenues sufficient to keep pace with the service and infrastructure demands placed on state or local government. The respected Florida Chamber Foundation sponsored a study of Florida's ranking among the fifty states on various public financial and quality of life indicators. Here is a summary of that study's findings:

- Property taxes, the major source of local government revenues, as a percentage of personal income ranks Florida 31st among the states.
- Florida's dependence on the sales tax is legendary in its cyclical and regressive characteristics.

Sustainable Governance

- Problems of poverty and income inequity persist in Florida. Just 12 states have a more unequal distribution of income than Florida.
- Access to high-quality jobs remains a problem in Florida, which ranks 29th among the states by this measure.
- Just 56 percent of Florida students entering ninth grade graduate in four years. Just five states have lower graduation rates than Florida.
- Just under half of high school graduates in Florida pursue higher education, placing the state 43rd in ranking.
- Florida ranks 38th among the states in expenditures per pupil in public elementary and secondary schools, and 34th in education appropriations for higher education.
- The state ranks 48th nationwide in the number of scientists and engineers per million workers.
- University spending on research and development in Florida ranks 45th among the states.
- Highway congestion in Florida's major urban areas has increased significantly in recent years. In Orlando and Miami, the average person spends 42 hours each year stuck in traffic.
- The crime rate in Florida is the highest in the nation.

Most of these trends are getting worse, when compared to a decade ago.[98]

The state of Florida Long-Range Financial Outlook Report in 2007 made the following observation:

> In each year, projected expenditures are growing faster than revenues. The available general revenue is insufficient to meet budget demands in Fiscal Years 2009-10 and 2010-11 unless prior actions are taken to reduce the recurring and non-recurring budget needs in subsequent years. At the end of the three-year planning horizon, expenditures funded by general revenue have fully exceeded revenues, and no balance remains ... Corrective actions will be required to bring the budget into balance.
>
> Furthermore, <u>RECURRING</u> general revenue demands exceed the amount of <u>RECURRING</u> general revenue available

in each year of the forecast. **This indicates that a structural imbalance is occurring.** *(Emphasis added).* This situation cannot be addressed within the parameters of the constitutional amendment limiting the amount of non-recurring revenues that can be spent on recurring programs unless an extraordinary vote of the legislature is taken ... The current reserve is inadequate to address next year's shortfall – over 7.5% of the projected budget need – and other actions will be needed to keep the budget in balance as constitutionally required.[99]

The state's report analyzes the main drivers causing the projected imbalance:

Typically, the two principal economic measures are income and employment growth. Compared to the October 2006 Estimating Conference, these measures have shown that Florida grew at a slower pace than originally thought. Personal income growth, initially estimated at 7.5%, ultimately reached only 7.3% for Fiscal Year 2005-06 and dropped to 6.5% in Fiscal Year 2006-07. Similarly, employment achieved only 3.7% growth in Fiscal Year 2005-06, even though the forecast called for 3.8%, and further declined to a modest 1.8% rate in Fiscal Year 2006-07. **While many near-term projections were revised downward in the February 2007 forecast for 2006-07, the final results proved to be generally worse than anticipated – particularly in the housing-related areas.** *(Emphasis added).* For example, the number of private housing starts was reduced by 6.6% in February and then by another 3.3% in the following July.[100]

By January 2008, the Legislature's Office of Economic and Demographic Research (EDR) reported that conditions had worsened since the 2007 Financial Outlook Report analysis. In a presentation to the House Policy and Budget Council, the EDR observed that decreased levels of consumer confidence and reductions in consumer spending were affecting sales tax, documentary stamp/intangibles taxes, and corporate income tax receipts. The following quote summarized the growing problem:

State legislators learned Tuesday that they may have to reduce the current year's budget by as much as $600-million for two reasons: a prolonged economic slump shows no sign of ending and previous revenue forecasts, while conservative, have turned out to be overly optimistic. "At this point it's definitely prudent to start building a reserve or a hedge, against any further reduction in the forecast," state economist Amy Baker said in testimony before the House Policy and Budget Council, the committee that assembles the state budget. Baker ticked off a series of unfavorable economic trends in Florida, such as a slowdown in population growth, falling home prices, record high oil prices and a credit crunch in the financial markets. She even used the R-word: recession. "Housing downturns are frequently a precursor to a recession," Baker warned. She suggested that lawmakers set aside $400-million to $600-million to get through the rest of the fiscal year through June 30 based on sales and other state tax collections in the past two months that have fallen $98 million short of earlier forecasts. Cutting current services is one way to do that, but there are other ways. For legislators, the scenario has become depressingly familiar. They made $1.1-billion in spending cuts in the fall to bring the budget in line with declining revenue, and the latest fiscal outlook for next year projects the need for another $2-billion in cuts to get through June 2009.[101]

A year later, the situation had deteriorated further. The 2008 Outlook Report, issued in December, contained the following dismal news: the revenue shortfall through June 30 is expected to be $2.2 billion in the current 2008-09 Fiscal Year. This represents a $150-million increase in just a matter of weeks due mostly to soaring health care costs. Without prompt action, Florida's bond rating could be downgraded, raising the cost of managing the state's debt by up to $150-million more a year.

The principal strategy offered by Governor Charlie Crist for addressing the crisis emerged as follows: Redirect trust fund dollars -- set aside to pay for programs such as affordable housing -- to the state's general-revenue checking account; make permanent the 4 percent holdbacks in agency budgets ordered earlier in the year; raid the Lawton Chiles Endowment Fund that pays for children's health care; and drain the last $681 million from Florida's "rainy day" fund.

Crist proposed more budget cuts, more borrowing, increased fees and some agency reorganization. In the language of a true "econo-thinker" Crist proclaimed: "Everybody knows we can be more efficient." Crist has said he wants lawmakers to return to balance this year's budget as soon as possible before the next regular legislative session, when law makers will be forced to consider cutting some $5.8 billion out of next year's spending plan.[102] A special legislative session was called for January, 2009.

Starving the Beast

The Republican leadership took the position as a matter of philosophy during the decade ending in 2009 that virtually any option that results in new revenues---such as removal of existing exemptions on the sales tax---amounts to a tax increase. If this logic is followed, the only "reform" option left as a practical matter is to do nothing but cut budgets, and let the "beast of government starve to death" as existing revenues and reserves bleed out along with the economic vitality of the state.

This seemingly draconian (in the eyes of more moderate thinkers) course of action is entirely logical to arch-conservatives who, in literal interpretation of the rhetoric of the inerrant Ronald Reagan, adhere to the bedrock principle that "government is the problem" and "the enemy." This fundamental position, according to arch-conservative ideology, will steal the lifeblood from the beast, render it impotent as a threat, and destroy the vitality of any counter belief that government can be a positive force in society if funding levels are not allowed to render its role irrelevant.

This is the species of "econo-think" contemplated in the last chapter that appears to be cut off from the American philosophical tradition of both political parties prior to the Reagan era. It is the ideological legacy left by former Governor Jeb Bush who governed from his principles, led others to do the same, and punished those who failed to toe the line.

If these arch conservative econo-thinkers began to retreat from principle during the heat of the present budget battles, they likely will be treated by their fellows as devoid of the courage of conviction.

Whether the change of direction signaled by the Florida public in the 2008 Presidential election will have any effect on the thinking of the state's Republican leadership remained to be seen. Perhaps the sheer intensity of the budget crisis would cause some change of direction, but this was not indicated in early 2009. The underlying consequences of this ideological approach for the new vision of a "sustainable Florida" will be examined in subsequent chapters.

A newspaper article reported the following key facts about Florida's budget crisis:

- Up to 147,000 state workers could face two-week furloughs for a savings of up to $300-million.
- Parts of prison yards are already being converted into tent cities.
- Crime is rising and so is the prison population, by about 6 percent yearly.
- Re-offender rate of ex-inmates is 32 percent, meaning one of every three inmates returns to a Florida prison within three years of release.
- The population of the Florida prison system will soon cross the 100,000 threshold for the first time.
- Florida is pitching tents at a dozen low-security prison work camps — most of them in rural North Florida — to house an excess of prisoners, and erecting four modular prison wings in northwest Florida.

Property values are forecast to plummet during 2009 by $266-billion. Schools statewide could lose $780-million next year, if property tax rates hold. Medicaid is costing the state $146-million more than anticipated this year.[103]

During the 2009 special session, legislators cut the budget an additional $2.4 billion, and were facing a $3.5 billion shortfall in the 2009-2010 budget. A slow turning of approach, examined in the next chapter, appeared to be in the making as the gravity of the crisis become clear.[104] Governor Crist, who observers suggest has a knack for accurately gauging political winds, vetoed $365 million of the legislature's cuts. A newspaper article reported, "Gov. Charlie Crist restored about $365 million in budget cuts Tuesday, sparing politically popular programs while straining relations with Republican legislators whose decisions he vetoed. Crist said he "resurrected" teacher merit pay, tourism promotion and the Florida Forever environmental land-buying program because the cuts the Legislature made "would have negatively impacted the people of our state."[105]

The 2009 legislature marked the first time since the Bush era of ideology began with his first election as governor in 1998 that increased taxes and fees were seriously considered. During that session, law makers balanced the budget with $5 billion in federal stimulus money, depletion of reserves and $2.2 billion of increases in scores of fees and taxes. [106]

Florida's budget woes have been latent for years. During the first half of the present decade it was averted by a robust construction industry driven mostly by spikes in the residential housing market. By mid-decade, there were signs of the impending crisis, which by 2008 had erupted.

A study sponsored by the Florida Chamber Foundation found the following:

- Strong population and economic growth is increasing the burden on Florida's transportation, energy, and water systems. Significant investments will be required to support present needs and future growth ... Sprawl threatens farmland, environmental resources, and water supply.
- State and local taxes as a percent of personal income in Florida are lower than all but twelve states.
- Increased transportation funding will still not able to reduce backlog; congestion continues to rise in urban areas and on interregional corridors ...The Florida Department of Transportation estimates that delay on the state's major highways is increasing about 6 percent per year. An estimated 34 percent of major urban roads are congested during peak periods, an amount that will only grow in future years. Major

airports and seaports also face capacity constraints, while rail and transit offer a competitive choice for moving people or goods only in limited parts of the state. High home prices, rising congestion, spike in urban crime rates raise concerns.
- Florida's quality of life has long been a key contributor to its success, helping attract new residents and visitors to the state. Rising costs and the negative impacts of strong population growth are raising questions about whether Florida's communities will remain livable in the future.
- Florida's health and wellness remains a concern. Florida ranks among the bottom quartile of states for employer health coverage, access to health professionals, and the number of uninsured low-income children; and among the bottom half of states for infant mortality.[107]

The Property Tax Debate

Local government spending practices in Florida have attracted much attention. Many state elected leaders and their staffs have developed a view of local governments as being wasteful. They point to the recent years' spikes in property valuations, suggesting that local governments received a wind-fall in revenues, and spent money irresponsibly.

While there may be exceptions in individual cases, the facts in general point in a different direction. A study of Florida county expenditure and revenue trends by economist Hank Fishkind found that in spite of spikes in home values in fiscal years 1999-2005 "... [The] combination of population growth and price inflation caused total expenses to increase by about the same amount as property taxes increased."[108] The same general trends likely hold true for Florida cities.

It is instructive that the state of Florida's total budget nearly doubled, from approximately $35 billion to $74 billion, during the economically strong eight years leading up to the election of the incumbent governor in 2006.[109] State government debt swelled from $13-billion to $24-billion in the decade ending in 2008. During the 2001-2006 period the legislature significantly cut taxes but also spent money faster than the state collected it. General revenue spending over this five-year period rose 8.8 percent; meantime, tax collections rose by 6.6 percent.[110]

State government experienced the same surge in revenues as local governments, and made the same decision to spend the money on services and infrastructure needs driven by population growth. State expenditures, like those of local governments, also increased in response to rising costs. Figure #11 shows the trends in the state's budget:

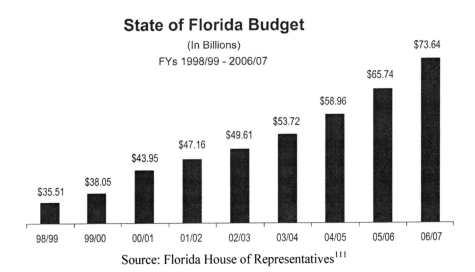

Source: Florida House of Representatives[111]

The inequities of the state's property tax policies are well-known. The combination of the homestead exemptions and Save Our Homes Constitutional guarantees shifts the tax burdens to business and commercial properties, and creates inequities among homeowners.

As the housing market began to sour during 2006-07, the swollen tax bases from the good times began to shrink. Predictably, calls for property tax reforms escalated. A Leadership Florida poll conducted in late 2007 found that property taxes were considered the most important statewide issue, and the least fair of Florida government revenue sources.[112] Legislative leaders responded with various property tax reform proposals, shifting the debate away from the general deficiencies of Florida's tax structure and the state's budget crisis.

One of these proposals, "Amendment 1," made its way onto the ballot in the form of a Constitutional amendment courtesy of the Florida Legislature. The measure was adopted by the voters of Florida on January 29, 2008. The amendment doubles to $50,000 the homestead exemption for city, county, and special districts. However, the original $25,000 exemption still applies to school taxes. It also grants the ability of homeowners who move to carry to new residences the assessment cap protections of the existing Save Our Homes Constitutional guarantee (up to $500,000). Businesses will receive a new $25,000 exemption for tangible personal property. Finally, the amendment grants the owners of non-homestead property a 10 percent cap on their annual assessments, but savings cannot be applied to school tax rates, nor is the savings portable. The amendment took effect in 2009.[113]

The story is worth telling of Florida's experience with property tax reform and the mounting budget crisis during 2008. The story includes lessons about the quality of leadership offered by Florida's business lobby, legislative leadership, and governor. The experience of the Taxation and Budget Reform Commission during 2008 will be told in the next chapter, where more insight into the character of the state's leadership will be seen.

During late 2007 it became clear that regardless of the outcome of the referendum on Amendment 1 (to be held the following January), the Florida business lobby would be back before the Legislature during the 2008 session wanting more property tax relief. Business and real estate interests poured $4.1 million into the campaign to persuade voters to support the amendment. Their opponents, including the Florida Education Association, the Florida Professional Firefighters and the Florida League of Cities, raised a little more than $2 million.[114]

According to a newspaper article, "... the prevailing strategy among the state's business establishment is to tacitly endorse the January ballot measure in hopes their needs will be addressed in the 2008 legislative session."[115] During the past two decades, property valuations for businesses have exceeded 10 percent only three times -- in 2004, 2005 and 2006. More double digit increases during the immediate years ahead are unlikely.[116]

The incumbent governor and speaker of the house supported the referendum aggressively on their conviction that tax cuts will help spur Florida's sputtering economy. Both are adherents of "supply side economics," a part of the "econo-think" ideological legacy left to Florida by former Governor Jeb Bush.

By January 2008, the new budget forecast may have prompted a change of strategy among some alarmed business leaders who had pushed for property tax cuts beyond the reform proposal:

> The situation became so dire that a series of business leaders, who in rosier economic times often plead for less government spending, urged council members to ramp up state appropriations for roads and economic development projects that they said would create jobs and kick-start the economy.[117]

Meanwhile, the property tax reform proposal was not received well by Florida newspaper editorial boards. An article in the Sarasota Herald Tribune summed up the problem with precision:

> ... (T)he proposal and process that led to it fail the tests of good government and effective leadership. The amendment would not solve the most pressing problems related to property taxes, yet it would compound other problems. Furthermore, it is designed to appeal to the self-interests of a specific group of taxpayers -- property owners with homestead exemptions -- at the cost of other taxpayers and with little consideration of the social and economic impacts statewide...TaxWatch, an organization funded by businesses, points to another shortcoming: If the tax cuts contained in the amendment are approved by voters in January, reforming Florida's antiquated, inadequate and unfair tax system will become more difficult, if not impossible ... "Quite frankly, we may have seen the best that this institution -- the House and Senate together -- can do on this," House Speaker Marco Rubio said. This may be the best the House and Senate and governor can produce, but Floridians and their constitution deserve better.[118]

The St. Petersburg Times wrote:

> A panicked, desperate Florida legislature squandered a golden opportunity to lead the way toward meaningful tax reform and significant relief for taxpayers who need it most. The constitutional amendment it placed on the January ballot costs too much for too little gain and creates more inequities in a property tax system that already is grossly unfair. It lacks vision and focus, and Floridians deserve better.[119]

The editorial concluded: "Unveiling a new constitutional amendment on Sunday afternoon and forcing an all-or-nothing vote before dark on Monday is no way to provide voters an opportunity to create a fairer, more reasonable property tax system. Floridians deserve better."

Meanwhile during January 2008, Florida House Speaker Mario Rubio, (R-Miami) expressed disappointment the Constitutional amendment failed to reduce property taxes sufficiently. He refused to support the consensus reached by the legislature, and advocated a citizen petition to amend the state Constitution and cap all property taxes at 1.35 percent of taxable value on any parcel of property.[120] Rubio's plan would offer a 26 percent average property tax cut statewide. "This plan is simple, it applies to all properties, it keeps Save Our Homes, and it cuts almost $8-billion in property taxes," Rubio said."[121] The plan would keep in place the existing $25,000 exemption on homesteaded property. Rubio's plan failed to meet a deadline to gain the signatures needed to call a referendum in 2008, but his petition drive could continue with a 2010 referendum target.

Rubio is widely perceived as a political protégé of former Governor Jeb Bush, known for his arch conservative political and economic philosophies. Rubio has been described as

> ...charismatic, quick-witted and a polished orator, [who] takes his philosophical cues from former Governor Jeb Bush, a fiscal and social conservative. They remain close ... Rubio wants to shrink government. The $2-billion deficit is an opportunity, he says, to cut government to a more manageable

size. He wants to eliminate some state agencies and has named his top priority as a cap on government spending and revenue. He is also helping gather support for a citizens' petition to cap property taxes at 1.35 percent of taxable value.[122]

Rubio drew a strong rebuke from the Tallahassee Democrat columnist Mary Ann Lindley:

> Rubio's lack of seasoning and public policy sophistication reared its head again last week when he commented that he saw "an opportunity for agency eliminations" during the economic slowdown we're experiencing. This had to be demoralizing for a state work force already squeezed to the bone, getting no pay raise last year and expecting the same expression of appreciation this year. Morale is so bad in agencies, which carry out state laws that the Department of Management Services is worried how it's going to hang on to high quality public-sector employees or recruit new ones.[123]

She characterized Rubio's positions as "... ideological sputtering that Rubio seems to think will sell well with his Coral Gables district — and with the party leaders, state and national, with whom he obviously likes to curry favor."[124]

Rubio's proposal would devastate many cities and counties, and likely place some of them in the same kind of structural imbalance facing the budget of the state of Florida.

A Departure from 'No New Taxes'?

On the eve of the 2008 legislative session, a new budget forecast was expected with more bad news. There were signs that a major lobbyist for business interests believed Florida's deteriorating economy needed stimulus from public sector spending. In this departure from strict allegiance to the tenets of supply side economics, the head of the powerful Associated Industries of Florida, Barney Bishop, expressed the following views: "Growth is really the fourth leg of our economy ... yet we have a $30 billion infrastructure backlog. At that rate ... the center cannot hold; economic stimulus is essential."[125] The forecasts continued to worsen through the balance of 2008. Budget cuts by September would rise to $6 billion during the year past with deeper cuts likely.

These business leaders may have been influenced by an analysis of state and local taxation and budget policy published in an article by the non-partisan Center on Budget and Policy Priorities:

> ...(E)conomists ...have argued that California, Florida and Nevada are already experiencing regional recessions ...Policymakers sometimes contend that the weakness of the economy means that a state should rely solely on cutting spending, rather than raising taxes. The aversion to raising taxes during a recession, however, rests on a misconception of economic effects. Two highly regarded economists -- Nobel Prize winner Joseph Stiglitz of Columbia University, and Peter Orzag, now the director of the Congressional Budget Office -- wrote during the last recession that spending cuts could actually be *more* harmful for a state's economy during an economic downturn than tax increases. This assertion still holds true, whether or not the nation is deemed to be in an official recession.[126]

The author of the article concludes by stating:

> As legislatures begin their 2008 sessions and begin to consider how to balance their budgets in difficult economic times, they should take seriously the Stiglitz-Orzag admonition that tax increases, particularly tax increases on higher-income families, may be the best available option.[127]

Stigliz expanded his argument in a newspaper article published in September, 2008. The exchange with the reporter's questioning reflected in the article indicates that while business leaders may be listening to him, state elected leaders are not. The article states:

> Economists say...that Florida's economic health may depend on state leaders' willingness to move beyond one of the most

fundamental fault lines dividing them...."Tax increases would not in general be more harmful to the economy than spending reductions," Nobel Prize-winning economist Joseph Stiglitz argued in 2001 during the post-9/11 economic downturn. A professor at Columbia University, Stiglitz said in an interview last week that his 2001 analysis holds equally true for states today - and where individual states go, so goes the country, affecting all taxpayers. "Congress enacted a $150 billion stimulus package. That will all be undone if the states contract their spending," he said. State spending flows directly into a state's economy, Stiglitz reasoned, supporting jobs and local businesses. Wealthy taxpayers, on the other hand, tend to save more of their incomes than other people do, bringing the economist to his next point. "If you increase taxes on upper-income individuals, it has the least effect on consumption," he said. "Poor people consume every dollar they get, unlike rich people who don't." Absent an income tax, Stiglitz said, one of the easiest ways to tax the rich is to increase property taxes on a state's priciest residences.

The response from incoming House Speaker Ray Sansom, R-Destin, is revealing: "I admire a Nobel Prize winner, but if he ran for office, I promise you, he'd change his mind."[128]
There are other indications that rethinking of the belief in the benefits of tax cuts in all situations may be occurring. The New York Times conservative journalist David Brooks offered the following insights in his column:

> Supply-side economics had a good run, but continual tax cuts can no longer be the centerpiece of Republican economic policy. The demographics have changed. The U.S. is an aging society. We have made expensive promises to our seniors. We can't keep those promises at the current tax levels, let alone at reduced ones. As David Frum writes in "Comeback," his indispensable new book: "In the face of such a huge fiscal gap, the days of broad, across-the-board, middle-class tax cuts are over[129]."

The tide seemed to have turned at the national level by January 2009 at a conference of the nation's top economists in San Francisco. A newspaper article reported from the American Economic Association conference:

> Frightened by the recession and the credit crisis that produced it, the nation's mainstream economists are embracing public spending to repair the damage — even those who have long resisted a significant government role in a market system... Hundreds of economists who gathered here for the annual meeting of the American Economic Association seemed to acknowledge that a profound shift had occurred..."The new enthusiasm for fiscal stimulus, and particularly government spending, represents a huge evolution in mainstream thinking," said Janet Yellen, president of the Federal Reserve Bank of San Francisco. She added that the shift was likely to last for as long as the profession is dominated by men and women living through this downturn.[130]

Apparently, Frum's book has not been widely read among Florida's top political leaders, nor do they appear to have internalized the shift in the thinking of the nation's economists. It is also doubtful that the analyses by Stiglitz, Orzag, and increasingly other respected economists will be heeded by the Governor, Speaker of the House of Representatives and other conservative leaders, as Samson's remarks confirm. Throughout 2008 and into 2009 they appeared to be so committed to the precepts of supply side economics that a change of direction was highly unlikely.

Consequences of the Economic Meltdown

Property tax reforms notwithstanding, during the period 2007-09, market forces hit state and local government and school district revenue streams hard. Declining sales of existing homes, increases in the number of mortgage foreclosures, and reductions in values devastated tax bases. The Florida Association of Realtors reported in December 2007, that existing home sales were down 30 percent statewide and the median price -- half sold for more, half for less -- fell 10 percent to $215,800.[131] Condo foreclosures were especially troublesome.

As this disturbing picture unfolded, another was in the making. Florida lost 17,500 construction jobs during 2007. It was the first time that sector has lost workers since 1992, according to the Florida Agency for Workforce Innovation. The Miami Herald reported, "In the Panhandle, the state's largest private landholder, St. Joe Co., announced that it was ending its new home construction efforts, laying off 760 workers -- more than 75 percent of its workforce -- and trying to sell 100,000 acres of land."[132] The same day the New York Times wrote:

> As construction and real estate spiral downward, the unemployment rate in Lee County has jumped to 5.3 percent from 2.8 percent in the last year. With more than one-fourth of all homes vacant, residential burglaries throughout the county have surged by more than one-third ... The county's Department of Human Services has seen a substantial increase in applications for a program that helps pay rent and utility bills for those in need. Half the applicants say they have lost jobs or seen their work hours reduced ... Many others are in similar straits, and the situation has had a ripple effect on the local economy.[133]

Lee County, located on the state's southwest coast, by 2009 had become Florida's "ground zero." The county lost a higher percentage of jobs (8.8 percent) from June 2007 to June 2008 than any other in the nation. Its unemployment rate had reached 9.8 percent by November 2008, up from 3.5 percent eighteen months earlier.

By February 2009, a newspaper article published a story about a section of that county reflecting the growing impact of the economic crisis: "In Lehigh Acres, homes are selling at 80 percent off their peak prices. Only two years after there were more jobs than people to work them, fast-food restaurants are laying people off or closing. Crime is up, school enrollment is down, and one in four residents received food stamps in December, nearly a fourfold increase since 2006."

The story captures the essence of the collapse of Florida's old growth vision and the public's desire for a new one: "...in church groups and offices, people call for "industry" and repeat one telling question: What do we want to be when we grow up?...That's one of the things we struggle with: What is our identity?" said Joseph Whalen, 37, president of the Lehigh Acres Chamber of Commerce. "We don't want to be...the foreclosure capital."[134]

Many other Florida counties report similar economic trends. By the end of 2008, the following economic indicators were reported:

- Home foreclosures remained the second-highest in the nation in October; home builders are sitting on a surplus of some 300,000 homes.
- Net migration into Florida has gone flat; after hovering around 2 percent through the 1990s, population growth has fallen to 0.7 percent this year.
- Statewide property values are forecast to plummet by a total of $266-billion — an 11 percent decrease — next year.
- If property tax rates hold the same next year, that could cost schools a total of $780-million statewide.
- Virtually all tax collections are falling, from sales to corporate income taxes.[135]

There was even more disturbing news. Florida was leading the nation in job losses as the national economy tanked.

> Florida lost more jobs in November than any other state as the pain that started in home construction continued spreading to other parts of the economy.
>
> The state's employment level fell by 58,600 workers from October, according to federal numbers released Friday. Florida's unemployment rate rose to 7.3 percent, the highest since June 1993 and well above the national rate of 6.7 percent for November.

That translates to 680,000 jobless Floridians out of a work force of 9.3-million.[136] By March 2009, Florida's unemployment rate had risen to 9.7 percent or 893,000 jobless out of a statewide workforce of 9.2 million.[137]

A news article reported in March 2009, "Florida's property values are crashing so precipitously that schools statewide will likely collect nearly $1 billion less next year, according to new economic forecasts."[138]

A snap shot of the state's construction industry was taken at the end of the second quarter of 2009 by the University of Central Florida's Institute for Economic Competitiveness. It reported that housing construction was down 87% from 2005 to the second quarter of 2009 and that the housing sector continued to lose jobs in 2009 at a double digit pace.[139]

Substantive tax reform that strengthens the state's tax structure by producing increased revenues from new, more stable, equitable, and sustainable sources apparently is politically counter-intuitive to many Florida elected officials. A predictable response is the one made by Speaker Rubio: slash existing taxes to jump start the economy.

The interesting thing about this ideological response is that the tax cuts being offered up are the major revenue source of politically vulnerable school districts and local governments. Cuts in taxes imposed by state government are not being proposed; nor has much attention been paid to the impacts of downgrades in state budget forecasts and the resulting spending reductions on local agencies. Some analysts have concluded that local agencies have become scapegoats as the harsh consequences of weaknesses in Florida's tax structure are experienced during a weak economy.[140]

The impacts of these cuts were being reckoned with in the wake of the passage of Amendment 1, the worsening crisis in the state budget, and the meltdown in the U.S. economy. After passage of Amendment 1, public dialogue and most media reports were focused on the impacts of property tax cuts in local areas, and the efforts of local governments and school districts to cope. The broader context of the impacts of taxation and budget policies and reforms at both the state and local levels and how these interrelate were not well appreciated.

State budget reductions have direct impacts on local governments and schools and through state revenue streams flowing to them for direct expenditure. These state and local taxation and budget interrelationships are complex and subtle. For example, reductions in the state corrections budget have cascading effects on county governments, which fund corrections facilities at the local level. If state prisons are over-crowded, the inmate population of local corrections facilities increases, along with costs.

Cuts in state health and human services funding affect county human services budgets and non-profit providers of services that are often funded by both county and state governments. The nature and degree of impacts also is influenced by the specter of increased state mandates requiring local governments to provide and pay for services that traditionally were state responsibilities.

Finally, a deteriorating economy results in impacts to both state and local services. Tax bases diminish, and often demands on law enforcement and human services increase when the economy takes a nose dive. All these impacts drive costs up while revenues decline, an unsustainable fiscal condition that ultimately must result in either increases in taxes or reductions in services. Neither choice is attractive.

Confronting the Consequences

A list of impacts from state budget cuts on state responsibilities began to take shape by the end of the first quarter of 2008, as that Florida legislative session began. One of the harshest debates surrounded the effects of reductions to budgets of the state's universities proposed by the governor. Conflict between the governor and university presidents escalated. The student-faculty ratio in Florida is the highest in the nation, the Bachelor's degrees production rate is 46th in the nation, and only one of the state's 11 universities is ranked in U.S. News & World Report's national top 100.[141]

An editorial in the St. Petersburg Times commented:

> The amount of money the state spends on each university student has dropped by a fourth in the past two decades, and the system is facing the additional loss of hundreds of millions of dollars. This crisis is no illusion ... The university presidents are telling the truth, every dispiriting bit of it. The governor and the legislature should listen.[142]

In an exchange that revealed the quality and intensity of the conflict over higher education spending, the editorial reported that "... Charlie

Crist told a Times reporter ... when asked about the presidents' financial worries, 'If they're unhappy, maybe they ought to turn the reins over to somebody else.'"[143] This exchange teaches that one of the negative impacts of Florida's taxation and budget crisis is on relationships among state leaders.

The crisis worsened during 2008. A newspaper article reported the following in November:

> Florida never will realize its potential and Floridians will never be competitive for high-wage jobs if the state's university system is allowed to continue to slip. Only the University of Florida ranks among the top 50 universities, and the state ranks near the bottom in the production of bachelor's degrees. The economic crisis and declining tax revenues already have forced more than $130-million in cuts to universities since last year and faculty members are fleeing to North Carolina and other states with stronger commitments to higher education. As college applications continue to rise, the universities have been forced to reduce staff, freeze or reduce enrollments and increase class sizes. It is not a prescription for success.

Governor Crist in response to intense lobbying from the Council of 100 and other business groups agreed in late 2008 to propose that the state's 11 state universities be granted the power to raise tuition by up to 15 percent a year without having to go through the Legislature.[144]

At the local level, property tax cuts likely will be counterproductive and abounding with unintended consequences. Slashing these taxes will do little to help Florida's construction and tourism-based economy or usher in the new economic development opportunities the state covets. If the analysis by Stiglitz and Orzag is correct, Florida's strategy probably will backfire.

If funding levels for basic services and infrastructure are substantially reduced at the local level, construction activity may slow down even further. This is because Florida's growth management law requires that infrastructure and services necessitated by new development must be made available concurrent with the developments' impacts. Local governments starved of revenue sources will have difficulty meeting these service and infrastructure requirements.

Provision of an array of services demanded by residents and visitors alike will be damaged. Local funding for new economic development incentives including infrastructure improvements will be diminished or lost altogether.

Meanwhile, the problems underpinning the state government's structurally imbalanced budget go unaddressed. The picture likely will get worse because downturns in construction in Florida reverberate through the economy, and choke-off the state's public revenues. In Florida, "the worse it gets, the worse it gets." The state's present taxation and budget strategy fuels the downward spiral, and is for that reason unsustainable.

The impacts will be experienced differently across Florida. There are pockets of urbanized Florida that will be able to weather the most intense impacts of property tax reform and reductions in the state's budget. Relatively high income areas with new housing stock, strong commercial and retail tax bases will embrace reforms that cut taxes. These areas can afford to answer the popular promise of lower taxes seemingly without suffering the consequences of damage to public services and infrastructure.

Many exclusive communities have private arrangements for basic services, including security, recreation, and infrastructure maintenance, and will not directly experience these service level reductions when property taxes are slashed. But much of Florida does not enjoy these advantages. The state's less fortunate residents are vulnerable to the consequences of public service delivery systems robbed of their capacity to meet serious human needs.

Some communities are highly dependent on property taxes as a percentage of all revenues. These jurisdictions often have an associated dependence on the residential housing component of the tax base. Others are less dependent on property taxes to fund governmental services, and may also enjoy relatively stronger commercial and retail tax base components.

These are reasons why a "one-size-fits-all" property tax reduction scheme imposed from the "top-down" is irrational for Florida, and likely will produce many unintended consequences. One consequence is that individual local governments that are well-managed, frugal, and in touch with the needs, aspirations, and values of local citizens are penalized by an indiscriminate policy.

The spirit of representative democracy is quenched when local self-determination is frustrated in this way. A "tyranny of the majority" is imposed when a statewide referendum authorized by the legislature and advocated by state elected leaders is adopted. This undermines the capacity of individual local government units to perform their responsibilities. This is especially true when the reform attempts exacerbate the deficiencies and inequities of existing policy problems, as is the case with Amendment 1.

The following relevant quote is taken from the classic essay *On Liberty,* written by the English philosopher John Stuart Mill (1806-1873) and published in 1859:

> Society can and does execute its own mandates; and if it issues wrong mandates instead of right, or any mandates at all in things with which it ought not to meddle, it practices a social tyranny more formidable than many kinds of political oppression …There is a limit to the legitimate interference of collective opinion with individual independence; and to find that limit, and maintain it against encroachment, is as indispensable to a good condition of human affairs as protection against political despotism.[145]

Americans decided long before Mills wrote his famous essay that taxation policy unchecked by direct election of the representatives who establish it is unacceptable. Those who promote establishment of local taxation and budget policies from the state level (no matter how popular, ideologically pure, or expedient these policies are) likely will learn this lesson of democracy when the full effect of their actions becomes apparent. When services and infrastructure needs go unmet in otherwise well-governed counties, cities, and towns across the state, the present obsession with tax cuts likely will lose its fascination. The relevant question is how much damage will be done in the interim.

Local governments and school districts that are not frugal and in touch with the needs, aspirations and values of the local citizenry, will be forced to re-evaluate their mode of governing. That may be a positive effect of property tax reforms. But even in those instances where school districts and local governments are spend-thrift and acting irresponsibly, the local political system should be trusted to do a better job of correcting unsustainable behavior than a top-down, state-driven approach.

Every citizen of Florida, regardless of wealth and place of residence, has a fundamental self-interest in ensuring that area-wide public infrastructure and especially health and human services and public safety do not decline to unacceptable levels. Existing cuts in federal, state, and local funds for health care, transportation of the sick and disadvantaged, community development of impoverished areas, treatment of substance abuse and the mentally ill, and child abuse and neglect produce consequences that affect all Floridians, regardless of wealth and station in life.

During 2007, 2008, and into 2009 we interviewed local government, school district and non-profit providers of many public safety, and health and human services about the impacts of state and local taxation and budget policies and reforms. A seize mentality had developed among many providers as the consequences of economic downturns (including escalating numbers of people without health insurance), funding cuts, and the impending tax and budget crisis formed a "perfect storm." School districts were being hit especially hard because of the combined effects of Amendment 1, declining state-shared revenues and flat-lined or decreasing student enrollments. In Volusia County, for example, school officials report they are at a "breaking point":

> "I fear for our children's future," School Board Chairwoman Diane Smith said. "We are at a point we cannot deliver the education these children deserve. We need to come up with solutions."
>
> The School Board cut $45.7 million in programs and personnel -- including 220 teachers -- this summer and wiped out its reserves to balance the $474 million operating budget in light of state funding reductions, declining enrollment and rising operational costs.

A continuing slide in tax collections because of the slumping economy sparked another $8.3 million state funding cut, and district officials are bracing for up to another $10 million in cuts before June with the financial prospects for the next school year even worse.[146]

Health care providers nationally, especially public hospitals that serve the medically indigent, are under severe fiscal duress. Many will be forced to reduce health services or compromise care. Some, as recently witnessed in Atlanta, (Georgia's Grady Hospital) and in Los Angeles, may be compelled to close their doors. "Once admired for its skill in treating a population afflicted by both social and physical ills, Grady, a teaching hospital, now faces the prospect of losing its accreditation," the New York Times reported. "Only short-term financial transfusions have kept it from closing its doors, as Martin Luther King Jr. - Harbor Hospital in Los Angeles County did last year. That scenario would flood the region's other hospitals with uninsured patients and eliminate the training ground for one of every four Georgia doctors."[147]

Florida certainly is not immune from this public health care nightmare.

By mid-summer 2008, Miami's Jackson Hospital was experiencing similar problems. An article published in the Miami Herald reported:

"Ongoing and future funding constraints on Jackson Health System are threatening its 90-year open-door mission. The health system needs to fill a $200 million gap in its budget this year. President and Chief Executive Officer Marvin O'Quinn believes it can be done. But next year, he said it's "highly unlikely." In 2010, he thinks it won't happen. And by 2011 or 2012, short of changing the public hospital's mission, "we won't be able to make payroll," Mr. O'Quinn said. Public hospitals nationwide face the same problems, he told Miami-Dade County commissioners this week: More uninsured patients, declining reimbursements and a souring economy. "People say county hospitals can't close. Well they can and they do," he said, pointing to DC General Hospital, Philadelphia General Hospital and others."[148]

Jackson Heath System's problems may be a harbinger of things to come in other Florida public hospitals. The state has the fourth largest number of non-elderly adults (under 65 and non-Medicare eligible) in the nation, and, among this population, the highest percentage (50.5%) of uninsured in the United States.[149] Florida is second in the nation in the percentage of the total population (21.2%) that is uninsured.[150]

Medicaid services are the primary driver of increases in the state's health and human services spending, the state match acting as a vortex that saps revenue from other needed health and human services. According to the state's 2008 Financial Outlook Report, Medicaid is the second largest single program in the state budget behind public education, representing 23.2% of the total state budget, and is the largest source of federal funding for the state. Medicaid recurring general revenue expenditures are consuming a growing share of recurring general revenue funds appropriated, increasing to 17.1% in Fiscal Year 2008-09.

The 2008 Outlook Report includes an increase in general revenue funds for Medicaid expenditures of $221.6 million in Fiscal Year 2009-10, $167.2 million in Fiscal Year 2010-11 and $404.1 million in Fiscal Year 2011-12.

The following trends were reported to state leaders by legislative staff on December 10, 2008:

- Medicaid rolls are skyrocketing during the 2008-09 fiscal year by 100,000 new recipients as the economy worsens, costing the state $146-million more than anticipated this budget year, which ends June 30.
- The higher Medicaid costs are to blame for the widening deficit.
- Next budget year, legislators could have to spend $346-million more than anticipated for Medicaid alone.[151]

Law enforcement and corrections personnel are reeling from the onslaught of increased criminal activity that routinely follows deteriorated economic conditions, and are bracing for more. Mental health providers report that lack of funds for counseling and medications are leaving many very sick people without the care needed to prevent the egregious consequences of mental illness, including suicide and violent criminal acts. Many mentally ill people are ending up in jails because alternative treatment programs have been cut with little hope of necessary increased funding commitments. According to research done by Florida Partners in Crisis, Florida's jails and prisons incarcerate more than ten times the number being treated in state forensic mental health facilities, at a cost fifteen times greater than treatment in the community.[152] (Refer to case example in Chapter VIII for more information).

Funding problems, especially for health and human services, have been around for a long time, so long that many public officials are numbed by persistent warnings and complaints. But this time the clouds on the horizon are especially dark, as weak revenue streams used to fund services begin to "trickle down" with no corresponding signs of the promised economic prosperity associated with that term. Add to that problem the fact that most federal and state revenue streams require local match.

The fiscal impact on health and human services is compounded when local governments can no longer afford those matching funds. Moreover, some county governments contribute to certain human services -- specifically community mental health and providers of substance abuse treatment -- at levels well-above state match requirements. These local funds likely will be among the first cut from county budgets when the full effects of Amendment 1 and other possible reduction schemes come to bear.

In sum, the misguided application of the ideological principle that all tax cuts serve as an economic stimulus and help float all boats evinces a naiveté detrimental to the sustainability requirements of Florida's new vision. There are signs that the intellectual fascination with the virtues of supply side economics may have begun to run its course, as discussed in the last chapter. But Florida leaders are so imbued with ideological fervor and, in the case of Governor Crist, living up to campaign promises to cut taxes, that there is little chance a counterview will prevail. As the dialogue on tax reform continued into 2009, the real impacts of revenue reductions at the state and local governments were unappreciated, and often dismissed by state leaders as complaints by the self-interested and ill-informed.

The Call for Transformative Leadership

It was clear during 2009 that the principles of econo-think ideology when applied to economic realities were wrecking havoc with Florida's budget. The only hope---and it was a vague one---lay in the possibility of uplift from the promised Federal stimulus package, itself a government-sponsored response at variance with econo-think ideology. Florida public leaders were showing no signs of adopting a more visionary and pragmatic strategy designed to help the state weather the storm or adapt effectively to future challenges.

As for his part, Governor Crist was contemplating vacating the governorship in favor of a run for the U.S. Senate. A respected columnist for the Orlando Sentinel newspaper wrote in February 2009:

> "Insurance rates are going to go up. Property taxes are going up. Amendment 1 did not revive home sales. His low-cost health-insurance program has fizzled. His global-warming initiatives are raising power bills. Florida's antiquated tax structure is strangling the economy. He sacrificed future budgets by plundering state trust funds. Legislators are getting tired of being set up -- most recently when they cut an environmental land-buying program with the consent of Charlie's staff, only to have Charlie make a grandstand gesture to restore it…And now respected University of Florida economist David Denslow says the state is headed for 'something reasonably close' to the Great Depression…Charlie's success depends on staying two steps ahead of accountability."[153]

The long-term consequences of budget reductions and property tax reforms for Florida's new vision are especially troublesome. Slashing budgets can decimate already stressed public service delivery systems in unexpected ways, and result in unintended and crippling consequences for years to come. Sam Bell, a former Chairman of the House Appropriations Committee, former Chairman of the Commission on Local Government Reform, and long-time advocate of higher education and of services to Florida's most vulnerable citizens, expressed his views in interviews during July 2008 and January 2009:

> The Chancellor of the North Carolina University system was quoted recently as saying that his desk was piled high with applications from top Florida University professors trying to get out of Florida. Not only are we not serving today's students, but we are laying the ground work for a less educated population, a sicker population (due to poor preventive care), a deteriorating infrastructure system since available monies must go for current services, a more lawless system because our prisons are doing no rehabilitation or job training. In other words, the current failures are going to be magnified in future years by our current neglect.[154]

Bell, a Democrat who is not known for mincing his words, continued:

> Our tax and funding problems are not accidental or the result of tight fisted tax policy. In fact, they are the result of a well funded and carefully orchestrated national effort backed by people who believe that government has no role in most of what it now does. These are people who believe in less government, personal responsibility and survival of the fittest. They work through organizations like the James Madison Institute that urge privatization, tax cuts and want to pay only for 'essential services'. They enjoy the current state of affairs in Florida for this is the opportunity to "starve the beast" and justify cuts due to lack of funds. Even if the economy were doing well, this group would still be moving us toward a down sized government that funded national defense and infrastructure construction and little else.

Bell concluded with the following observations: "I think there is more hope for change at the local level than at the state level. The state problem is that the state is so mal-apportioned that the legislature is not really representative of the people. The right wing has the legislature by the throat."

As we will see in the next chapter, there were signs during the first quarter of 2009 that some Florida public leaders at the state level were beginning to consider a more moderate course. But the mental image of that time was of leaders bunkered down during a fierce Category 5 hurricane, lifting their heads to see which way the wind was blowing. Governor Crist, who is well-known for his ability to judge wind direction, appeared to be testing them, unsure of his heading as the debate between Republicans and Democrats heated up nationally over the Obama stimulus package and his Green New Deal.

Through the din of the current conflict and controversy, one conclusion is abundantly clear: an entirely new way of defining and solving the taxation and budget problems facing Florida is needed. This requires transformative public leadership which has yet to materialize. Adaptation to the forces and trends bearing down on Florida, the bellwether state, were showing no signs of sustainable governance as what was rapidly becoming the worst disaster in the state's history unfolded.

It is useful to conclude this chapter with an examination of the nature of the problems facing the state from the perspective of the theory of sustainability. This will show that the problems are highly complex---systemic is the term we use---and that the solutions will have to be far reaching, multi-dimensional and developed over a period of time adequate for people to come to grips with the serious challenges facing the state and the strategies for adapting to them.

Systemic Solutions to Systemic Problems

Florida's taxation and budget challenges are systemic, as the following graphic demonstrates. Their contemporary consequences cannot be blamed on any one leader or political party because they have developed over many decades. But present and future leaders and party platforms will be judged on how well they adapt their performance to the challenges bearing down on the state. Adaptation begins with understanding and acceptance of responsibility.

An economy driven by "old vision" pursuits supported by antiquated taxation and budget policies fails to produce sufficient revenues needed for investments in the state's quality of life and in the protection and restoration of natural resources. This, in turn, prevents emergence of a "new vision" economy capable of producing the fiscal means needed for "new vision" public services and infrastructure.

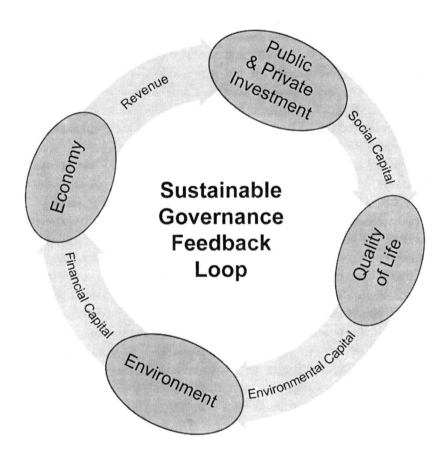

The availability of fiscal resources for private investment also is involved because the old economy is not producing the capital for innovative private contributions to Florida's sustainability vision. Quality products and services that produce sustainability are not cheap. As suggested in the next chapter, private capital availability and lower costs for these "green" products and services are linked to scale production of them. Also needed are public investments in innovative technologies, in strategic planning and management approaches and in regulatory policies that create incentives for sustainable private investment.

Neither the nation nor the state can continue to borrow its way to sustainability. This borrowing takes three main forms: more financial debt, depleting scarce reserves, and irrational attempts to avoid true downstream costs by cutting programs and services to balance budgets short-term. The well-being of the present and of future generations in all three cases is put at risk in direct contravention of the goals and objectives of sustainability.

Additional "negative feedback loops"---like tornadoes from a hurricane---are spinning off from the one depicted. The same dynamic is at work in growth management policy, as we will see in Chapter VI; and in health and human services, justice and virtually every area of public policy. Continued deployment of the intellectual, social, environmental and fiscal capital of the old vision is producing unsustainable results precisely because the means of producing these forms of capital are unsustainable.

These "negative feedback loops" are complex and difficult to break. Solutions that halt and rationalize these cycles are equally as complex and difficult. The entire public policy and leadership framework of the state must be radically altered for the overall "system" to produce different results consistent with a vision that aspires to sustainability.

Taxation and budget policies carry overriding systemic importance, but attempts to reform these in isolation will not be sufficient to turn the ship of state in the direction of Florida's new vision, as the next chapter clearly shows. Albert Einstein once defined insanity as doing the same thing over and over again and expecting different results. This is what Florida leaders have been doing with taxation and budget reform for decades, as the next chapter teaches.

The ideology that maintains the old vision must be abandoned as well, as examined further in Chapter VII. Florida's new vision requires a new governance approach---a new dominant philosophy of governance, broadly defined---capable of aligning initiatives with public aspirations, needs, and values in favor of sustainability. This new governance approach must replace eco-think with public action organized around sustainability-thinking and grounded in the principles and practices of democracy. The ways and the means of governance are at play---both public policy and its administration, as shown in Chapter VIII. This is what the "renewal of the search for sustainable governance" from public sector perspective is all about.

At play also is the state's means of creating wealth, which must be turned to producing sustainable products and services consistent with market demand. The emergence of the new "Green Economy" is much more than a marketing gimmick or political slogan, as the next chapter affirms. It is a way a creating wealth that serves the tenets of sustainability consistent with market and citizen demands. It extends to virtually every sector of the economy from construction and tourism and agriculture to life sciences and the way we value and price insurance and real estate and other services---the way we live, work and play.

It is at this juncture---the hopeful transition from the old to the new vision---that the interests of the public, non-profit and private sectors converge, which is why all three must be involved in solution seeking in pursuit of the common good. The sectors must learn to work together effectively, and see that their fundamental self-interests are interdependent.

Those who persist in old ways of governing merely cause the negative feedback loops to increase in speed and intensity, spiraling toward systemic collapse with dire consequences for the state's future. The performance of state public leaders during 2008 and 2009, especially the Florida House of Representatives, amount to a continuance of the old ways of governing with a tired, worn-out econo-think ideology and virtually no new creative thinking or innovative action. The same may be said for the efforts of the 2008 Taxation and Budget Reform Commission, whose work is chronicled and analyzed in the next chapter.

We return to this topic in Chapter VII, and, as in the last chapter, fix the responsibility for introducing econ-think ideology into Florida politics with the Republican Party under the leadership of former Governor Jeb Bush. By any standard of comparison, he was an activist governor who helped to usher in many innovative governance approaches that now should be refashioned around sustainability principles. Former Governor Bush would do both Florida and America a great service by recognizing this opportunity. As a respected private citizen-leader, hopefully he will seize it in the spirit of bipartisan patriotism that marks the best of his remarkable family's legacy of public service to the nation.

A Return to Practicality and Necessity

Meanwhile, local governments, non-profits providing public services, school districts, public colleges and universities and other public agencies are furiously running against the wind. These providers of public services and infrastructure are reeling from the dizzying speed at which revenue streams are evaporating and service levels and planned capital projects are being devastated. The monster hurricane of unsustainable systemic activity with its many egregious feedback loops is wreaking havoc. The local community level is where most of the damage is being done, and where citizens and their public leaders will have to pick up the debris and deal with the victims.

One example that helps tell the story of these consequences for a major Florida city was reported in May 2009 when the Mayor of Orlando, Buddy Dyer, announced the probability of a 10% cut in the city's workforce, some 342 positions, including 100 police and firefighters.[155] This comes at time when the city's homeless population was expected to increase 17% during 2009 over the 2008 number, rising to some 10,000 homeless in the metro-Orlando area, and when crime statistics reflect alarming levels of violence. Orlando's story was being repeated throughout the state as county and municipal budgets were being developed. School districts, as noted earlier in this chapter, were taking severe financial hits as well.[156]

The "starve the beast", anti-government approach to governance has had its effects; and, in Florida's case, has gone too far in its successes. It should now be abandoned in favor of a more practical answer to the philosophical question about the proper role of government in society. Florida's era of ideology served the purpose of ensuring that individual responsibility exercised through civil society as opposed to government-centered activity is the American way. But the American way, as discussed in the last chapter, also includes an activist role for government as practicality and necessity demand through time. We live in such a time.

The requirements of a turning away from the present direction strike at the heart of the state's political system. Campaign finance and lobbying reforms, prohibition of gerrymandering as new legislative districts are created, revisiting term limits and length of terms for elected officials, election laws that ensure fairness and accessibility for all voters and other changes to the mechanics of the political system will be needed.

But much more is demanded: the soul of the body politic must be stirred for a meaningful and sustainable change of direction to occur.

There is perhaps no stronger generator of this stirring than a cold, hard confrontation with the real world dynamics and consequences of the present course.

The most important question facing Florida is whether the turning will be given real energetic momentum as citizens experience these consequences in their businesses, social, civic and private lives. From the continuing impacts of climate change to the consequences of under-serving the needs of the mentally-ill and drug addicted to failing the meet health care requirements of the working poor in an effective and cost-efficient manner, the public's response to the present day of reckoning will define the political and moral character of the state and its future direction.

The level of transformative change demanded will require a bona fide social movement centered on the goals and objectives of sustainability. Participating citizens must give no quarter to those who stand in the way, while reaching out to all people---regardless of political philosophy or party affiliation---who show signs of understanding and aspiring to join the cause being served: realization of the vision of a sustainable Florida.

The ultimate responsibility for the turning lay squarely on the shoulders of civil society, which in our "system" is sovereign. This is why we argue that Americans and Floridians must learn how to transition from a cultural emphasis on consumption to an ethos of sustainable production grounded in stewardship. This means, as suggested in the opening chapter, we will have to learn once again how to become *citizens* and not only *customers*; producers, not merely consumers.

Divorced from ethics, leadership is reduced to management and politics to mere technique.
—James MacGregor Burns

Chapter V

THE RE-INVESTMENT:
TAX AND BUDGET REFORMS AND THE GREEN NEW DEAL

The TBRC: Background

Theoretically, strong leadership during 2008 could have come from the potentially powerful Taxation and Budget Reform Commission (TBRC), a relatively new addition to Florida's institutions designed to address the state's public budget and finance problems and its strategic direction. The TBRC was established by amendment to the Florida Constitution, and has strong powers that are best explained by the Constitutional language itself:

> The commission shall examine the state budgetary process, the revenue needs and expenditure processes of the state, the appropriateness of the tax structure of the state, and governmental productivity and efficiency; review policy as it relates to the ability of state and local government to tax and adequately fund governmental operations and capital facilities required to meet the state's needs during the next twenty year period; determine methods favored by the citizens of the state to fund the needs of the state, including alternative methods for raising sufficient revenues for the needs of the state; determine measures that could be instituted to effectively gather funds from existing tax sources; examine constitutional limitations on taxation and expenditures at the state and local level; and review the state's comprehensive planning, budgeting and needs

assessment processes to determine whether the resulting information adequately supports a strategic decision-making process.[157]

The Commission was established in 1988 by this Constitutional amendment, and met for the first time in 1990. It did not get off to a good start. Its first session was constituted on the heels of an aborted attempt to broaden the sales tax to advertising and other services. The 1987 legislature passed and newly elected Governor Robert Martinez signed the services tax. It lasted in Florida law a grand total of five months before being repealed prior to its scheduled implementation at the New Year.

Martinez reversed course, called for a September special session to repeal the tax, and got his way. The TBRC met in 1990 as required and did nothing about tax reform. Two years later, Martinez, a Republican with a Democratic Legislature, lost his seat to Lawton Chiles, a Democrat, who would lose the Legislature to the Republicans during his two terms. Chiles tried to re-energize the services tax debate, but gave up. In 1998, the Constitution once again was amended, this time mandating that the TBRC meet again in 2007, and each twenty years thereafter.[158]

The Constitution provides that the TBRC consist of 29 members, 11 appointed by the Governor, seven appointed by the President of the Senate, seven by the Speaker of the House and four non-voting ex officio members, all of whom are members of the Legislature. Members began meeting in early 2007 and were required to submit any proposed constitutional amendments by May 4, 2008.

In early 2008 the TBRC was in the process of its review of state government tax structure, budget process, revenue needs and collections, and constitutional limitations on taxation and expenditures at the state and local levels. It carried authority to offer recommendations to the Legislature, and to take its proposals directly to the voters by Constitutional amendment.

The TBRC has the necessary authority to help craft a new tax structure and establish a new strategic direction for state and local government in accord with the outlines of the vision for a sustainable Florida. But, as the follow account reports, its inauspicious beginning in 1990 was replayed during 2008.

The McKay Battle: Blindsided from the Right

Two substantive reform proposals were being deliberated by the TBRC by February 2008. One of them, proposed by member John McKay, a former Senate president, would have removed certain exemptions from the sales tax. The other proposed a cap on government revenues and expenditures, explained below.

The deliberations of the TBRC were summarized in the following quote:

> The battle lines have been drawn once again on the future of Florida's sales tax system, and they look very familiar. On one side is John McKay, a Bradenton real estate broker and former Senate president who has argued for years that Florida's sales tax base is much too narrow for such a big state. McKay wants to expand the sales tax base by closing exemptions and taxing some services, using the new money to eliminate local property taxes that pay for schools, reducing property owners' tax bills by 40 percent or more.[159]

McKay defended his proposal by saying, "If we don't broaden the tax base ... there's going to be a huge, huge train wreck." He said, "Florida keeps piling more demands atop a narrow sales tax base, and the Legislature's growing reliance on local property taxes to fund schools illustrates the problem."[160]

McKay's plan was drawing strong opposition from Florida business interests, which dominated the Commission. McKay needed persuade 16 of 24 members of the Commission to place his proposal before voters. He ran into a major obstacle in early February 2008 during a meeting of the TBRC:

> McKay was blindsided Tuesday by an economic study that was approved without his knowledge and conducted by a former economic adviser to [former Governor Jeb] Bush. It claimed his plan would cost the state 53,000 jobs, a questionable assertion considering that McKay seeks no net increase in taxes. The McKay plan is only one idea about how to make Florida's tax

system more equitable and stable, but the commission appears headed in the opposite direction. The day before his plan was delayed; a committee unanimously endorsed a revenue and spending cap that sounds more like a constitutional rant than a prescription for responsible government spending. For cities and counties, the cap would call for increased budgets to be submitted to voters ... For the state, it would enact spending limits that are, at best, superfluous for a government whose payroll already ranks the lowest in the nation.[161]

McKay's plan appeared dead by late February. A committee of the TBRC adopted an amendment to his proposal with the following features:

The Legislature would have to eliminate $8 billion a year in mandated property taxes for public schools by 2011 (school taxes account for about 27 percent of property taxes statewide). The proposal would have required lawmakers to recover the $8 billion from various sources: increasing the 6 percent statewide sales tax by up to a penny; reductions in spending and eliminating up to $4-billion in sales tax exemptions.

Lawmakers could dedicate any increased tax revenue attributed to economic growth against the $8-billion requirement. In essence, the proposal offered legislators a range of options, from more spending cuts and no new net gain in revenue to up to a one cent increase in the sales tax with elimination of $4 billion in exemptions. The one certain outcome would be a reduction in property taxes for schools.[162]

McKay reacted strongly to the amendment to his proposal: "'If you want the Legislature to modernize the tax system, then you can't give them an out by letting them cut the budget.' ... He said excluding services from the sales tax benefits special interests at the expense of other taxpayers."[163]

In the end, a version of McKay's proposal would receive the approval of the Commission for placement on the November 2008 ballot. This proposal (labeled Amendment Five to the Florida Constitution and the "tax swap") would eliminate $9.3 billion in state-required property taxes on schools, but would mandate that the Legislature replace the lost revenue with other sources, including a one-cent sales tax increase and possible elimination of some existing sales tax exemptions. The plan would take effect in 2011, if approved by the voters.164 There was a catch. The replacement revenue was required for one year only; in other words, the Legislature after one year of appropriating replacement revenue was unconstrained in subsequent years, causing much concern from advocates for education funding.

Meanwhile, near the end of the 2008 legislative session, the Florida Senate began discussion of sales tax exemptions, and their purpose was to avoid raising taxes. Senator Mike Haridopolos, Republican-Melbourne, chairman of the Senate Finance and Taxation Committee, said his committee's effort would be "to preserve exemptions that promote the state's economy, not to create more revenue for government programs."165 The Senate did not pass such legislation.

Hardopolos, the incoming Senate President, strongly opposed the Taxation and Budget Reform Commission "tax swap" proposal in the knowledge that he would be required in future legislative sessions to raise new taxes. Much of the Florida business community, concerned the measure will result in a services tax and removal of sales tax exemptions favorable to business, also opposed the measure. Realtors and homebuilders associations supported the tax swap, banking on an upsurge in homes sales linked to reduced property taxes.

The Bush Agenda: A Supreme Court Rebuke

The TBRC also would pass forward two additional amendments for placement on the November, 2008 ballot. Both of these related to school funding and were tied to the battles of former Governor Jeb Bush to promote vouchers for public schools, which would enable students to attend private and religious institutions and pay tuition costs with state revenue. Amendment 7 would remove the "no aid" language that bars state money from going to religious institutions. Amendment 9 would soften language mandating a "uniform" system of free public schools. It also would have required school districts to spend at least 65 percent of their money in class rooms; a feature some policy experts believed was a ploy to develop support for vouchers.[166] By mid-summer the fate of Amendment Five was in the hands of a Leon County circuit judge, who ruled against its placement on the ballot, citing its lack of clarity. The Daytona Beach News Journal editorialized on August 17, 2008:

> In the end, the proposed amendment cloaked substantial facts in order to aim for an emotional response from purposefully misinformed voters anticipating lower taxes and no harm done. Give those voters a clearer picture. They're likely to react less emotionally and more rationally once they discover that overall taxes won't necessarily be lower, considering the shift to the sales tax, while overall services in the state will almost certainly be poorer, beginning with the already begging education system.[167]

The Florida Supreme Court, hearing the case on appeal, issued a stunning rebuke of the TBRC proposal. It upheld the lower court decision, ruling unanimously within five hours of closing arguments.

Steve Bousquet, Tallahassee Bureau Chief for the St. Petersburg Times made the following observations about the tax and budget policy record of the Florida Legislature, and the work of the Taxation and Budget Reform Commission:

> Florida's part-time Legislature lurches from crisis to crisis, constrained by its annual 60-day timetable, a lack of vision exacerbated by term limits, and the political pressures of the next election. Comprehensive tax reform has proven much too daunting a task for legislators. The taxation commission is expected to be free of those shackles, so that its members can peer beyond the political horizon and act decisively. But after nearly a year of deliberation, it's still too soon to tell if they will.[168]

One month after Bousquet's article was published, his newspaper wrote:

> In theory, the Taxation and Budget Reform Commission is insulated from the cruder election politics that work against genuine and thoughtful reform on taxes. The reality is looking

not so different from the Legislature itself. This is an opportunity that comes along once every 20 years, and it should not be hijacked by pandering and surprise economic studies.[169]

His newspaper editorialized seven months later, after the TBRC had finished its ill-fated work:

> The tortured language that led the Florida Supreme Court to remove Amendment 5 from the November ballot is a window into the crass politics that shaped the Florida Taxation and Budget Reform Commission. The appointed commission is supposed to be an alternative to the elected Legislature, where tax issues often are held captive by special business interests who tell lawmakers how and whether to vote — or face the consequences in the next election. This time, the commissioners behaved all too much like legislators…Crist and legislative leaders act as though tax cuts should be the only priority in a state whose taxes rank 47th lowest in the nation. The only "tax reform" in the past decade has been the piecemeal creation of more tax breaks, the reduction of business taxes and the elimination of taxes on wealthy stockholders. Instead of achieving fairness, lawmakers have only made a bad tax system worse.[170]

TBRC Summary Observations and Conclusions

It is useful to examine Florida's taxation and budget policies and the attempts to reform them through the lens of the sustainable governance analytical model presented in Chapter I. The model suggests the features of sustainable policy-making, leadership, and governance, and the political behaviors demanded of sustainability.

Not since the failed attempt to enact a services tax two decades before has unsustainable governance been more blatantly obvious in the performance of the State of Florida than when the 2008 Taxation and Budget Reform Commission proposals were summarily struck from the ballot by the Florida Supreme Court. The conduct of the TBRC, including its attempts to resurrect school vouchers, displayed the entire menagerie of Florida's conservative leadership.

The tax swap amendment was viewed variously as the impetus to force the Legislature to enact a services tax and repeal sales tax exemptions, and as a way to further cut property taxes and "starve the beast" of public school funding. The voucher related amendments were attempts by arch conservatives influenced by the hand of former Governor Bush to promote school choice and religious education.

Nowhere were the marks of sustainable public leadership in evidence. Every where there were signs that political ideology had trumped sound public decision-making grounded in the principles and practices of representative democracy and the rule of law---everywhere, except the judiciary, which held that the public interest is not well served when narrow and confusing ideological policy agendas are placed before the voters to amend the state's Constitution.

It is instructive to study how leaders can witness the same phenomenon and draw strikingly different conclusions. Allan Bense, the Chairman of the TBRC, said of the Supreme Court decision: "We gave it our best shot," he said. ``I thought that was Florida's best chance ever for real tax reform." He blamed the requirement for approval of 17 of the TBRC's 25 members for placement of an issue on the ballot. This allowed too much "horse trading" to occur: members held out support for one proposal contingent on garnering sufficient support for others.

Former Governor Bush expressed a measure of contempt for the Supreme Court's ruling, calling it "extremely disappointing." He feared for other voucher programs that have not faced a legal challenge. "Now, more than ever, Floridians should have a voice in determining -- not just how much they are taxed -- but how their tax dollars are spent," Bush said.[171] A St. Petersburg Times article quoted Bush as calling the decision "heartbreaking." Both vouchers and charter schools "will remain in limbo," he wrote in a statement, "under the real threat of litigation from individuals who want to centralize all education decisions within government bureaucracies."[172]

A Miami Herald article by Ellen Klaus reported other reactions: "In rejecting the measures, the court backed clear, unambiguous constitutional amendments, not proposals that mask their true meaning," said Florida Education Association President Andy Ford. Gov. Charlie Crist was "disappointed the people will not have the opportunity to vote to lower their property taxes."[173] The same journalist posted a comment on the Miami Herald website September 3, 2008, quoting John McKay, the chief architect of the property tax amendment, "I'm disappointed in the Supreme Court's denying Florida the opportunity to decide how they are taxed to pay for the education system and the services they reasonably want and deserve." The post continued: "The TBRC wandered far afield of its tax reform mission by advancing the voucher amendments," said Miami Rep. Dan Gelber, a non-voting member of the tax commission, "Further, in its over zealousness to seek passage of these measures, the TBRC tried to trick our citizens into voting for something that otherwise would have little chance of passage. The Court's ruling treated these measures with the contempt they deserved."[174]

When so many different leaders see the same outcome from such divergent points-of-view, there is indication that the process leading to the result was badly flawed. Each point of view purports to represent the public interest. The problem, from the perspective of the sustainable governance analytical model, is absence of a connection between the way the TBRC policy proposals were developed and a genuine, well-supported understanding of public needs, aspirations, and values and a sense of balance among the components of sustainability. The process was focused on education and property taxes, with no clear understanding of how the state would address its long-term funding problems associated with other major issues of concern, including health and human services, natural resource, economic development, transportation or growth management.

One reading of the impact of the proposals was that the elimination of property taxes for school funding -- with replacement revenue to be made up by the legislature from unspecified sources (if at all) -- would have had the practical effect of taking needed revenues away from all components of sustainability to make up the education shortfall. There was virtually no constituency in support of the combined effects of the failed proposals precisely because they were imbalanced and out of alignment with the needs, aspirations and values of Floridians.

Bense, a former Speaker of the Florida House of Representatives, is widely respected for his abilities as a consensus-builder and for his integrity. His conclusion that the TBRC structure and process presented difficulties is insightful, but the problems went deeper than his quote in the newspaper article suggests. Some members of the TBRC, many of whom were loyal to Bush and his protégé House Speaker Rubio, appeared to equate their individual ideological agendas with the public interest. The virtues of open-minded decision-making based on the principles of democracy are deadened when this happens. It is impossible to provide sustainable leadership to a commission when a substantial number of its members are not committed to its precepts.

Sustainable governance does not demand that all involved leaders agree with or comprehend a policy outcome in the same way, but it does require that their perceptions of the public interest be grounded in a well-informed understanding of public needs, aspirations, and values and a degree of balance among the components of sustainability. There is no place in sustainable governance for forced ideological positions, especially when the voters are asked to consider amending the Constitution. Ours is a representative and not a direct democracy. On those occasions when constitutional amendments are offered for consideration by the citizenry, leaders must be particularly mindful of the need for the clarity of ballot questions. Proposals also should be devoid of attempts to advance narrow ideological preferences and unfinished political agendas.

Bense may be on the right track now that the TBRC is finished with its failed effort. According to the September 4, 2008 Miami Herald article, Bense said he hopes "a citizens' group will pursue tax reform now that the commission's signature issue has been killed." Hopefully, if such a citizens group forms, it will design a decision-making process that employs tools and techniques grounded in the principles of democracy and mindful of the requirements of sustainability. All options should be explored thoroughly, including the repeal of the constitutional provision against a state income tax. Martin Dyckeman, a retired associate editor for the St. Petersburg Times and respected analyst of Florida politics and governance, wrote in a column published September 11, 2008:

> Martha Barnett, a commission member who voted for Amendment 5, says that "with the wisdom of hindsight," she

wishes she had asked the commission to consider a personal income tax referendum as well.

"I do not think it would have passed," said Barnett, the prominent Tallahassee lawyer-lobbyist who had raised the income-tax issue as a member of the 1988 tax commission and of the 1998 Constitution Revision Commission. "But I do think the discussion and debate would have informed the members of the commission and hopefully the public, and that it would have moved the ball forward. I believe that Florida will one day lift the constitutional ban on a personal income tax, but it will likely be in response to a crisis."[175]

Legislators were lining up after the Supreme Court decision with ideas of their own. Tax cuts, not tax reform, appeared to be the order of the day among key Florida leaders, including the legislative leaders and the Governor. A newspaper article published September 5, 2008 reported:

> In the wake of a state Supreme Court ruling removing a major tax initiative from the Nov. 4 ballot, legislative leaders vowed Thursday to again make property taxes a top issue in their annual spring session. The target: put a plan on the 2010 ballot calling for a strict spending cap on government expenditures... Also gaining currency is the government spending cap, which would tie local and state spending to the growth in family income. That idea could be put before voters in the next statewide election in 2010, Republican leaders say.[176]

If McKay is right and Florida does not act to broaden its tax base, the resulting "train wreck" will be devastating. State government will be unable to correct its budget's structural imbalance without causing major disruptions in the state's service delivery systems. Local governments and school districts will need to prepare for more major expenditure reductions as well; and, if past legislative behavior is any guide, could face even more problems as the state seeks to pass on to local government mandates to provide services the state refuses to fund. These developments may well provoke the "crisis" Martha Barnett and others believe will be needed for meaningful taxation and budget reform.

In sum, the state's tax structure is widely perceived as inadequate, unfair and inequitable. Tax policies are strategically out of alignment with the present needs, aspirations and values of Floridians as the state transitions from the old vision to the new, as we shall see in the next three chapters. This misalignment is the root cause of the political acrimony and intergovernmental tension facing state and local governments. Until leaders move to align tax policies accordingly, the new vision for Florida's future will remain an illusion.

Moreover, tax and budget policies are established with no intelligent attention to the need for balance among the components of sustainability: governance, economic, social, and natural resource. There is no evidence of a leadership framework designed to advance Florida's emerging new vision. There are no signs that meaningful tax and budget reform will occur under the present state leadership.

The Road Ahead: The Green New Deal

It is time to find out in the interests of leadership alignment and balance what Floridians really want, need, and value; and what public leaders from all sectors and political persuasions mean when they advocate for a "sustainable Florida". Misaligned and imbalanced leaders themselves are not sustainable; and neither is the brand of governance they orchestrate, as the property tax reform fiasco and the 2008 TBRC debacle clearly teach.

During the period studied, 2007-09, it appeared Florida leaders were doing little more than repeating the same mistakes over again. They should listen to Allan Bense who suggests that the entire direction of taxation and budget policy should be placed in the hands of the citizenry. Bense now understands from bitter first hand experience where unsustainable governance leads, and seems also to understand that the only way out of it is to consult with the people themselves.

Thinking clearly about the Florida public's message sent in the 2008 national presidential election may be a good place to start. President-elect Obama's speech on the economy made on January 9, 2009 points to the new national vision that helped power him to victory. A proposed American Recovery and Reinvestment Plan was outlined. A close study of this speech reveals much "sustainability-thinking" and much food for thought that should be digested by all interested and engaged citizens and especially by elected leaders regardless of political party. Some are calling Obama's plan the Green New Deal. We will return to an examination of the Green New Deal after looking first at the opportunities facing Florida for true taxation and budget reform.

The key questions for Florida become, "What will help avert the collision of trains that appears to be on the horizon and achieve the alignment between tax and budget policy and the needs, aspirations, and values of Floridians and help realize the vision for a sustainable Florida?" We suggest two insights that may prove helpful in answering this question. First, the support for broadening the tax base must come from the "bottom-up"; that is, until sufficient numbers of citizens become engaged and energized to demand a change of direction, the trains will continue to roll down the track on their present course. Secondly, the best way to engage citizens is with modern communications and opinion research tools as part of a new leadership framework that communicates with them about their preferred vision for the future. Armed with accurate information and the public support that comes with quality participation in civic affairs, policy-makers may devise fundable policies, programs, and projects consistent with citizens' vision.

Tax and Budget Policy-making: A Fresh Approach

As noted, Florida with its extraordinary diversity likely would have the best experience with the tools of a new leadership framework at the regional and local levels. The role of state government in this regard will be examined in Chapters VII and VIII of this book. There we offer ideas about how to go about tackling the monumental challenge, calling for serious attention to the need for new governance structures and approaches. We introduce the notion of "fiscal home rule" or "fiscal decentralization" whereby local government sponsored initiatives (including regional initiatives) enjoying strong public support may receive the authority to implement new revenue sources. We also examine the ramifications of blind allegiance to the tenets of supply side economics and other precepts of post-Reagan era econo-think in Florida's distinctive circumstance as we analyze the leadership style and approach to governance of former Governor Jeb Bush, whose legacy lives on.

The problems of his leadership style and aspects of his ideology notwithstanding, Jeb Bush was right that long-term and sustainable solutions will demand much more than new taxes, regardless of the level of government that imposes them. This is one point of agreement between econo-think and sustainability-think, as we shall see.

In his report for the Century Commission Stephen Mulkey turns his attention to Florida's present economic and social condition, and makes these observations:

> ...(E)conomic incentives for creation of a future where sustainable resource use and economic development go hand in hand. Far preferable to a limited strategy relying solely on near-term regulation and damage control would be a longer-term vision of Florida's future in which the social, economic, and environmental components of sustainability are mutually reinforcing. Inherent to a comprehensive design strategy is the potential to capture efficiencies that would truly enhance the quality of Florida's environment and the quality of life for its citizens, rather than merely maintain the status quo. An overarching design for long-term use of the state's resources would provide a defined set of economic and conservation objectives, and thus provide business incentive for innovation and entrepreneurial development. In this approach, the solutions for Florida's growth problems can become, in part, the market drivers for economic development projected over a 25 year and 50 year time horizon.[177]

This very powerful concept can serve as a point of synthesis between the seemingly opposite views that the answers lay in stronger and more activist role for government with higher levels of public funding versus strict reliance on private market forces. Both points-of-view are accommodated in Mulkey's conception. Public goals are met and the best of the entrepreneurial spirit is unleashed when public policy and funding commitments work in tandem with private investment to achieve consensus-based sustainability objectives.

For example, taxing environmentally destructive activities to create revenues or tax credits for natural resource restoration and conservation initiatives and renewable energy technologies promotes both public sustainability goals for natural resources and private economic development.[178] Likewise, raising revenue from broad based sources and investing it in sustainability objectives in ways that leverage private investment is far more likely to result in public support for additional tax revenue than current governance approaches have been able to do.

Governments can use the power of the purse and regulation to advance sustainability objectives in other ways. Existing dollars now going to economic development incentives can be linked to agreements with recipient entrepreneurs for achievement of sustainable outcomes such as green building standards and use of innovative renewable energy technologies.

In similar fashion, government growth management and environmental regulation can be used to ensure development of sustainable communities and redevelopment of existing ones. When large public projects are undertaken, community benefit agreements with project developers can help ensure that people who most need jobs are brought into the design and construction process.[179]

The key point is to use "strategic sustainability-thinking" as the guiding principle for taxation and budget, growth management and other public policies. This approach would respect the language in Article XI Section 6 of the Florida Constitution that authorizes the TBRC to "...review the state's comprehensive planning, budgeting and needs assessment processes to determine whether the resulting information adequately supports a strategic decision-making process."

The spirit of this provision ought to apply to all policy-makers who have the authority to raise and to spend public revenues. It seems to contemplate use of strategic planning, which carries with it a sense of overall direction or "vision." This is a far superior approach to policy-making than the use of a popular ideology such as "econo-think" or policy-makers' personal religious views as the basis for establishing policy.

True visioning and strategic planning as demonstrated in subsequent chapters becomes a way of doing the business of governance and a key element of the new leadership framework. This approach is grounded in alignment between citizens' needs, aspirations and values, and pubic policies and initiatives. When these are aligned with the way taxes are levied, and public revenue and private capital are spent, meaningful leadership results. When balanced attention to all components of sustainability is present through a truly comprehensive visioning and strategic planning and decision-making process, Florida's new vision is given real energy.

One wonders whether the drafters of the relevant Constitutional language intended that this strategic approach be used by policy-makers; indeed, whether such an approach is mandated. If government's core purpose is interpreted to be protection of public, health, safety and welfare, this purpose becomes a mandate that could be understood as grounded in "sustainability thinking" with its parallel emphasis on the economic, natural resource stewardship, and social welfare components of society.

Article XI Section 6 could well be interpreted to mean that this core function of government be conducted in a comprehensive and strategic manner. If it does mean this, the entire Florida public policy-making apparatus is acting outside the boundaries of the requirements of the Constitution! Regardless, comprehensive and strategic policy-making grounded in sustainability themes is far superior to the reactionary, ideological and short-sighted approaches now being employed; and clearly is contemplated in the Constitution as such.

A Call for Innovation

Florida's experience demonstrates that attempts to reform taxation and budget policies are a waste of time without this alignment and sense of balance. Bold, new and innovative thinking and leadership must replace narrow-minded ideologically-based approaches to governance.

New York Times journalist Tom Friedman penned a column published September 7, 2008 that could well have been aimed at

Florida. He wrote, quoting Chuck Vest, the former president of the Massachusetts Institute of Technology:

> The irony of ignoring innovation as a theme for our times is that the U.S. is still the most innovative nation on the planet. But we can only maintain that lead if we invest in the people, the research that enable it and produce a policy environment in which it can thrive rather than being squelched. Our strong science and technology base built by past investments, our free market economy built on a base of democracy and a diverse population are unmatched to date; but we are taking it for granted.

Friedman continues, quoting Curtis Carlson, chief executive of SRI International, a Silicon Valley research company:

> Our competitiveness…is based on having a broadly educated work force, superb research universities, innovation-supportive taxes, immigration and regulatory policies, a productive physical and virtual infrastructure, and a culture that embraces hard work and the creation of new opportunities. America is still the best place for innovation," said Carlson. However, we are falling behind in K-12 education, infrastructure and in tax, regulatory and immigration policies that no longer welcome the world's most talented minds. "These issues must be at the top of the national agenda because they determine our ability to provide health care, clean energy and economic opportunity for our citizens."[180]

Innovation is at the core of the capacity to adapt society to the challenges it faces, and from this perspective becomes a key element of sustainability.

Broad consensus in support of a goal to unleash sustainable and entrepreneurial innovations provides the incentive to create the framework necessary for meaningful public policy reforms, and to mitigate partisan bickering and polarization. It appears that the administration of President Barack Obama understands this necessity, and likely will attach "Green Strings" to the receipt of federal funding. The new administration likely will press for legislation that will incorporate achievement of sustainable outcomes in a variety of policy areas, including health care, climate change and energy.

ICLEI, an organization of local governments dedicated to sustainable development, tracks President Obama's "sustainability thinking." Its website contains the following:

> In June 2008, at a speech before a U.S. Conference of Mayors gathering, Obama expressed his commitment to urban revitalization and offered to form new partnerships with urban leaders.
>
> "We need to stop seeing our cities as the problem and start seeing them as the solution," said Obama. "Because strong cities are the building blocks of strong regions, and strong regions are essential for a strong America. That is the new metropolitan reality and we need a new strategy that reflects it. As president, I'll work with you to develop this kind of strategy and I'll appoint the first White House Director of Urban Policy to help make it a reality."

ICLEI also notes that "Obama articulated an equally impressive vision on climate protection and clean energy. 'To completely revamp how we use energy in a way that deals with climate change, deals with national security, and drives our economy, that's going to be my number-one priority when I get into office," said Obama in a recent *Time* interview.'" The organization notes that, "A Zogby post-election survey of 3,357 voters nationwide found that 78% believed investing in clean energy is important to revitalizing America's economy. In July, a nationwide poll conducted by the nonpartisan Presidential Climate Action Project found that 62% of respondents believe it is important that the next U.S. president initiates strong action to address climate change soon after taking office."[181]

Some Florida cities and counties are out in front of this national consensus. ICLEI is sponsoring a "Cities for Climate Protection Campaign" in the wake of the U.S Mayor's Climate Protection Agreement was launched by the Mayor of Seattle in 2005. A report grounded in sustainability themes prepared for the City of Naples in 2008 states:

> Cities can achieve the goals laid out in the Mayor's Agreement, by participating in ICLEI's 'Cities for Climate Protection (CCP) Campaign. Over 350 cities across the US (and 1000 worldwide) participate. So far, at least 17 communities in Florida join Naples in CCP, including Key West, Tampa, and Gainesville, and Miami-Dade, Orange and Sarasota counties. A study of approximately 100 ICLEI members in the year of 2005 showed that by following CCP action plans, these governments and their communities cumulatively saved $535 million in 2005 fuel and energy costs. Additionally, this group cut 23 million tons of GHG, which is equivalent to eliminating the emissions from 4 million cars each year (ICLEI, June 2007). This movement by local municipalities presents significant opportunities for information sharing and collaboration on emissions reduction strategies.[182]

Taxation and budget practices and reform attempts devoid of sustainability themes amount to tinkering around the margins of an unsustainable status quo, and continuing to make the same divisive mistakes. The same holds true for growth management, environmental, education, energy, health and human services and other areas of public policy. Only sustainable governance with aligned leadership that advances sustainability objectives in a balanced manner can produce sustainable public policy.

The key challenge facing the state is about bridging the gap between existing realities and the requirements of the bold, new vision for a sustainable Florida. Leadership that continues to concentrate on "no new taxes" and "starving the beast" of government or scoring points with social conservatives will not rise to the standard of sustainable governance, and will miss out on the promise of what some are calling "The New Green Deal."

Florida local governments, like those participating in the ICLEI effort, are showing signs of getting the "green message" from the public. Examples abound of communities and their local governments pulling together in support of local option sales taxes or major bond finance initiatives with the voters responding favorably at approval referenda. These success stories, as examined in Chapter VIII, have been built around environmental, social, and economic sustainability themes such as land acquisition for conservation, restoration and recreation; arts and entertainment venues; and funding for schools.

We are beginning to witness other examples reflecting inter-sector innovation with sustainability themes, such as the current wave of "green building" initiatives and the growing interest in renewable energy technologies that serve environmental and economic development objectives. The U.S. Conference of Mayors has begun a "Green Cities" program designed to promote sustainable policies at the local level. The International City Management Association is developing similar resources for its members.

The emerging "Green Economy" holds much potential beyond natural resource challenges. Innovative ways to manage health care costs, including models for reducing the spiraling escalation in employee health insurance, are beginning to enter the market place. A model using work site clinics with robust medical management systems for primary care is proving to be a winner throughout the private, non-profit and public sectors. Florida public leaders as we shall see in Chapter VIII also are beginning to develop plans for tackling the tough interconnected problems of drug abuse, mental health, and crime. Job creation resulting from Green Economy innovation holds much promise for workers coming from all skill and income levels.

There are many examples of practical ideas for like-minded sustainable public policy-making at the state government level. Among them are developing an agreement with universities that links spending levels with performance standards; purchasing more environmentally sensitive land while prices are low, and investing in restoration of existing conservation lands; and providing health insurance for more children to reduce impacts on hospital emergency rooms. These approaches to public policy share a common theme: they make public investments in human and physical resources to protect, enhance, and sustain them through time.

Obama's Commitment to Sustainability

The capstone for this bold initiative is found in the American Recovery and Reinvestment Act. The details of this Act, which was signed into law in February 2009, were unfolding as this book was nearing completion. The outlines of the various grant programs were breath-taking in scope and the quantity of funding involved, some $787 billion.

After an in-depth study of the emerging policy framework being used to develop the various grant opportunities under the *American Recovery and Reinvestment Act*, we have concluded that sustainability has been chosen as an organizing principle by the architects of the Act and those charged with its implementation. The Act appears to be based on the aspiration to leverage initiatives that address all three of the major components of sustainability simultaneously: economic development; quality of life; and energy and the environment. It is our belief that communities which demonstrate in grant applications an understanding of this policy framework will be in a position to maximize opportunities for acquisition of grant and low interest loan funds. The following graphic shows how these grant-funded initiatives may be categorized around the components of sustainability.

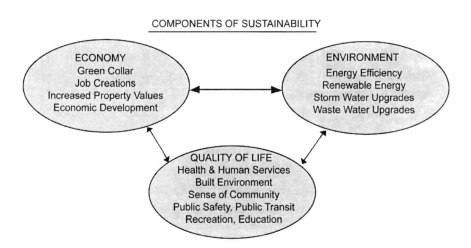

We will return to further examination of what it takes to produce aligned, balanced and sustainable governance and leadership; and summarize the necessary intellectual platform, case examples, core competencies, tools and techniques in the remainder of this book. We will emphasize the importance of a new leadership framework that alters the present roles and relationships between civil society and government.

Here is a sampling of Obama's roll out of the Green New Deal and how it reflects the features of sustainable governance. The following excerpts are from the prepared text of Barack Obama's speech at George Mason University near Washington on January 8:

> Now, the very fact that this crisis is largely of our own making means that it is not beyond our ability to solve. Our problems are rooted in past mistakes, not our capacity for future greatness. It will take time, perhaps many years, but we can rebuild that lost trust and confidence. We can restore opportunity and prosperity. We should never forget that our workers are still more productive than any on Earth. Our universities are still the envy of the world. We are still home to the most brilliant minds, the most creative entrepreneurs, and the most advanced technology and innovation that history has ever known. And we are still the nation that has overcome great fears and improbable odds. If we act with the urgency and seriousness that this moment requires, I know that we can do it again... It is time to trade old habits for a new spirit of responsibility. It is time to finally change the ways of Washington so that we can set a new and better course for America.

Obama here accepts responsibility on behalf of Americans for the mistakes of the past, and characteristic of sustainable governance, points to the opportunities for adapting the present challenges, relying on the nation's past greatness at adapting to tough demands. He takes stock of the nation's major assets, and offers a hopeful message.

> It is true that we cannot depend on government alone to create jobs or long-term growth, but at this particular moment, only government can provide the short-term boost necessary to

lift us from a recession this deep and severe. Only government can break the vicious cycles that are crippling our economy – where a lack of spending leads to lost jobs which leads to even less spending; where an inability to lend and borrow stops growth and leads to even less credit... It's a plan that recognizes both the paradox and the promise of this moment – the fact that there are millions of Americans trying to find work, even as, all around the country, there is so much work to be done. That's why we'll invest in priorities like energy and education; health care and a new infrastructure that are necessary to keep us strong and competitive in the 21st century. That's why the overwhelming majority of the jobs created will be in the private sector, while our plan will save the public sector jobs of teachers, cops, firefighters and others who provide vital services.

Here Obama points to the American philosophical heritage that relies on practicality and necessity in crafting the role for governance. His remarks about not depending on government alone point to his understanding of the need for strong free enterprise and entrepreneurship, consistent with the strand of econo-think that connects with Lincoln's vision of the role of using government to leverage economic development. All components of sustainability are addressed in his remarks: environmental, economic, social, and governance.

(T)he American Recovery and Reinvestment Plan won't just throw money at our problems – we'll invest in what works. The true test of the policies we'll pursue won't be whether they're Democratic or Republican ideas, but whether they create jobs, grow our economy, and put the American Dream within reach of the American people.

Obama in these remarks touches on a major tenet of sustainable governance: searching for consensus across philosophical boundaries and differences of opinion. His reference to the "American Dream" suggests that he understands that sustainability demands leadership with a sense of vision aligned with citizens' needs and values as well as strategies to realize broad aspirations.

> This must be a time when leaders in both parties put the urgent needs of our nation above our own narrow interests...that's why I'm calling on all Americans – Democrats and Republicans – to put good ideas ahead of the old ideological battles; a sense of common purpose above the same narrow partisanship; and insist that the first question each of us asks isn't "What's good for me?" but "What's good for the country my children will inherit?"

These remarks indicate that Obama understands a cardinal requirement of sustainable governance: understanding self-interests, rightly. This understanding, consistent with the goals and objectives of sustainability, is mindful of the overarching requirement to meet the needs of the present generation without compromising the ability of future generations to meet their own needs.

> More than any program or policy, it is this spirit that will enable us to confront this challenge with the same spirit that has led previous generations to face down war, depression, and fear itself. And if we do – if we are able to summon that spirit again; if are able to look out for one another, and listen to one another, and do our part for our nation and for posterity, then I have no doubt that years from now, we will look back on 2009 as one of those years that marked another new and hopeful beginning for the United States of America.[183]

The notion of renewal of the American spirit is clearly evident in Obama's approach. Sustainable governance, as we have suggested, demands the "can do" spirit of patriotism that has been present in response to crises during every great period of U.S. history.

In a poll sponsored by CNN released Christmas Eve 2008, more than eight in 10, or 82 percent, of those questioned approved of the way Obama was handling his presidential transition. Fifty-six percent of those questioned said they favored the stimulus package that President-elect Barack Obama is proposing; 42 percent were opposed.[184] A Gallup poll conducted during early January 2009 showed 65 per cent public approval of Obama's leadership.[185] Obama clearly was enjoying his honeymoon.

The political debate began soon after his inauguration. In an opinion piece published in the Washington Post in early February 2009, Obama, in defense of his economic stimulus plan, made these observations:

> In recent days, there have been misguided criticisms of this plan that echo the failed theories that helped lead us into this crisis -- the notion that tax cuts alone will solve all our problems; that we can meet our enormous tests with half-steps and piecemeal measures; that we can ignore fundamental challenges such as energy independence and the high cost of health care and still expect our economy and our country to thrive.
>
> I reject these theories, and so did the American people when they went to the polls in November and voted resoundingly for change. They know that we have tried it those ways for too long…So we have a choice to make. We can once again let Washington's bad habits stand in the way of progress. Or we can pull together and say that in America, our destiny isn't written for us but by us. We can place good ideas ahead of old ideological battles, and a sense of purpose above the same narrow partisanship. We can act boldly to turn crisis into opportunity and, together, write the next great chapter in our history and meet the test of our time.[186]

Clearly, the battle whose outcome will do much to set the course of the nation for the foreseeable future was underway. But by mid-2009, Obama was still enjoying broad public support nationally and in Florida. A Quinnipiac poll released in April 2009 found the following:

> Florida voters' enthusiasm for President Barack Obama is waning a bit, but his 60 - 32 percent job approval remains

strong, according to a Quinnipiac University poll released today. Voters approve 55 - 36 percent of the President's approach to fixing the economy. President Obama's job approval rating among Floridians is down slightly from 64 - 23 percent in a February 19 Quinnipiac University survey. The biggest change is the increase among those who disapprove of what he is doing. Obama goes from a negative 33 - 47 percent score among Republicans in February to a negative 22 - 70 percent today.

"The movement away from President Barack Obama, not surprisingly, comes from those who are Republicans and consider themselves to be conservatives," said Peter Brown, assistant director of the Quinnipiac University Polling Institute. "But the President's support remains strong, and the numbers show that tens of thousands of Floridians who didn't vote for him last November like what he is doing in office."[187]

By mid-summer 2009, Obama's honeymoon period was at its end. Unemployment continued to rise and was expected to reach 10 percent during 2009, the federal stimulus notwithstanding. His supporters generally fell into two camps: those who defended his plan and believed it would stimulate the economy after its full effects take hold; and those who believed the plan was not enough and needed more revenue, a second round of stimulus. A third camp consisted of the loyal opposition in the Republican Party, who believed that the plan was wrong from the start, and should be scrapped in favor of tax cuts.[188]

Meanwhile, the national debate on health care reform had heated up. An ugly "fourth camp" developed in late summer after Congress failed to adopt a health care reform bill before taking its usual recess, knowing the debate would resume the following month. As members returned home, several Democrats held town hall meetings to discuss health care reform issues with constituents. Many of these public meetings turned into venues for protests by angry citizens.

New York Times columnist Paul Krugman wrote that the protesters were organized by two right wing groups, FreedomWorks, run by the former House majority leader Dick Armey, and a new organization called Conservatives for Patients' Rights. The latter group, Krugman noted, is directed by Rick Scott, the former head of Columbia/HCA, a for-profit hospital chain. "Mr. Scott was forced out of that job amid a fraud investigation; the company eventually pleaded guilty to charges of over billing state and federal health plans, paying $1.7 billion — yes, that's "billion" — in fines. You can't make this stuff up," Krugman wrote.[189]

Florida's U.S. Representative Kathy Castor, a Tampa Democrat, faced some 1,500 people at a town hall meeting in Ybor City on August 6, 2009. According to a news article published by the St. Petersburg Times, Castor was asked to leave the meeting by its organizers because protestors were shouting so loud she could not be heard.

The article reported:

> The spectacle at the Children's Board in Ybor City sounded more like a wrestling cage match than a panel discussion on national policy, and it was just the latest example of a health care meeting disrupted by livid protesters. Similar scenes are likely to be repeated across the country as lawmakers head to their home districts for the summer recess...Hundreds of vocal critics turned out, many of them saying they had been spurred on through the Tampa 912 activist group promoted by conservative radio and television personality Glenn Beck. Others had received e-mails from the Hillsborough Republican Party that urged people to speak out against the plan and offered talking points.[190]

Whatever else this political behavior may say about American and Florida politics, it certainly affirms the observation referenced in Chapter III by Fareed Zakaria that, "It is fear that has created a climate of paranoia and panic in the United States and fear that has enabled our strategic missteps...Too many Americans have been taken by the rhetoric of fear."

Krugman shares this view in his August 7, 2009 column:

> The driving force behind the town hall mobs is probably the same cultural and racial anxiety that's behind the

"birther" movement, which denies Mr. Obama's citizenship. Senator Dick Durbin has suggested that the birthers and the health care protesters are one and the same; we don't know how many of the protesters are birthers, but it wouldn't be surprising if it's a substantial fraction. And cynical political operators are exploiting that anxiety to further the economic interests of their backers.

Krugman concludes his column by noting, "But right now Mr. Obama's backers seem to lack all conviction, perhaps because the prosaic reality of his administration isn't living up to their dreams of transformation. Meanwhile, the angry right is filled with a passionate intensity. And if Mr. Obama can't recapture some of the passion of 2008, can't inspire his supporters to stand up and be heard, health care reform may well fail."

The general political conundrum Obama faced with his stimulus plan as well as his health care reform proposal was described by Nicolo Machiavelli in 1513, the same year Ponce de Leon discovered Florida. Machiavelli observed, in his classic work, The Prince:

"There is nothing more difficult to take in hand than to take the lead in the introduction of a new order of things...the innovator has for enemies all those who have done well under the old conditions, and lukewarm defenders in those who may do well under the old conditions, and lukewarm defenders in those who may do well under the new."

Were Machiavelli observing American politics in the 21st Century, he likely would conclude that the "fourth camp" consists of people gripped by fear and anger, whose emotions are stirred by commentators and organizers. While a minority of the general public, this camp is able to generate widespread attention with the intensity of the conflict generated.

This political condition is a far cry from Obama's soaring inaugural rhetoric calling for placing "...good ideas ahead of old ideological battles, and a sense of purpose above the same narrow partisanship." Even so, with Obama's bold willingness to press ahead with his ideas, he showed during his first eight months in office a willingness to step into the fire of controversy with the sense of vision and strategy sustainable governance demands. Whether he will win the health care and stimulus battles and otherwise show transformative leadership remained an open question. But this much was certain: the larger war for the soul of the American body politic had begun.

A Contrast of Vision and Leadership

The 2008 Florida Taxation and Budget Reform Commission by comparison with the federal approach did not elevate its deliberations to such a visionary and strategic level. It failed to imagine a role for government that contributes to "a new order of things" with respect to Florida's tax and budget practices. Instead of helping develop a new leadership framework, the Commission merely "played it safe," failed to innovate, and continued to rehash old arguments about the taxation and budget conditions of an unsustainable status quo, using inept leadership practices.

Likewise, legislative leaders in the wake of the Commission's failure appeared to be devoid of leadership in favor of the conditions needed to give meaning to the new vision for a sustainable Florida. Two St. Petersburg Times editorials written almost a year apart tell the story of leaders maintaining fixed ideological positions at a time when much more was required. The first editorial was written in February 2008:

> All it would take to brighten Florida's future is a grasp of reality and a vision that stretches beyond the next election. But those qualities are in terribly short supply in Tallahassee, where politicians see the sun always shining and good times just around the next budget cut.[191]

The second editorial was written in January 2009 at the end of the special session called to address the state's mounting budget crisis:

> The Florida House and Senate are poised today to pass separate plans to reduce the state's $2.4-billion deficit. Both lack vision and creativity. The Republican leadership refuses to raise

new revenue beyond court fees and traffic fines, and relies too heavily on spending cuts and reducing reserves to dangerously low levels. It is a short-term strategy that inflicts more pain than necessary on schools, social services and health care and leaves the state in a financially precarious position... (L)awmakers are postponing tough decisions and digging next year's budget hole even deeper by raiding trust funds and draining reserves. The only hope is that this painful special session serves as a reality check and that lawmakers will be more willing to honestly confront Florida's financial crisis in the spring.[192]

It appeared as the first decade of the 21st Century neared its end that a new way of providing leadership -- a new leadership framework and new governance arrangements---would be needed before Florida began to move in the direction of sustainable governance.

President Barack Obama is sketching the outlines of a renewed search for sustainable governance that will demand the participation and support of well-meaning citizens acting as Americans first. Whether his example will be followed by the leaders of state and local governments nationally remained an open question.

Obama's hopeful promises will be dashed if the nation's public leaders persist in divisiveness, stubborn ideological approaches to governance that have failed, and politics as usual. It is time, once again, for Americans in civil society to dream big, and to be bold in devising new ways and means of governing grounded in that distinctive combination of idealism and pragmatism that has characterized the best of the nation's experiment with democracy.

Before turning to the challenges of governance and the requirements of the new leadership framework, it is necessary to examine Florida's growth management track record, and the thinking and action concerning its reform. There, too, we find many helpful lessons in the search for sustainable governance.

We are limited, not by our abilities, but by our vision.
—Source Unknown

Chapter VI

THE RE-PLANNING: GROWTH MANAGEMENT, HISTORY AND FUTURE

Introduction

Florida's attempts to "manage growth," which began in the early 1970's, reflects the tension that occurs when major public policies do not address the components of sustainability in a balanced manner: economic, social and natural resource. Former Florida Governor Reubin Askew, who held office from 1971-79, understood this dynamic when he taught long before sustainability became a popular concept that managing Florida's growth was about "balancing equities."[193] When this imbalance is coupled with misalignment with public needs, aspirations and values, the result is unsustainable policy, leadership, and governance.

The "winner" among the components during the 20th Century clearly was the economic. Inheritors of the old vision during this period--- with their ambition to grow Florida's population base---were unapologetic about this dominance of economic interests, equating it with prosperity itself. As examined in Chapter I, they defined government's role as being the hand-maiden of the old vision, to provide infrastructure and services required by Florida's growth ambitions and little else. Florida failed to provide the public funding necessary to build and maintain service delivery systems and infrastructure at adequate levels. The "Perfect Storm" with its tornadic "negative feedback loops" examined in Chapter IV is the result.

Concerns about resulting damage to the natural and social ecologies were muted during much of this period. But as the dawn of the new century approached, these concerns were expressed with louder voice. The consequences of Florida's massive and sprawling growth and its stingy public spending practices increasingly had entered the everyday experiences of residents and visitors. Traffic congestion was the most obvious, but there were many other consequences, from environmental degradation to over-crowded schools to high crime rates. The attempt to manage the state's growth during the intervening years since the early 1970's is understood best against this backdrop.

Fast-forward to contemporary Florida, and we find a chaotic chorus among advocates for each of the components of sustainability in seeming conflict with the others, and a widespread failure to recognize interdependencies among advocates for the economy, the social ecology, or the natural environment. None of the components appears to enjoy clear dominance.

Nowhere is this imbalance among the components of sustainability more apparent than in Florida's experience with growth management. In no area of public policy is there more evidence of unsustainable governance with its unhealthy conflict, intellectual confusion, intergovernmental hostility, and directional uncertainty. There is increasing evidence examined in this chapter that growth management policy is cut off from the needs, aspirations, and values of citizens.

There is no sustainable leadership occurring when the components of sustainability are out of balance, isolated, and in conflict with each other; and public policies are out of sync with the citizenry. Tom Pelham, a chief architect of Florida's growth management policies, in 2007 during his second tenure as Secretary of the lead state's growth management agency, the Department of Community Affairs, aptly described the situation as "a mess."[194]

Florida Growth Management Chronology

Florida's experience with growth management is summarized here:
The Florida Legislature in 1971 enacted the state's first growth management legislation and revised it in 1975 to require comprehensive plans for local governments to manage development and address capital needs. A decade later the Legislature enacted the 1985 Growth Management Act considered at the time as the nation's

most progressive attempt by a state to manage growth. The planning principles of consistency, concurrency, and compact development were at the heart of the attempt.

The goal was to have within comprehensive plans internal consistency of policies with development approvals, and consistency among local, regional and the state's plans. Concurrency would ensure that the services and infrastructure demanded by new development would be made available "concurrent" with the impacts of the development, measured by established levels of services set in the local plans.

The Act sought compact growth as opposed to urban sprawl into rural areas. Comprehensive plans were built around various planning elements, and were tailored to established population projections to ensure that new population growth correlated with density allocations, and the infrastructure and services demanded.

An elaborate approval process for comprehensive plans and amendments was established. Local municipal plans were to be evaluated for consistency with the plans of adjacent jurisdictions and the county plan for unincorporated territory. Regional planning councils were established to review plans before sending them on to Tallahassee for evaluation, including determination of consistency with an over-arching state plan. Plans were to include "capital improvement elements" that demonstrated the jurisdiction's ability to pay for the services and infrastructure needed to pass "concurrency tests" against established levels of service. Large developments with regional impacts had their own elaborate review procedures, and certain areas of the state -- most notably the environmentally sensitive Florida Keys -- were deemed "areas of critical state concern." These received closer scrutiny by state agencies and oversight by the Florida Cabinet.

1972	State Comprehensive Planning Act: Created Division of State Planning, called for creation of state comprehensive plan; Established Areas of Critical State Concern (ACSC) and Development of Regional Impact (DRI) planning processes.
1980	Regional Planning Council Act: Regional Planning Councils (RPCs) required throughout the state.

1984	State and Regional Planning Act: Required the development of a State Comprehensive Plan. RPCs designated as the primary agent to address regional issues, with a requirement that they prepare Regional Policy Plans.
1985	Local Government Comprehensive Planning and Land Development Act (Growth Management Act): State mandates certain elements in local comprehensive plans; Concurrency policy mandated; State-Regional-Local planning framework established.
1985	State Comprehensive Plan adopted: A directions-setting document with 27 goals across a broad array of issues.
1986	Growth Management "Glitch Bill": Refinements and clarifications to the 1985 GMA.
1986	Chapter 9J-5 FAC: Detailed rules on the content and form of comprehensive plans and criteria related to compact development established by DCA.
1993	Growth Management Act: Restricted the powers of the RPCs and reduced the scope of regional policy plans; Phased elimination of the DRI process.
1995	Reinstatement of the DRI process.
1999	Urban Infill and Redevelopment Areas legislation: An attempt to promote redevelopment in the state's urban cores through reduced state oversight and financial incentives.
2005-2007	"Pay as You Grow" legislative package: This legislation included an increase in state funding for infrastructure, relaxed transportation concurrency standards, required concurrency for schools, and greater planning for potable water supplies.

Source: The FSU Department of Urban & Regional Planning

Calls for Change: From a "Mess" to Sustainability

By 2007, newly-appointed as Florida Secretary of Community Affairs, Tom Pelham, made these remarks about the state of growth management in Florida Trend magazine: "It's badly in need of an overhaul," says Pelham. "We're trying to manage growth with an unmanageable statute. ... It's a mess. It spraawwwls."

In another article, this one penned by Pelham as a guest columnist and circulated to Florida media, he notes, "Originally, the Growth Management Act allowed local plans to be amended only two times each year. Subsequently, however, the Legislature has enacted 32 exceptions to the twice-a-year limitation. Additionally, many local governments have developed a habit of considering and adopting dozens of plan amendments every six months. For example, in 2005 alone, Florida's local governments adopted more than 8,000 plan amendments." He continues, "As a result, the local plan is constantly changing, offers little stability or predictability, and has diminished credibility with the public. Instead of the 10- or 20-year visions they were supposed to represent, local comprehensive plans are in danger of becoming little more than six-month suggestions."[195]

In a report completed in 2006, prepared for 1000 Friends of Florida by the Center for Quality Growth and Regional Development at the Georgia Institute of Technology, the following broad observation is made:

> Florida, like other fast growing southern and southwestern states, is at a critical juncture. Such population and job growth, and the corresponding changes to the built environment, make it imperative that state leaders and decision makers establish a policy framework that prepares for the expected growth, maintains the state's economic progress, enhances livability for all people, and protects the natural environment. The expected demand for construction presents a tremendous opportunity to shape the state's built environment—the land use patterns, transportation systems, and aesthetic qualities that influence how we live. Unfortunately, this impending growth also presents a potential threat. If not done well, it could exacerbate existing

challenges, like traffic congestion, natural habitat encroachment, and deterioration in the quality of life for residents.[196]

The report calls for a new, more regional policy framework to manage the state's growth, with a stronger oversight role for Pelham's department. We will return to this perspective on growth management at the conclusion of this chapter, and examine it further in Chapter VIII.

Richard Mulkey's report Toward a Sustainable Florida (cited earlier) includes the following observation:

> The present situation is not new, and since the early 1800's the history of Florida has been characterized by periodic land speculation. What is different about our unfolding predicament is the high degree of consensus among policy makers, developers, land managers, and conservationists that a limit to development is rapidly being approached, beyond which the state's economy and natural resources will suffer possibly unrecoverable damages.... Most would agree that it is time for a different vision of Florida.[197]

One concept that is central to this book is reflected in the 1000 Friends report's title "A Time for Leadership": "*A Time for Leadership* builds on the 2003 report by the Florida Chamber Foundation..., which called for a shift from growth management to growth leadership. Growth leadership is described as a proactive approach to plan for future growth that is both sustainable and environmentally-friendly. To support the *New Cornerstone* call for growth leadership, (the 1000 Friends report) offers a policy framework and recommendations for land development and preservation planning in Florida.[198]

Assessing Growth Management

In 2007 a book was published entitled *Growth Management in Florida: Planning for Paradise* edited by three professors from the Urban and Regional Planning Department of Florida State University.[199] The book was hailed as "...the most comprehensive and detailed assessment of Florida's far-reaching growth management legislation ever done."[200] An excellent overview of the book entitled "Pain in Paradise: Florida's Failed Fix All" was written by Parker Neils, and posted on the website of Research in Review, an academic journal published by Florida State University.

Neils points out that two major problems with the Growth Management Act of 1985 arose in the immediate years after passage. First, the state plan that was supposed to serve as the overarching blueprint for Florida's growth management ambitions was largely ignored by local governments and by state agencies. Quoting the contribution to the book made by Tom Pelham, Neils writes:

> Ultimately, the state plan—perhaps because it was never linked in any way to the state *budget*—became largely ignored by planners throughout state government. Through various amendments "and administrative neglect," Pelham writes that the plan "never became a factor in the implementation of the (larger growth management) process." With no playbook to go by, local governments had nothing to make their plans "consistent" with, and thus a key tool that Pelham believes could have been a powerful agent against the worst elements of urban sprawl went by the boards. His summation of the status quo:
> "Consequently, the state Plan currently is the object of criticism and even ridicule because it is seldom used (and) has little or no effect on governmental decisions; and, except for DCA's urban sprawl policies, has little impact on the review and approval of local plan amendments."[201]

A second major problem arose during the immediate years after passage of the Act, and has worsened since: the costs of public services and infrastructure requirements needed to ensure concurrency outstrips the public funding available to pay for them. The attempt to enact a services tax during the late 1980's, examined in Chapter V, was viewed as a way to produce the public revenue needed to give meaning to Florida's newly-crafted growth management approach. The failure of the services tax was assessed by University of Florida public finance expert James Nicholas in *Planning for Paradise*: "The repeal of the Services Tax brought an end to broad-based and state funding of infrastructure. Since then, the burden has been shifted largely to local and *increasingly narrow sources of revenue.*"[202]

These narrow sources of revenue include local optional gas and sales taxes and impact fees. Local governments (and school districts in the case of the optional sales tax and impact fees) during the past two decades largely have exhausted these sources.

Impact fees imposed on new construction have been widely used because they are technically not a tax requiring legislative authorization. These fees have sparked much conflict and litigation, and have not served as an adequate or equitable source of revenue to help meet concurrency requirements. Like the other local option revenues mentioned, impact fees cannot be spent on operating and maintenance needs, which have shifted these costs to other local revenue bases, including the property tax.

Various special assessment fees, which also must be spent primarily on infrastructure and other capital needs, also have been widely used by local governments through creation of special improvement districts. Many local governments have used these local option sources to fund projects backed by revenue bonds, which require pledges and debt service that exhaust these revenue streams and mitigate their future use.

In similar fashion, many local governments have established Community Redevelopment Areas (CRAs), which use tax increment funds accumulated as values increase within these areas. Because the "tax increment" revenue generated from the base year of establishment of these areas is plowed back into them, other jurisdictions that normally would receive these revenues (principally counties) often object. This creates much intergovernmental tension.

The combined effect the state's failure to overhaul its tax structure and the use of these local government financing schemes has resulted in a hodge-podge of approaches to meeting concurrency requirements that overall has failed. Meanwhile, the development community came up with its own creative ways to meet concurrency requirements. Voluntary infusion of private capital into public infrastructure required to meet concurrency tests has been made through development "exactions." Also, the use by developers of privately financed community development districts has shifted the burden of public infrastructure for concurrency to future residents of new developments.

Developers have been known to pay for public roads and schools with private capital, and take back bonds placed by local governments, which require repayment over time, often at discounted interest rates. The combination of these public and private strategies kept the growth machine running, until the housing boom burst in 2007-08.

Weak Policy "Reforms" and Public Reactions

The main public policy response to the looming concurrency infrastructure funding crisis by the late 1990's was to postpone the deadline for having the infrastructure in place to meet the impacts of new development. As long as the funds were budgeted in five-year plans, the new rules enabled development to proceed. Often, however, the needed revenue would not materialize during the five year period and after the permitted development was well underway or completed.

The next public policy responses came in 2005 and 2007, when the Growth Management Act was amended by Senate Bill 360 and 800, respectively to enable developers to move forward, so long as they paid their "fair share" of the costs of concurrency requirements for schools and roads. This "pay, go" approach has produced much confusion about how the fair share is calculated, and other concurrency requirements are to be met. Also, the Legislature has placed the responsibility to come up with the necessary revenues on local governments, which do not have the legal authority, financial or political wherewithal to come up with new tax sources or sufficiently increase existing ones.

SB 360 also required that local governments demonstrate through a "financial feasibility test" that adopted levels of service for required concurrency facilities can be met and maintained. Failure to pass the test results in local governments being unable to amend comprehensive plans. Such amendments often are required when new development is permitted.

So, not only is the state pressuring local governments to produce revenue they do not have, but the development community likely will pressure local governments as well when it becomes clear that plan amendments necessary to the regulatory entitlement process will be halted because local governments cannot demonstrate financial feasibility. The combined effects of SB 360 and SB 800 have exacerbated long-standing concurrency funding deficiencies, with no relief in sight.

1000 Friends a Florida summarized the effects of Senate Bill 360 as follows:

> It requires that by December 1, 2007, all **Capital Improvement Elements** must demonstrate through a "financial feasibility test" that adopted levels of service for required concurrency facilities can be met and maintained; thereafter an annual update by comprehensive plan amendment must be performed. If this is not done, no comprehensive plan amendments may be adopted, and sanctions may apply. A similar enforcement process is required for [other] plan **amendments**.
>
> A **"pay and go" provision** requires developers to pay their "proportionate share" of the cost new roads and schools needed for new development, and water must be available at the time of occupation. 1000 Friends lobbied unsuccessfully to require that roads and schools also be available at the time of occupation. We remain very concerned that this provision could prove to be a major loophole, as once the proportionate share is paid, development is allowed regardless of concurrency shortfalls.
>
> Other provisions make **school concurrency** mandatory, except for built-out or no-growth areas. Local governments are encouraged to adopt a **vision** and **urban service boundary**; if done, state and regional map amendment reviews are waived.[203]

A sense of panic took hold of law makers during the 2009 session of the Florida Legislature. Proposals to loosen the growth management requirements in the name of economic stimulus were the order of the day in the Florida House of Representatives. One of these proposals would have abolished the Department of Community Affairs altogether and shifted its responsibilities elsewhere in the state's bureaucracy. This anger-driven proposal was made in response to criticisms launched against legislators by Secretary Pelham. This proposal was withdrawn, largely because wiser heads prevailed in the Florida Senate.

The bill that passed out of the Legislature was a compromise of the various interests engaged in the debate. 1000 of Florida joined by Audubon of Florida and the Sierra Club of Florida provided the following summary recommendations in the wake of the session:

- The bill's definition of "dense urban land area" promotes unchecked and inappropriate urban development in vast tracts of fringe and rural lands
- It automatically qualifies 245 cities and the entire territory of eight of our largest counties for transportation concurrency exemptions and Development of Regional Impact (DRI) exemptions.
- It runs counter to Governor Crist's goals to address climate change.
- Instead of being an economic stimulus strategy as proponents argue, it would allow massive new development to the already over-allocated and over-approved development already in existence in our state.[204]

A host of other interest groups, including the Florida Association of Counties and Florida League of Cities, and many of the state's newspaper editorial boards expressed strong opposition to SB 360. Crist signed the bill into law unceremoniously, and sparked a torrent of criticism that may haunt him as he vacates the governorship to seek election to the U.S. Senate in 2010.

The underlying intent of the new law's advocates is to promote economic stimulus by de-regulating the private sector and allowing development to move forward unencumbered by transportation concurrency requirements. This policy approach is grounded in econo-think. Its emphasis on short-term economic gain is blind to down stream negative effects on the quality of life and environmental components of sustainability. This approach to growth management is likely to produce many unintended consequences for existing and future Floridians. It is roughly analogous in philosophy to schemes that maximize profits in the nation's financial services industry by avoiding the public oversight and accountability of government regulation.

The 2009 treatment of SB 360 stands as an excellent example of the old vision econo-think leadership framework clashing with the new vision sustainability leadership framework. It teaches that no matter how well intended policy-makers may be, they inevitably fail the test of sustainability when they allow ideology and a misguided focus on the economy to guide decision-making. The sad irony is that this approach redounds to the detriment of the economy ultimately precisely because it undermines the vitality of the quality of life and the natural environment.

The thrust of SB 360 also runs counter to public needs, aspirations and values, as shown by the best public opinion research into Floridians' views on problems attendant to population growth reported later in this chapter. SB360 is misaligned with the needs, aspirations and values of Floridians, the opposite of the character of public leadership sustainability demands.

There is little question that adopting SB 360 as law will stoke the fires of the Home Town Democracy movement. This ballot initiative (which was gathering petition signatures as this book was completed), if adopted by Florida voters at referendum, will require that all comprehensive plan amendments, now routinely approved by local governments, be subject to local voter approval. The truth is that many comprehensive plan amendments involving properties that enjoy long-standing, existing development entitlements often produce better and more sustainable developments as a result of the amendment process.

The Home Town Democracy initiative would turn Florida's approach to growth management into an experiment in direct democracy with unknown and risky consequences for the state's economy and future vision. Its approval at referendum may become the most egregious of all the unintended consequence of SB 360.

If so, the damage will have been borne out of frustration with failed leadership at the state level, lending credence to David Brook's insight---quoted earlier and repeated here---about similar failure of national political leadership: "...(L)eaders have been fixated on short-term conventional priorities...There is no evidence that the power brokers understand the fundamental transition ahead. They are practicing the same self-indulgence that got us into this mess."[205] SB 360 amounts to an attempt to re-inflate the bubble that created the present chaos.

1000 Friends of Florida, which has advocated for a new leadership framework, has developed recommendations for changes to the Growth Management Act. The Florida Sustainable Communities Act embodies this change of direction, and will be examined later in this chapter.

The lack of a responsible state plan and leadership role in growth management coupled with the lack of public funding for concurrency is likely why Pelham describes the overall growth management situation as "a mess." But the problem gets worse: the ambition to promote compact urban development, which in theory would help hold down costs and provide substantial environmental benefits as it mitigates urban sprawl, also has failed to live up to its promise.

The New Urbanism

Attempts to promote compact urban development and reduce sprawl have been given labels that now are popularly familiar: "Smart Growth" and the "New Urbanism." The theoretical case for this approach to growth management is strong.

Smart growth carries the potential to address a variety of sustainability issues within a single framework. The Smart Growth Network, a national organization dedicated to these sustainable planning principles, offers the following insight:

> In communities across the nation, there is a growing concern that current development patterns -- dominated by what some call "sprawl" -- are no longer in the long-term interest of our cities, existing suburbs, small towns, rural communities, or wilderness areas. Though supportive of growth, communities are questioning the economic costs of abandoning infrastructure in the city, only to rebuild it further out. Spurring the smart growth movement are demographic shifts, a strong environmental ethic, increased fiscal concerns, and more nuanced views of growth. The result is both a new demand and a new opportunity for smart growth.
>
> The features that distinguish smart growth in a community vary from place to place. In general, smart growth invests time, attention, and resources in restoring community and vitality to center cities and older suburbs. New smart growth is more town-

centered, is transit and pedestrian oriented, and has a greater mix of housing, commercial and retail uses. It also preserves open space and many other environmental amenities.[206]

A summary of the principles of smart growth was prepared by Smart Growth America, a coalition of national, state and local organizations dedicated to improving planning of towns, cities and metropolitan areas. The organization defines smart growth by the outcomes it achieves, claiming the results of its planning principles reflect the values of Americans. Six broad goals are identified: 1) enhancing the "livability" of neighborhoods by developing them as safe, convenient, attractive, and affordable; 2) mixing land uses, clustering development and providing multiple modes of transportation to reduce traffic and trip lengths; 3) placing emphasis on new development near existing cities, suburbs and towns where infrastructure investments exist; 4) promoting "shared benefits" across income and racial lines by mitigating sprawl; 5) lowering costs and taxes, which are driven upward by sprawling development patterns; and 5) preserving open space.[207]

The synopsis of Planning for Paradise offered by the Department of Urban and Regional Planning at Florida State University offers the following:

> Regarded as the key element of what planners now call "smart growth," compact development, at least in theory, has powerful potential for doing much for the common good, such as protecting Florida's natural environment, conserving energy, even enhancing safety, livability and a sense of community... In 1990, the idea was hailed by DCA Secretary Pelham as "a model for a new area of urban design in Florida." New Urbanism soon became grafted into the fiber of Florida's growth management policy.
>
> Twenty years on, Florida has become the veritable incubator of New Urbanist projects for the nation. The state is home to more communities and downtown revitalization projects based on New Urbanism principles than any other. In 1996, the Walt Disney Company rolled out a $2.5 billion, 5,000-acre town—

Celebration, near Orlando—that was touted as a New Urbanist utopia of sorts. Last year, a coalition of Orlando citizen groups and corporations launched "2050 Future Vision," an ambitious blueprint for Orlando's projected growth. The plan places a third of the city's future population into New Urbanist-style town centers and compact neighborhoods.

But the movement has never been without its critics. Despite their optimistic buzz, New Urbanist projects have so far captured only a fraction of the national residential market. Developers have rarely opted for a New Urbanist plan when they had a choice, mainly because they tend to be more costly and take longer to build than the standard strip mall.[208]

There are other problems the authors learned about when Arrington-Marlowe developed a 20 Year Vision Plan for the City of Naples in 2007. In focus groups and community forums with Naples residents, "smart growth" was perceived negatively as promoting unwanted higher density development inside existing single family residential neighborhoods and commercial areas. Smart growth meant to these residents more traffic congestion, more noise, and more people. The primary beneficiaries of smart growth, according to the popular view in these community forums and focus groups, were developers and the very wealthy.

A few months before, up Florida's west coast from Naples in our strategic planning work for Pinellas County Government, planning and environmental staff suggested that Pinellas citizens, already living in the most densely populated county in Florida, would oppose attempts to grant higher densities in developed areas as an incentive for redevelopment. Their reasoning mirrored the Naples experience. The City of Ormond Beach in Volusia County at the other end of the I-4 Corridor received a similar negative response to a failed referendum proposal to increase building heights inside the City as an incentive for more compact development and less sprawl.

These experirnces are part of the mix of reactions to smart growth initiatives. Several communities, as in the Orlando experience cited earlier, continue to promote compact development and praise the virtues of the New Urbanism, but the struggle to bridge the gap between theory and reality is not easy; and many of fallen into this chasm.

Smart Growth Struggles: The Volusia Example

Volusia County, for example, struggled to figure out how to promote smart growth. There was much "blood on the table" as the various proposals were vetted, including a failed attempt to establish a smart growth planning tool known as urban growth boundaries. Owners of large tracts of rural lands outside the proposed boundaries were wary of efforts to change land use designations without knowing the practial effect of such an approach. City officials were skeptical about promoting higher densities inside urbanized areas, a political matter that changed from hypothetical concern to concrete reality when the Ormond Beach referendum failed.

Volusia's experience with urban growth boundaries is consistent with the observations of an author of a chapter of *Planning for Paradise*, Randall Holcombe, a Florida State professor of economics. Holcombe surmises that attempts to promote compact urban development often run head-on into resistance from another formidable source in addition to rural land owners, city residents and their elected local officials: consumers. Neil writes in his summary article:

> ...[Urban growth] boundaries are planning tools ostensibly aimed at curbing some of the negative aspects of urban sprawl. An unavoidable side effect of boundaries is that they reduce the amount of developable land and thereby force prices up on what's left. Developers and buyers can escape such traps by running to suburbs and rural areas, which they eagerly do. Holcombe told *Research in Review* that even for people with the wherewithal to live in denser neighborhoods, many simply choose not to.[209]

The Volusia County Council, working in concert with the Volusia Council of Governments, continued to struggle with various smart growth tools, including a scheme to develop transfer of development rights from rural to urban areas that sparked much confusion. Another proposal akin to urban growth boundaries, but without the same force and effect, would adopt an "Environmental Core Overlay" on 296,000 acres in unincorporated Volusia County as high-priority for conservation and limited development. The County Council in August 2008 voted unanimously to transmit the so-called ECO -- Environmental Core Overlay -- to the State Department of Community Affairs for its review. The policy framework governing lands in the ECO will be devised at an unspecified future time through adoption of land development regulations, prompting some critics to claim that the County has the "cart before the horse."[210]

One problem encountered in the Volusia experience, common in other parts of the state, involves what to do with existing development rights of exempted subdivisions and other lands in rural areas. In Volusia, these exempted subdivisions have long-standing "vested rights," legal entitlements to develop, many at densities of 1 unit per 2.5 acres. Others require more land per residential unit but may still be able to develop. Still other rural lands that do not enjoy vested rights as exempted subdivisions may also have the potential to develop, albeit at very low densities.

Any policy that prevents these rural lands from developing may run head on into a major problem: the so-called Burt Harris Act. Enacted by the Florida legislature in 1995, this Act requires that local governments must pay landowners if regulations "inordinately burden" their rights to develop their land. One potential policy response Volusia considered is to permit clustering of density entitlements on rural lands, enabling compact development in exchange for creation of conservation lands on the remaining portion of the property. As Volusia discussed this idea, it was unclear precisely how this scheme would work.

Attempts to meet these challenges to smart growth policy can provoke the law of unintended consequences: some owners of rural lands, fearful of impending and unknown restrictions, may choose to develop their properties in sprawling, low-density rural subdivisions, precisely the opposite effect proponents of compact urban development seek to achieve. Moreover, even if Volusia's ECO is adopted as policy, it is unlikely that development of these entitled rural subdivisions and other rural lands will be prohibited.

The conflict, confusion, and political crosscurrents Volusia faced exemplify the difficulties that confront local policy-makers who try to enact smart growth policy. In Volusia during the 2005-2007 period, a county manager and, ultimately, growth management director and principal planner were victims of the political fallout, and resigned in frustration or were forced out.

All the while, Volusia held in its hands what many observers believe to be the smartest growth management tool of all: buying large tracts of undeveloped property fee simple or restricting its development through purchase of conservation easements. Volusia got in the business of acquiring environmentally-sensitive lands in the mid-1980s. In 2000 the program was expanded through creation of Volusia Forever. The County's website states:

Volusia *Forever* was created in 2000 when the citizens of Volusia County voted to tax themselves .2 mills over 20 years to protect the County's natural biodiversity. Over the life of the program it is anticipated that $191 Million will be raised through this ad valorem tax. In order to stretch these dollars as far as possible Volusia *Forever* will attempt to form partnerships with federal, state, water management district and local agencies that are committed to protecting natural resources. Approximately 30,000 acres (fee-simple and less-than-fee) have been acquired since the beginning of the program.[211]

Neils article in *Research in Review* concludes with observations about land acquisition programs as a growth management tool:

The authors provide considerable evidence that Florida's future isn't all bleak. For one thing—a *big* thing, in fact—Florida has preserved more natural lands than any other state in the past two decades. On the theory that outright land purchases trump even the best land-use regulations—subject to political vagaries as these inevitably are—no harder line may ever be drawn in the battle over Florida's growth than locking away land forever from the clutches of development.[212]

Clay Henderson, a well-known environmental lawyer and activist, was instrumental in establishing Volusia's first land acquisition program when he was a member of the County Council in the 1980's, and went on to help establish the state's Florida Forever Program. In 2000, he was a major supporter of the Volusia Forever referendum. Later he would serve on the County's smart growth committee. Henderson offers the following perspective on Florida's and Volusia's experience with growth management generally, and smart growth specifically:

Volusia was the first in the nation to adopt a bond issue for acquisition of environmentally sensitive lands. In 1986 and again in 2000 voters approved $20 million and $160 million respectively for acquisition of environmental lands, water recharge areas, and lands for parks. The programs were both pro-active and reactive. They were proactive in the sense that it gave the county tools to partner with the state and water management districts to acquire large swaths of natural areas and take them out of the path of growth. They were reactive in the sense that the county was able to acquire lands in sensitive areas where development approvals had already been authorized.[213]

The Growth Management Verdict

The authors of *Planning for Paradise* cite several positive outcomes of Florida's experiment with growth management, in spite of all the problems. Their conclusions as summarized by Neil:

"The art of comprehensive planning has been advanced in Florida and the state and is seen as a model for comprehensive plan development in the United States," the writers assert. In the bargain, Florida has also become a nationally recognized leader in transportation planning, as well as in finding innovative, local means of financing it.

Furthermore, there's evidence that growth management laws still enjoy plenty of popular support in Florida, even among developers…Florida's epic struggle to deal with a human flood unmatched in U.S. history should be seen as a work in progress, the writers conclude. Given the number and enormity of challenges the state faces, giving up the struggle now makes no sense in the middle of what they see as an evolutionary process. The "final verdict" on whether the struggle has produced any lasting benefits they write, is still "decades in the making."[214]

One legacy of the growth management experience is that Florida has become a state with many plans, and much capacity to plan in the future. Highly-qualified planners can be found not only in public agencies, but importantly in the many non-profit organizations and universities dedicated to advancing Florida's growth management understandings and approaches. Many of the state's best planners are in the private sector, well-positioned to influence developers, policy-makers, and the Florida public in positive ways. Planners' knowledge, skills and abilities will be needed in the immediate years ahead as the state seeks to over-haul the growth management act; and to deal with problems long-neglected like water supply, climate change and energy policy.

One problem with Florida's prolific public planning efforts at the state and local levels is the lack of integration among plans and strategies to implement them. When Arrington-Marlowe helped develop the Pinellas County strategic plan in 2005-06, we were struck by the sheer number of existing plans current in the County organization.

In addition to the Pinellas County Comprehensive Plan, there were more than 100 separate plans, covering topics as varied as economic development, parks and recreation, and public transit. These plans neither served nor shared a well-articulated vision; and there was no strategic integration or management system to guide implementation.

The County's leadership to its credit recognized this problem, which is why they saw the need for a strategic plan. We had a similar experience with our strategic planning effort for the City of Orlando in 2007. We expect we would find similar situations in virtually every local government of any size and in many state agencies.

Clearly, Florida's planning profession can produce well developed plans. What's missing is the vision, strategies, and will to implement them in ways that serve sustainability themes. There is much work to be done by the planning profession to improve the state-of-the-art of comprehensive *sustainability* planning, and much education of public policy-makers and administrators about how to develop and implement visions and approaches to implementing them that will be meaningful and lasting. The state-of-the-art in this regard is in its infancy.

One criticism of the existing public growth management scheme is that it has become too focused on land development, physical infrastructure, and natural resource issues at the expense of the state's social ecology, existing urban problems, and future "new vision" economic development aspirations. Education, health and human services, criminal justice and economic development opportunities, especially those associated with the emerging "Green Economy," deserve excellence in planning.

In the language of sustainability, Florida growth management system needs to be better aligned with the goals and objectives of sustainability, which demands that integrated planning resources be put to all the components: natural resource, economic, social and governance.

Also demanded is alignment of public policy and approaches to governance with the needs, aspirations and values of the Florida public. This will require advancing the state-of-the-art in visioning and strategic planning, citizen engagement; and development and execution of public policies and initiatives in new and innovative ways.

Proponents of "smart growth" recognize these deficiencies, and have sought to address them intellectually. But practical experience with these concepts reflects a dearth of public understanding and trust that smart growth policies serve the public interest. These problems notwithstanding, "smart growth" holds promise to provide a new planning framework grounded in sustainability thinking. The current top-down growth management system with all its attendant bureaucratic requirements, funding deficiencies, and intergovernmental tensions is ill-equipped as a platform to launch smart growth in a meaningful way.

Probing the Purpose of Growth Management: A Basic Flaw

The problems run deeper than the difficulties with crafting smart growth policies onto the present bureaucratic system. There is a basic flaw in the current approach that deserves much public understanding and debate. Awareness of this flaw begins with understanding that the existing growth management system is limited to planning and development regulation of growth as it happens. It has little to say about addressing yesterday's urban problems today or the effects they will have on the new vision for tomorrow.

The growth management arrangement forces scarce public resources -- when they are available -- into projects and programs designed to accommodate new growth, and away from those needed to deal with existing over-burdened infrastructure and service delivery systems. The idea that concurrency requirements enforced through time have kept infrastructure and service levels concurrent with the impacts of growth and to acceptable levels is a myth. Infrastructure and services have been declining, not improving through time in spite of the fact that growth has resulted in much new valuable infrastructure and increases in the level of commitment to services.

This overall deterioration of service levels has occurred because most of Florida's growth has been residential, which does not pay for itself, especially when it sprawls into outlying areas. Also, much of Florida's infrastructure is aging. Some of it was not built well to begin with, as exemplified by the flooding problems suffered by residents in many parts of the state after a hard rain. Costs have been going up, while service levels have been going down. Meanwhile the state's taxation policies continue to produce frustrating inequities.

The public is aware of this trend toward decline and inequity because citizens live it. The best of the opinion research affirms that the public not only is concerned with the rate of growth; citizens also blame growth for most of the problems facing the state.[215]

The "Smart Growth" movement inches the system toward a more enlightened approach grounded in the theory of sustainability. But even with this improvement, the state's growth management and tax and budget policies continue to be built on the assumption that the role of government essentially is to provide the infrastructure and services required of new growth. The fact that the revenue base of state and local governments and schools is hard-wired to new growth exacerbates this fatal flaw, and causes the whole system to collapse when the economy turns south.

Missing are the vision and the will not only to plan and regulate, but to *govern* in a sustainable manner. The existing system has become a 21st Century extension of the traditional view of the role of government as the handmaiden of the old growth vision. This insight helps explain why smart growth initiatives are mistrusted, and lack public credibility. They are associated with the status quo arrangements for managing growth, which are not aligned with the needs, aspirations, and values of citizens who envision a sustainable Florida. It is not hard to understand why Floridians are angry with their governments, some of them are threatening to take matters into their own hands.

What is needed is a new *leadership* framework for *governing* -- not merely planning and regulating -- in a sustainable manner; and recognition that "growth management" through "comprehensive planning" is a means to an end, and not an end in itself. Sadly, much of Florida's planning; public management and legal talent are dedicated to keeping an unsustainable system in operation. Would it not be much more productive to divert this talent to helping policy-makers construct a new leadership framework, including a new growth management approach?

We offer in the next two chapters and throughout Part II ideas about how to advance the state-of-the art in planning and public policy-making, including in depth examinations of best practices for visioning and strategic planning, citizen engagement, consensus-building and other tools necessary to bring to life the features of sustainable governance and policy presented in Chapter I. Others are beginning to think in the same direction by figuring out ways to identify and use the tools of sustainable governance.

Offered next is a summary of related and promising work by the Century Commission, 1000 Friends of Florida and the Central Florida visioning and planning effort known as MyRegion. These serve as examples of the direction true "comprehensive planning" built around sustainability themes should head: away from only planning for and regulating new growth as it occurs to a broader emphasis on sustainable governance that gives meaning to the word "comprehensive" and content to the word "sustainability."[216]

Lawrence W. Arrington and Herbert A. Marlowe, Jr.

Understanding Public Needs, Aspirations and Values

In a report prepared for the Century Commission entitled "Engaging the Future through a State-Coordinated Regional Visioning Initiative," Dr. Tim Chapin, Department of Urban & Regional Planning Florida State University, calls for a more regional, less technical, and more visionary approach to growth management. He makes the following observation:

> ...(I)n Florida comprehensive planning was designed primarily as a technical process in which a local government was to demonstrate how it would accommodate its population growth and provide urban services at or above a minimum level of service. Regional visioning offers a tremendous opportunity to reestablish planning as a normative process, whereby a desired future state is envisioned and policies and programs are designed to work towards that vision. A regional vision can provide longer-term, big picture guidance to government actions, something that comprehensive plans have struggled to do given their relatively near-term time frames (10-20 years) and onerous administrative processes (hearings, amendments, EARs).[217]

One research effort sponsored by the Century Commission in 2006 deserves special attention. Chapin and Heather Khan, Florida State University reviewed existing statewide survey data, including thirty-four surveys, reports and other material on the attitudes of Florida citizens toward growth and growth-related issues over time.

The Executive Summary of their report to the Century Commission states:

Two questions guided our work:

1. Is there a sufficient body of sound survey data available to provide a clear understanding of Florida citizen views and values regarding growth and how it is managed in Florida?
2. Does the available evidence indicate an ability by the Century Commission to determine what Floridians like and don't like

about growth and development, what their related concerns or desires are, and whether they perceive their quality of life to be getting better or worse over time?[218]

Our review of these materials yields four conclusions of interest to the Century Commission:

1. *A great deal of information on citizen attitudes is available*, offering a detailed picture of citizen views towards ongoing population and economic growth in the state, impacts associated with this growth, and perceptions concerning the effectiveness of the state's growth management approach.
2. *Florida's citizens express major concerns about the pace and form of growth in the state*, with many of the issues associated with growth identified as major problems facing the state. There is some limited evidence that Floridians perceive their quality of life to be declining, in large part because of growth-related issues.
3. *There appears to be a set of five "core values"* that receive broad-based support: Environmental Protection, Safety and Security, Personal Time, Affordability, and Commitment to Collective Action.
4. Despite the large number of surveys, survey reports, and articles that have investigated citizen attitudes, *our current state of knowledge regarding these attitudes remains incomplete*. Areas where our information base remains incomplete are: north Florida resident attitudes, rural county resident values, insights into what citizens want (versus what they don't want), and insights into tradeoffs when pursuing those state and local attributes valued by citizens.

In a related research effort, those charged with leading the Central Florida regional planning effort MyRegion chose to conduct an analysis of the values held by Central Floridians. The MyRegion effort is an excellent example of a regional and local leadership initiative designed to articulate and develop strategies to advance toward a new vision.

It is likely that the findings, conclusion, and recommendations of MyRegion are equally applicable to other areas of Florida. Harris-

Interactive, a strategic research organization, conducted the study, which identified the key values held by Central Floridians. Guiding principles associated with the region's growth and quality of life were developed and tested, using the values as a foundation.

According to a September, 2006 MyRegion report entitled "Central Florida Growth Vision: Mid-Project Report", Harris-Interactive identified the "...shared, core values Central Floridians associate with quality of life, growth, and the development of their ideal community. The study explored the attitudinal differences among key stakeholder groups, such as citizens, business leaders, and local political and regulatory personnel." The report identified three "value pillars": nature and outdoors, safety and security, and education. According to the My Region Mid-Term Report, "By surveying attitudes, the study finds that 70 percent of concerns about the future are directly related to growth. These values have fed directly into the development of the principles identified to guide the regional vision..."[219]

The principles are presented in the following graphic:

Guiding Principle	Percentage Of Respondents Who Chose Principle As One Of Top Five
Preserving open space, recreational areas, farmland, water resources and critical environmental areas	77%
Provide universal access to the highest quality of education, healthcare, and cultural amenities	72%
Provide a variety of transportation options	57%
Foster distinctive, attractive and safe places for people to work	45%
Encourage a diverse, globally competitive economy	42%
Create a range of obtainable housing opportunities and choices	41%
Create walk-able neighborhoods	33%
Strengthen and direct development toward existing communities	28%
Make development decisions predictable, fair and cost effective	28%
Encourage community and stakeholder collaborations	21%
Mix land uses	17%
Take advantage of compact building designs	9%

Source[220]

The Century Commission also engaged Harris-Interactive to conduct a qualitative values analysis of the Tampa-St. Petersburg Region.[221] Understanding values (as well as needs and aspirations) of citizens is critical to aligning public policies, programs, and projects that will be supported by the Florida public.

Taken together, these recent efforts offer many ideas for improving Florida's growth management approach. Various principles and guidelines are offered, and calls for restructuring intergovernmental roles and relationships are made. The work of the Century Commission and MyRegion effort stand as excellent examples of mining for solid data about growth management values. They point to the need for more related research. Hopefully, new applied research will be given the support necessary to tackle all the components of sustainability. This is the kind of information a new leadership framework must be based upon. Florida's new vision will require this comprehensive effort.

A de-centralized and regional approach unfettered by burdensome "top-down" bureaucratic rules and procedures will be needed to unleash the level of creative energy demanded of such a new framework. Florida's local governments working closely with state and regional agencies, non-profit organizations and the citizenry at-large can become true laboratories of democracy, full of experimentation, creativity and excellence in planning and execution of sustainable public policy.

The MyRegion effort with its de-centralized and collaborative framework informed by high-quality citizen engagement---including focused efforts to understand citizen needs, aspirations and values---reflects the features of sustainable governance. This case example suggests that regional and locally-driven planning efforts are producing much success, and points to a framework in which accountability for results primarily would be with the public itself; and not with Tallahassee level planning bureaucrats.

The Florida public today is highly concerned about growth management issues, much more so than when the Growth Management Act was made part of Florida law. The public expresses these concerns most frequently and intensely at the local level. State budget cuts, shameful compensation treatment of state planners and incessant reorganizations has diminished the planning capacity of the Department of Community Affairs as regional and local planning capacities and competencies have increased. Today, state planners likely possess far less seasoned knowledge of the real problems facing Florida than the combination of talent that is found in any of Florida's regions among public, non-profit, and private sector planning professionals.

This could not be said when Florida's experiment with growth management began in the 1970's. Then, there was little planning talent outside state government and the universities. Compared with state government where the power and authority over growth management were placed, there was much apprehension about the capacity of local government to plan well and to resist the political pressures of development interests. Today, thanks to the strides made by the planning profession during the intervening years and the performance of the Florida Legislature, the concern about the level of government best equipped to plan and resist narrow special interests has reversed direction.

Growth Management Reform: The Role of Sustainability

This line of analysis leads to the conclusion that the future growth management role of state government under a new framework should be less rules-driven and top-down command and control. A better approach would be for the state to steer the process by establishing and measuring the achievement of sustainability goals and objectives, and to reward successful performance at the local level, reserving punishing penalties as a secondary strategy for local governments that act irresponsibly. This approach could give real meaning to the so-called "State Plan".[222] The role of state government is examined further in the Chapter VII.

One option is to recognize that the present Growth Management Act has become so unwieldy that a new framework should be developed to replace it altogether. The Act's ultimate repeal would enable the state to proceed with lessons learned from its experience with growth management, a clean slate to create a better way, and present mistakes left behind.

1000 Friends of Florida in a report issued in March 2009 provides much rich insight into the quality of growth management reform needed. In a proposal entitled, "The Florida Sustainable Communities Act," 1000 Friends provides a blueprint containing the following goals:

- Save money for the citizens of Florida
- Promote sustainable community development
- Create health, sustainable communities
- Protect the state's rural and natural lands
- Offset the impacts of global climate change
- Ensure that growth and development pay for themselves
- Restructure the state's economy to be less dependent on growth

In language that strikes at the heart of the authors' motivation for writing this book, 1000 Friends concludes: "Strong and decisive leadership is needed to bring Florida into the 21st Century. In this time of economic hardship and declining natural resources, no longer can we afford to pay the high costs associated with sprawling, automobile-dependent development. The basic tools are in place. We must now focus on better use of them."[223]

Conclusion

Such is the state of growth management in Florida. It is such a "mess" that it is questionable whether the legislature and ultimately the Governor will be able to develop the "new policy framework" replete with "growth leadership" called for by 1000 Friends of Florida and others and conceptually favored by Pelham. If the growth management policy-making experience during the 2007-2009 legislative sessions is any indication, state elected leaders appear to be moving in the opposite direction.

The track record of growth management policy-making, like that of taxation and budget policies, contains many object lessons in misaligned leadership and unsustainable governance. Florida's growth management experience fails the test when the features of sustainable governance arising out of our *analytical model* are applied.

The system is not broadly *visionary and future conscious* with its limited emphasis on land development. Growth management policy does not reflect that developers, citizens or local communities perceive and advance their *self-interests, rightly*. The planning and development process is so narrowly focused on issuance of land development orders that it fosters imbalance among the components of sustainability and fails to address correction of urban problems associated with deteriorating infrastructure and over-burdened service delivery systems.

The growth management approach is clearly *misaligned with the needs, aspirations, and values* of Floridians, and is widely perceived as favoring development interests. Rightly or wrongly, many citizens, as evidenced by the Hometown Democracy movement, perceive they are treated as spectators in the development and administration of growth management policy with no meaningful opportunity for *citizen engagement* in key growth decisions.

The tools and techniques of citizen engagement---the public hearing or local planning or governing board workshop---do not capture an accurate picture of citizens' needs, aspirations, and values, and too often result in a few citizens affecting decisions in ways that do not advance the public interest. The system is perceived by all the major stakeholders and the citizenry as neither *transparent nor trust worthy*.

The history of patchwork fixes to the problem of funding concurrency requirements demonstrates that the growth management approach overall *is not grounded in the realities* of the problems being left in its wake. The system is unmindful that public problems are *complex, multi-dimensional, and interconnected*. It fails to address the need for a comprehensive approach to integration of multiple plans and strategic initiatives in service to the goals and objectives of sustainability, focusing instead on goals, objectives, and policies in individual elements of comprehensive plans that, taken together, leave much unplanned and unaddressed. The system is often attacked by those involved with its administration as *uncreative, rigid, and lacking in basic commonsense*.

Growth management administration is *not results or performance oriented*. It focuses on process, not outcomes. When specific and definitive accountability for results and compliance with the law are sought for planning and development regulatory actions, the venue is all too often a court. There is little performance measurement geared to determining whether the goals, objectives, and policies of comprehensive plans---including concurrency requirements---are being met as permitted developments are built out.

Finally, the cumbersome intergovernmental evaluation, appraisal, and approval processes are not administered in a *meaningfully collaborative* manner by the agencies and stakeholders involved. These processes too often result in more intergovernmental and inter-sector tension, turf protection and unhealthy conflict than cooperation, mutual support and understanding of shared service to agreed-upon goals and objectives. Local governing boards and top administrative staffs in our experience hardly ever actually read these reports, much less use them for strategic decision-making

Yet, the system "keeps on keeping on" because only a few public leaders have displayed the intellect and courage to stand up and demand the mess be fixed. Secretary Pelham, to his credit, is among them.

Surely, Florida is better off because of its growth management experience than it would have been without it. Even with all its problems, the past quarter century's massive population growth provided a proving ground for advancing the art of planning and development regulation. This experience is invaluable as the state now seeks a new vision for a sustainable Florida. The knowledge, experience, and resources developed by virtue of the Growth Management Act at all levels of government and throughout the private sector will well serve the state in the years ahead.

We agree with the assessment in *Planning for Paradise* that the jury is still out, and the final verdict on growth management efforts will be years away. Meanwhile, it is clearly time to regroup, honestly assess the performance of present growth management arrangements, and take the art to its next level: sustainability planning within the context of a new leadership framework that seeks sustainable governance comprehensively.

The new leadership framework we describe in this book and other calls for new leadership will be useful in achieving better balance and alignment of growth management decisions with the tents of sustainability and the needs, aspirations and values of Floridians. The call here is consistent with those of 1000 Friends of Florida, Florida Chamber Foundation, and the Century Commission for a Sustainable Florida, Florida Audubon, Florida Sierra and the Central Florida MyRegion effort.

But much more is needed than merely reforming the existing Growth Management Act, although substantial reform certainly is warranted in the near term. Demanded are new de-centralized and regional ways and means of governing Florida through which new leadership may be exercised. Growth management must move away from being a technical top-down process for providing infrastructure and services and regulating new growth to a broader framework for providing leadership needed to advance the state's new vision of a sustainable Florida.

As this slow turning of the "Ship of State" takes place, the traditional approaches of state and local governance must be transformed to produce the quality of public leadership demanded by the new vision. No one has all the answers; and there are no quick fixes. There is much work to be done over many years in crafting new approaches.

The Moral Imperative

The final concluding observations here seek to articulate this sense of high purpose and to square with the "moral compass" sustainability provides. It will be well for engaged public leaders to connect with this larger sense of purpose as they undertake changes to Florida's taxation and budget; and growth management approaches.

Just as the state's forebears through the aegis of democracy forged a practical and necessary role for governance suitable to the old vision, today's leaders must craft civic roles, relationships and management and financial arrangements suited to the new vision. The old vision by world standards -- despite all the problems it created for the present day -- produced a magnificent place full of opportunity to live, work, and play in the pursuit of happiness and prosperity. The hope of the new vision is that it will move society to a more humane level of existence full of opportunity for people to pursue a good life serving human values and purposes beyond mere pleasure and profit. Realization of this hope demands the same commitment to hard work and sacrifice made by those who brought the old vision to fruition, but with the understanding that the places we inhabit are on loan to us and demand a strong ethic of stewardship to fulfill great purposes beyond our own self-aggrandizement.

The capacity to adapt to complex challenges and transcend them in the spirit of the "citizen-as-steward" is required, just as it was for the best of our forbearers, on whose shoulders we now stand. This cannot be done if large numbers of Florida's most fortunate and talented citizens continue to act as crowd of consumers on an extended vacation or a self-centered and civically-blind retirement, passing away the time in life-style enclaves cut off from fellow citizens unlike themselves. And it cannot be done either with public leaders who wallow in this malaise, pander to its cynicisms, fears and distractions; and offer shallow-minded, ideological responses issuing from either extreme of the political spectrum.

The search for sustainable governance -- in honor of our forbearers and love for our children -- is about mustering the sense of civic responsibility and balance, community identity, and of place demanded to ensure that Florida remains for future generations a proud *home* of opportunity for a good life. We are confident that Floridians, as Americans first, will rise to the occasion if they are presented right choices by leaders who consult with them and earn their confidence and trust; leaders who will help them become citizens once again and good stewards anew.

A new era of sustainable governance must replace the present era of ideology. The new era must demonstrate the capacity to adapt to the challenges of a time in history when the state's public institutions are put to work to do what is practical and necessary to advance toward the new vision of a sustainable Florida.

It is to this governance challenge that we turn in the next two chapters, where will learn that there is much evidence in case examples that the turning to the proper heading already is underway. It is being steered by regional and local citizen-leaders who have learned how to assess, understand, and forge public initiatives aligned with what their fellow citizens need, hope for, and value.

If there is one thing we should have learned in the past few decades, it is that social, environmental, and economic challenges facing Florida are interwoven. The attempt to deal with neatly defined problems in isolation from one another---itself a product of the industrial-age mentality---creates only confusion and unhealthy conflict. Yet the organizational structure of government mirrors precisely this approach to reality. The arrangements for governing must undergo transformative change. It is to this challenge that we now turn.

Nowhere is obsolescence more advanced than in our political life. And in no field today do we find less imagination, less experiment, less willingness to contemplate fundamental change.

—Alvin Toffler

Chapter VII

THE REFORMING: GOVERNMENTAL REFORM, NECESSITY AND HISTORY

Introduction and Background

The most daunting challenge facing the state's public agencies as the transition from the old growth vision to the new vision for a sustainable Florida takes place involves shifting their roles, relationships, organization, and management approaches. These must be aligned with the requirements of a new vision that sees Florida's public agencies working collaboratively among themselves and with the private and non-profit sectors to produce a globally competitive state. We have labeled this as a shift from "government" to "governance."[224]

This chapter will examine the necessity for congruence of roles, relationships, management and organizational approaches among what traditionally has been viewed as three separate sectors: public, private and non-profit.

We argue that the three sectors must work in concert to serve the goals and objectives of sustainability. This will require changes in the nature of their interrelationships with an emphasis on collaboration as the major public challenges facing society are addressed. The ways and means of organizing and managing the "business" of each of the sectors must be sufficiently in accord with each other to enable public, private and non-profit organizations to work together to solve public problems in a sustainable manner.

While the organization and management approaches of all three sectors will have to continuously adapt and restructure, the most profound changes must occur in the public sector. Traditional public sector jurisdictional and bureaucratic approaches have been relatively slow to adapt to the demands of social, technological and economic changes associated with the emerging global economy. Government agencies can no longer function as separate and fragmented jurisdictional and bureaucratic "silos", separated from each other and performing their roles apart from the non-profit and private sectors. The intergovernmental system itself must be transformed, as federal, state and local agencies learn how to work together effectively.

Sustainable governance requires that the talents and resources of the private and non-profit sectors be brought into the development and administration of public policies, programs, and projects in new and innovative ways. Sustainable governance also demands that public sector resources and the auspices of official authority be used to leverage private and non-profit sector talent and investment in the public interest.

This blending of sectors in the interests of advancing society toward the goals and objectives of sustainability cannot occur unless the three sectors learn how to work together harmoniously and efficiently. The transition from the old to the new vision for a sustainable Florida depends on this shift from "government" to "governance", recognizing that devising new inter-sector roles and relationships, and appropriate organization and management arrangements and systems of accountability will pose significant challenges.

Governance arrangements and public policies suited to the old vision must give way to the requirements of the new vision. This demands solutions that "fit" both the threats to the state's sustainability and the opportunities to advance it. New governance arrangements, public policies and leadership practices are needed to forge sustainable solutions. This means that top-down, command and control intergovernmental practices with power centralized at the state level must be altered to recognize the diversity and complexity of the problems the state faces. State government leaders must see the wisdom of de-centralization of power within broad directional guidelines, and learn to trust the democratic processes at work at the regional and local levels.

It also means that the hodge-podge of fragmented public agencies at the local level must forge productive relationships among themselves and with the non-profit and private sectors. This new governance process also requires new ways of forming strategically planned and networked interrelationships for development and administration of public policy. These new approaches and arrangements for governing must be grounded in the goals and objectives of sustainability, and aligned with the public's needs, aspirations, and values. No ideology can meet this standard. A combination of sustainability-thinking and democracy well practiced forms the basis for creating sustainable governance.

The chapter begins with observations about the necessity for forging productive interrelationships among the sectors, drawing on the insights of respected social critic, futurist and author, Alvin Toffler, who points the way to a key element of his "anticipatory democracy." Special emphasis is placed on the relationship between business and government, keying first on the difficult governance problems associated with lobbying and campaign finance practices of contemporary political culture.

We argue that the way the private sector understands and advocates its interests must change to a broader and more intelligent definition, recognizing that campaign contributions and lobbying are essential parts of the political process that condition the way the two sectors relate to each other. Sustainable governance demands that the private sector understand its economic interests rightly by recognizing the critical implications for business of the natural resource, social, and governance components of sustainability.

The non-profit sector serving the public interest also has a stake in lobbying and campaign finance issues. Many public interest non-profits are affected by private sector lobbying and campaign finance, and are often at odds with private interests. Some of these public interest non-profits participate in financing campaigns for referenda (and sometimes, but not in all cases, candidates for political office), and hold great sway in the halls of government. Sustainable governance demands better relationship building and collaboration between non-profit and private sectors as they seek to interface with and influence the public sector.

Next, we turn attention to an overview of Florida's attempts to reform government, with special emphasis on the structure, organization, and management approaches of local government, where most of the reform effort has been directed. Traditional attempts to reform the fragmented nature of the state's governmental architecture enjoyed only modest success. These structural reforms were "echoes" of the Progressive Era influences, and began to take hold at mid-20th Century.

A major lasting feature of these reforms was the rise of the Council-Manager system at the city and, to some extent, the county levels, and the increasing use of corporate-bureaucratic organizational forms throughout state and local governments. The failure of traditional structural reforms to change significantly the state's fragmented Jacksonian system coupled with the negative reactions to aspects of Progressive Era reforms gave birth to Florida's version of the "reinvention of government" movement which arose in the 1990's. This movement had some effect on Florida State and local governmental structure, organization and management practices.

The self-proclaimed "passion for reform" of former Governor Jeb Bush was an outgrowth of the reinvention movement alloyed with his distinctive ideological approach to governing and leadership style. Bush's reforms involve the role as well as the structure (organizational forms and management practices) of government. As noted, his ideological approach stands in contrast to traditional Jefferson-Jacksonian philosophies and Progressive Era influences, and helped bring the state to its present crisis. We argued in Chapter III that Bush's approach is also a departure from the great heritage of the Republican Party.

Paradoxically, the reforms of the Bush "Era of Ideology" also have helped lay the groundwork for the promise of the government to governance shift. This is because the best of so-called "econo-think" ideology understands the importance of a strong economy and how to organize and manage entrepreneurial activity in profitable ways. Public agencies must learn more about how to interact, support, and, in some cases, emulate these approaches. Jeb Bush understood this, and despite many failures and setbacks in trying to bridge the gap between theory and reality, accomplished much good work.

The "shift from government to governance" is treated as a progression from the traditional structural reforms, the reinvention movement and the Bush reforms and approaches. The emphasis is on understanding how the governance roles, relationships, management and organizational approaches of the past and present may be transformed into those needed to advance the search for sustainable governance. A summary discussion is presented of the features of the sustainable governance public organization of the future based on current trends and necessary characteristics demanded by the book's analytical model.

Sustainable governance must move beyond these normal conceptions of governmental reform to include collaboration among the branches of government generally as each performs its lawful role, recognizing that ours is a system of *sharing* as well as *separation* of powers and responsibilities within checks and balances. For example, the need for cooperative and concerted effort in the Florida case study is especially acute among all three branches in the administration of social-criminal justice programs. This dimension of inter-governance relationships deserves special attention. It involves the roles and relationships of the judiciary, law enforcement, prosecution (States Attorney) and public defender in working with the executive and legislative branches at the state and local levels in the development, funding, and administration of programs at the interface of the criminal justice system and human services.

This problem illustrates how sustainable governance requires that each branch re-evaluate its roles in relation to the other branches and involved private and non-profit stakeholders as solutions are forged to multi-dimensional, interrelated and highly-complex problems. These inter-governance relationships are highly significant in the search for sustainable governance, and point to the larger problems of re-conceptualizing the traditional administration of civil and criminal justice to include not only social, but environmental and economic spheres as well.[225] This effort is a part of the shift from government to governance as we define it.

Consensus must be forged about what these concepts mean and how they will be applied in concrete circumstances. Many of the leadership tools described in this and the next chapter and in Part II of our work will be helpful in arriving at the conceptual definitions and sorting out the roles and relationships each branch and agency will play.

The next chapter presents case examples of the shift as it is taking place at the regional and local levels, where, we argue, a renewed emphasis on de-centralization and "home rule" are necessitated if the shift is to reach its full potential. The emerging use of "public-private partnerships" and "public management networks" is explored in several areas of public policy, including water supply, green energy and environmental policy, and the interface between criminal and social justice. These are organization and management approaches that integrate the public and private sectors (and sometimes the non-profit sector) in ways that exemplify the shift from government to governance. A more in depth discussion of public management networks is included in Part II of our work in digital and web-based formats because we believe this approach will become an essential element of the new leadership framework, and will help advance sustainable governance.

The Challenge of Congruence Among the Sectors

Futurist Alvin Toffler provides guiding insight to the necessity for congruence among the private, public, and non-profit sectors: "In any system ... there needs to be some congruence between the way a people make wealth and the way they govern themselves. If the political and economic systems are wildly dissimilar, one will eventually destroy the other."[226] He continues:

> Few seem to have considered that if we change the structure of business and leave government unchanged, we create a gaping organizational mismatch that could damage both. An advanced economy requires constant interaction between the two. Thus, like a long-married couple, government and business eventually must take on some of each other's characteristics. If one is restructured, we should expect corresponding changes in the other.[227]

According to the new vision, tourism, construction, and agriculture must be joined by knowledge and technology-based, high-wage generators of wealth in the new global economy. If Toffler's insight is true, there must be mutual understanding, support, and a degree of harmony among the ways the public, private and non-profit sectors interact; the way they "do business". As the nature of wealth generators change, so must associated business practices and inter-sector relationships.

The ways of doing business in construction, tourism, and agriculture have changed dramatically in recent years. All three are much more technology dependent, knowledge-based, and reliant on global networks of providers of goods and services; and all three seek and are affected by international markets. This change in business practices will be even more pronounced as new high-wage and technology-based businesses are recruited and developed in various parts of the state.

Moreover, the nature of the "competition" is changing. No longer is it this or that city within the state or the farmer or grower down the road. Today's real competition includes major international destinations, entire metropolitan regions like Shanghai, London, and New York; citrus growers in Brazil, cattle ranchers in Argentina, and suppliers across the developed world.

All these trends point to the necessity for the public sector to change its ways of doing business. The shift must involve the ways public agencies relate to each other, and interact with the citizenry at-large. The shift must occur in the spirit of Toffler's prophesy about the need for "congruence" between the ways wealth is generated and the ways government is purposed, organized and managed. The shift also is in the spirit of sustainability, which requires concordance between governance systems and economic, social, and environmental systems.

Any honest assessment of the relationships among these sectors, especially between business and government, would conclude that words like "congruence, mutual support, concordance and harmony" do not always apply. In the focus groups we have conducted in recent years, and in our professional experiences and observations generally, business people often view government as inefficient, overly-bureaucratic, full of duplication and waste, slow to respond, and worse.

Many public administrators, especially those with no private sector experience, have trouble understanding why business people criticize and complain so much about government. Public officials often perceive those in business as unconcerned about the public interest, self-absorbed, and motivated strictly by profit. We have witnessed specific instances in which a negative cycle of recrimination has developed between the two sectors, with each seeing the other as "the enemy."

These sentiments have been building for years in American political culture, and appear to have reached a crescendo in Florida recently. While there are many examples of the two sectors working together well, business and government, to use Toffler's analogy, often act like a long-married couple in deep trouble, damaging each other in the midst of a nasty estrangement. The new vision for Florida demands reconciliation among business and government, and inclusion of many non-profit organizations in collaborative leadership initiatives.

Lobbying and Campaign Finance: Self-interest, Rightly Understood

One feature of the relationship between business and government deserves special attention: the use of lobbyists and campaign contributions by businesses at state and local levels of governments as ways to influence law-making, public policy development and administration. In this regard, it is "business" that must change in the interests of sustainable governance; which as defined here includes realtors, homebuilders, developers, medical, legal, agriculture, and insurance as well as those usually labeled business and professional interests.

Attempts to reform these aspects of the relationship between government and business usually center on campaign finance laws designed to limit, disclose, and otherwise regulate contributions; and regulation of lobbying activities, including registration, disclosure of clients and fees, and gift-giving. These rules-driven approaches may have had some positive effect on the most egregious practices, but they have not worked to change the political culture fundamentally. Reform attempts also have sparked much resentment and serious litigation.

This is not the place for a full-blown policy analysis of campaign finance and lobbying reforms. But it is appropriate to examine how the practice by businesses of investing private funds in the political process must change to suit the requirements of the search for sustainable governance.

Seasoned state and local elected officials and public administrators, when pressed on this subject, often view lobbyists as indispensable resources. While there are certainly exceptions, lobbyists usually are highly-educated and experienced in complex policy areas. They are sources of information about how various public initiatives can be made to serve the public interest without crippling litigation or negative reactions that can lead to difficulties in enforcement and administration of policy.

Campaigns for office and to advance referenda are expensive and require contributions from various special interests. While complaints about the quality of these campaigns are justified, they are nevertheless a permanent part of the political system. Changes in campaign style and substance may be possible if the root of the problems we examine next is addressed effectively.

The problem arises for sustainable governance when investments in lobbyists and campaigns are limited to the advancement of the narrow special interests of specific clients. It is the way these interests are defined by businesses that is the root of the problem. Business interests often pay little attention to the social and natural resource implications of public policy, and end up defining their economic interests too narrowly. Many businesses using lobbyists and making campaign contributions are owned and managed by people who are located outside Florida. This absenteeism is in the nature of the economy, and likely will increase in practice as Florida's new vision begins to bear fruit.

The number of lobbyists has increased dramatically at both the national and state levels during the past quarter century, a trend that seems to be escalating. One cause of this increase in business funding of lobbyists and campaigns can be traced to the changing nature of the economy. Globalization, de-regulation and technology have intensified competition for customers and investors. Many lobbyists are hired and campaigns financed to ward off the influence of competitors. The public interest and notions of corporate civic responsibility and the common good get lost in the shuffle.

In Florida politics the wars between the telephone and cable industries come to mind as an example. Sometimes, these lobbyists will join forces against the public interest when broader issues, like tax reform, are on the table. In any event, the influence of often narrowly-defined special interest groups is increasing with emphasis on advancing the interests of consumers and investors and not citizens.[228]

Sustainable governance requires a broad definition of individual interests, and an understanding of its relationship to the common good of society as a whole. This means that businesses ought to be participating in advocacy of sustainable social and natural resource initiatives, and in defining their economic interests in broad terms.

Businesses will not flourish where there exist low levels of investment in education, congested highways, polluted waterways and bad air quality, and high crime rates. Communities are not good for business that cannot offer decent and affordable housing, quality and affordable health care, substance abuse and mental health treatment, and other public initiatives designed to address social, natural resource, and economic problems.

An equal amount of attention should be paid to advocacy of ways to address these broad community problems as has been paid traditionally to lobbying for the latest tax cut or supporting so-called "business-friendly" candidates, legislation and referenda. Business people who participate in Florida politics regardless of their location and competition should educate themselves about the public problems facing the state, and ensure that their interests are defined properly. The most dangerous "competitors" to businesses are a declining quality of life and deteriorating natural environment.

Lobbying and campaign finance practices often are attacked because relatively wealthy business interests carry undue influence when compared with advocacy groups for social, environmental, and other public interest causes. One way to achieve a counter balance would be for wealthy interests to divert some of the private money now spent on contributions to campaigns and excessive lobbying fees to advocacy and other support for initiatives that advance the state's social and natural ecologies. This is the path to being truly "business-friendly"; and a way for businesses to build positive relationships with the many non-profit organizations whose mission involves education, advocacy and support for progressive social and environmental policy.

If sustainable governance is to have any chance of success in Florida, the candidates who receive campaign contributions in the future must be those who demonstrate the capacity to understand the basic precepts of sustainability, and the willingness to pursue aligned leadership initiatives.

The transition from the old to the new vision may prompt a parallel changeover in the nature and power of interest groups themselves. The groups that carry the most influence and have the most interest in the old vision's success may find themselves weakened as new enterprises, non-profits, and citizen-based efforts motivated by realization of the new vision emerge.

New vision interest groups, by definition, would be congenial to the requirements of sustainability, and more likely to press for public policies and initiatives that foster sustainable governance. Moreover, if the general public truly aspires to a vision for a sustainable Florida, the power and influence of these new groups would be considerable and possibly transforming of the existing lobbying and campaign finance culture.

A "clean break" from the old to the new vision is not likely; nor is a rapid parallel transfer of power and influence from old vision interest groups to new vision interest groups. More likely is a slow turning of the way existing powerful groups define their interests coupled with the emergence of new vision groups through time. Either way, more emphasis on sustainable governance would be involved, recognizing that the status quo campaign finance and lobbying practices, like the public policies they produced, have proven themselves unsustainable.

The Opportunity of Crisis

The turning may be accelerated if the state's economic and social conditions continue to deteriorate in response to the global economic crisis that gripped the nation in 2008-09. These conditions may unleash the dynamics necessary to energize taxation and budget, growth management and other policy reforms mentioned in preceding chapters. The reach of this crisis could extend to the lobbying and campaign finance culture as well.

Moreover, the nature of campaigns and post-election lobbying tied to them is changing. The 2008 Presidential election reflected a growing trend toward more "grass roots" involvement, much of it powered by the Internet and associated networked activism among politically-minded citizens. Coupled with the more de-centralized approach to governance mentioned earlier, this new activist style could dilute the power and frustrate the influence of traditional old vision interest groups.

We are reminded here of the insight offered in the introductory chapter that "(r)eal visions for change rarely come from government or from the marketplace, but from civil society."[229] An article published in the New York Times Magazine in early 2009 sounded the same theme, and describes the conditions precedent to transformative change. Citing a book published in the early 1980's by a University of Maryland professor, Mancur Olson, entitled, "The Rise and Decline of Nations," the article's author notes:

> In Olson's telling, successful countries give rise to interest groups that accumulate more and more influence over time. Eventually, the groups become powerful enough to win government favors, in the form of new laws or friendly regulators. These favors allow the groups to benefit at the expense of everyone else; not only do they end up with a larger piece of the economy's pie, but they do so in a way that keeps the pie from growing as much as it otherwise would.

When economies in crisis are forced to rebuild, interest groups are "wiped away," according to Olsen's study. The article quotes MIT professor Frank Levy, an Olsen admirer, as observing: "In a crisis, there is an opportunity to rearrange things, because the status quo is blown up." The article continues, "(i)f a country slowly glides down toward irrelevance, [Levy] said, the constituency for reform won't take shape. Olson's insight was that the defeated countries of World War II didn't rise in spite of crisis. They rose because of it."

In words that well describe contemporary Florida, the author observes, "The parallels to the modern-day United States, though not exact, are plain enough. This country's long period of economic pre-eminence has produced a set of interest groups that, in Olson's words, 'reduce efficiency and aggregate income.' Home builders and real estate agents pushed for housing subsidies, which made many of them rich but made the real estate bubble possible." He continues: "In good times — or good-enough times — the political will to beat back such policies simply doesn't exist. Their costs are too diffuse, and their benefits too concentrated. A crisis changes the dynamic. It's an opportunity to do things you could not do before."[230]

Finally, lobbyists are often treated as "hired guns" that do the work of interfacing with public officials without the direct involvement of clients. Sustainable governance demands that business owners, chief executive officers, members of boards of directors and other business and professional people roll up their sleeves and get directly involved in public service and with crafting public policy at all levels of government.

One hopeful sign emerged when the authors interviewed several key business leaders in the Central Florida region in preparation of a strategic plan for the City of Orlando in 2007. A government relations director for a major business made an insightful comment during a focus group session. He noted that formerly the extent of participation in public affairs of the corporation he worked for and others he knew about was writing checks to candidates at election time or lobbying an issue when the corporation was directly impacted. That changed a few years before when corporate leadership began to understand that fundamental business interests are affected by deteriorating social conditions and physical infrastructure occurring in the Orlando area. A board level decision was made calling for direct corporate involvement in solving community problems. Corporate executives began to volunteer for public service in a variety of ways, including participation in advisory boards and committees designed to develop public policy recommendations.

One keen observer of the Tallahassee business lobbying corps, Allison DeFoor, reports that tangible efforts have been made in recent years at the state level to achieve "cross-fertilization" of various interest groups traditionally at odds with each other in an effort to increase dialogue and promote understanding among them. For example, attempts have been made to diversity the memberships of Florida Audubon and 1000 Friends of Florida by recruiting members who represent development interests. These groups traditionally have supported strong environmental and growth management policy. DeFoor, a well-known environmental and political activist, now serves on the Board of Associated Industries, Florida's most powerful business lobby, a development he describes as "unthinkable five years ago."[231]

During summer 2009 such a coalition was formed to develop and advocate ways to curb the inmate recidivism rate of the state's prisons. DeFoor was instrumental in bringing together the president of Associated Industries of Florida; the president of Florida TaxWatch; the executive vice president of the Florida Chamber Foundation; a former state corrections secretary; three former Florida attorneys general; the executive director of the Florida Police Benevolent Association; and the executive director of the Florida Catholic Conference.

According to a news article[232], members of the coalition signed "An Open Letter to the Governor, Legislature and People of Florida," urging the state to develop alternatives to prepare inmates for reentry into society. The open letter states, "Too many ex-offenders (are) going back to prison because, while behind bars, they received little or no job training, mental health and substance abuse treatment, and the necessary life-skills tools to legitimately re-enter civil society." The letter continues:

> About 33 percent of inmates released in Florida are back behind bars within three years. This is costing us a fortune and will cost more.
>
> We have just over 100,000 people in prison. The budget of the Department of Corrections this year is $2.4 billion.
>
> And if we keep zipping along, we'll need 15 or more additional prisons over the next five years (on top of the 60 we have), costing a couple of billion more in construction, not including the money to run them.

These improvements in relationships among public, private, and non-profit sectors, and in the quality of civic dialogue about the public problems facing Florida are small, but important steps in the search for sustainable governance. These opportunities for dialogue among interests help educate those involved in crafting public policy from different perspectives—social, economic, and environmental—essential to sustainability. If coalitions are formed among these diverse groups, substantive policy reforms will be made possible.

A Dysfunctional System: Lessons from California

These efforts present an opportunity to go further than mere dialogue, and to strike at the heart of a deeper problem with Florida and American politics. Fareed Zakaria, in his acclaimed book, *The Post-American World*, observes:

> The American political system has lost the ability for large-scale compromise, and it has lost the ability to accept some pain now for much gain later on. [The United States] has developed a highly dysfunctional politics. An antiquated and overly rigid political system…has been captured by money, special interests, a sensationalist media, and ideological attack groups. The result is ceaseless, virulent debate about trivia—politics as theater—and very little substance, compromise, and action. A "can do" country is now saddled with a "do-nothing" political process, designed for partisan battle rather than problem-solving. By every measure…the political process has become far more partisan and ineffective…[233]

These trends accurately describe Florida's governance arrangements, public policies, and politics. Only time will tell whether the emerging examples of powerful groups redefining their interests more broadly and opening productive dialogue with others indicates a new directional change in the political culture. If so, this effort must include the capacity to build coalitions for change, and to replace partisan bickering and ideological approaches with sustainability-thinking.

At the core of adaptation to these challenges are the rediscovery of the virtues of democratic decision-making, the tradition of bipartisanship, and a renewed respect for the public service. Failure to adapt in this way could unleash highly-destabilizing political forces, as the state of California has learned. An intensification of the current Florida movement toward "government by referendum", political gridlock on decisive issues, and further deterioration of public services are likely consequences of maintenance of the status quo.

By summer 2009 California was in a bona fide governance crisis. Serious consideration was being given to calling a Constitutional convention to address what was termed the state's serious structural problems. The following statement posted on the web site[234] of a respected economic development organization, the Bay Area Council, provides a description that could easily apply to Florida:

> We believe California's system of government is fundamentally broken. Our prisons overflow, our water system teeters on collapse, our once proud schools are criminally poor, our financing system is bankrupt, our democracy produces ideologically-extreme legislators that can pass neither budget nor reforms, and we have no recourse in the system to right these wrongs. Drastic times call for drastic measures. We believe it is our duty to declare that our California government is not only broken, it has become destructive to our future. It is time to repair our system of governance.
>
> Our state's founders gave us the tool to take this step — with a constitutional convention. We can either be led to a convention by our elected leaders in the Legislature, or we can bypass any gridlock in Sacramento with a "citizen's Constitutional Convention."
>
> When we initially floated the idea of a convention we were met by waves of support from the public and lots of interest from groups around the state. It is now time to take this concept to the next level.

Florida Governmental Reform: An Overview

It is useful to survey prior efforts to reform the structure, functions, and relationships among Florida governments, especially at the local level, where much of the governmental reform activity has taken place. The attempt is to understand the broad strokes of the history that has brought Florida to the government to governance shift. Observations are offered about the relations between state and local government in Florida, keying on the evolution of home rule powers. We critique the philosophical underpinnings of the "reinvention of government movement" of the 1990's and how they were interpreted and applied during the administrations of former Florida governors Lawton Chiles and Jeb Bush.

Our views are based on observations of political behavior, statements, speeches, and dialogue with key political actors, respected academic analysts, journalists, lobbyists and engaged business and civic leaders. We have tried to proceed objectively in a non-partisan manner, and to maintain our personal philosophical fidelity to belief in the principles of democracy and the call for sustainable governance and leadership framework we have described. We hold that both governors examined made positive contributions to governmental reform, and that former governor Bush, although we criticize aspects of his approach to leadership, was particularly committed to meaningful reforms. He helped set the stage for the hopeful promise of the government to governance shift that is currently under way.

These summaries lead to observations about the emerging new approach to "reform": the shift from government to governance. Since we believe the full benefits of this shift have the highest chances of success at the regional and local levels, we concentrate on regional and local approaches to plan and implement features of the new governance shift, and cite a few case examples.

Florida's traditional governmental architecture was designed like many separate factories. State agencies, cities, counties, school districts, and an array of independent authorities and special taxing districts were created to produce the physical infrastructure and services to be consumed by ever-increasing masses of newcomers and visitors.

The state's tax policies – no income or inheritance taxes coupled with homestead exemptions (and later Save Our Homes) were designed to help fuel the growth machine. The role of government was viewed as limited to helping the respective jurisdictions achieve their grand visions of a high growth economy based on construction, tourism, and agriculture. The new vision will demand a different role for government, and reform of the old vision's governmental arrangements.

There have been frequent calls for reforms of Florida's local government arrangements for at least fifty years. During the 1950's and 1960's, Dade and Duval Counties enacted significant local reforms. Home rule for Florida's counties and cities was given constitutional and legislative boosts during the late 1960's. These provisions granted cities and counties significant leeway to reform local government structure and relationships and to sort out which type of local government should provide specified functions.

Some 19 counties have adopted their own governing charters. However, these reforms have spawned more unhealthy conflict and litigation than substantive change.[235] The Metro Dade County charter, authorized by Constitutional amendment in 1957, led the way. Other county charters were adopted after a constitutional revision in 1968 that authorized their creation. The successful Jacksonville-Duval city-county consolidation effort stands as the state's sole example of the merger of municipal and county governments.

Since the Jacksonville-Duval experiment, there have been numerous attempts to consolidate cities and counties in Florida. All have failed. There have been no mergers of cities. The creation of new municipalities has escalated during the past two decades. The Florida local governmental reform landscape is mostly bare.

There have been a number of non-binding inter-local agreements, some of which put in place consolidations of local functions; a few county charter amendments resulting in minor county structural changes, consolidated services and countywide regulatory authority. Many new special taxing districts and authorities have been created.

One trend has been clear in Florida history during the past five decades: as the state urbanized, calls for local home rule intensified. When the Florida Constitution was revised in 1968, cities and counties were given a measure of local self-determination, as mentioned. We will examine the home rule trend and its implications for the government to governance shift in the next chapter.

Why has the appetite for reform been so weak? One answer is that the traditional arrangements served so well the old vision for Florida's economy, and its ways of doing business, that reforms were generally considered unnecessary, even risky to those holding political and economic power. Moreover, it is generally accepted as a broad proposition that citizens are suspicious of governmental reform, and while there appear to be preferences for local home rule, consolidation and centralization of governmental power and responsibility are mistrusted.

The Reinvention of Government Movement: Florida Influences

The traditional approaches to governmental reform did not produce much fruit. Those interested in governmental reform in Florida recognized during the 1990's that a different approach was needed. Governor Lawton Chiles and Lt. Governor Buddy McKay expressed strong interest in the emergent "reinvention of government" movement, prompted by a national bestselling book published in 1992 by authors David Osborne and Ted Gaebler, and entitled *Reinventing Government: How the Entrepreneurial Spirit is Transforming the Public Sector*.[236]

The book owes much to the Democratic Leadership Council, a reform-minded organization linked to the Democratic Party, and influenced by former President Bill Clinton. Osborne and Gaebler's "principles for reinventing government" served as the basis for Al Gore's attempt to "reinvent" the federal government, and are to be found at the heart of attempts throughout all levels of American government to privatize, out-source, de-centralize, re-mission, foster accountability and competition, and otherwise unleash the spirit of entrepreneurship in an effort to banish government "bureaucracy"[237] and "politics as usual."

These "reinvention" themes are attractive philosophically to any serious analyst concerned about the self-aggrandizement and cumbersome inefficiencies that have plagued so much of American politics and public administration at all levels of government, especially since the end of World War II. Republicans and Democrats found common ground in advancing reinvention ideas, but inevitable philosophical disagreements arose. The partisan conflicts became evident when reinvention themes were alloyed with anti-government "Reaganomics" and "econo-think" and hard core conservative religious positions on social policy.

The Chiles administration certainly did not "reinvent" Florida state government. Some progressive steps were taken, but overall, our observation is that Chiles either lost interest or concluded that implementing the kinds of complex and controversial reforms advocated by Osborne and Gaebler weren't worth the political costs and difficulties.[238]

As participants and observers in Florida state and local government, we know that many Florida local governments were influenced by the reinventing government movement, and have implemented a wide variety of innovative practices. But early enthusiasm has abated in what is best understood as an on-going and evolutionary process to change the way governments do business.

A Passion for Reform

When Jeb Bush was elected in 1998, he shaped his own approach to "reinventing government," grounded in his self-proclaimed "passion for reform." His philosophy of government and economics, leadership style, and, to some extent, his religious views combined to form the foundation from which his reform ideas were launched.

He held a strong philosophical belief in a marginalized role for government, and in cutting taxes to stimulate economic growth, the practice of supply side economics. A statement made in his inaugural address in January 2003 was instructive: "There would be no greater tribute to our maturity as a society than if we can make these government buildings around us empty of workers; silent monuments to the time when government played a role larger than it deserved or could adequately fill."[239]

In an article written by Bush during his last months in office, he assessed his view of the role of government and his reform record as governor. His perspectives recognize the need to reform governments in response to the demands of the emerging global economy. He writes:

> Economies are emerging every day to challenge our dominance in the global marketplace, where innovation and ideas are as commonplace as goods and services. Yet, government, with few exceptions, still works like it did in the

1950s, with a pyramid-style, top-down bureaucracy that moves with tortoise-like speed. For America to succeed in the increasingly competitive global economy, our government needs to be able to quickly adapt to this new, changing world."

Bush writes that the role of government is to promote public safety, create opportunity that fuels the economy, and care for the vulnerable. Roles beyond these will cause government to grow beyond the ability to pay for it.

He cites his many outsourcing projects, claiming that he reduced the government workforce by 9,570. He claims his administration saved more than $741 million in actual dollars and "prevented" an estimated $1.4 billion more, presumably through cost avoidance. Bush also notes his use of a public-private partnership to establish a statewide radio system that allows emergency responders and law enforcement to communicate with each other.

The hallmark of Bush's reform agenda was in public education. He instituted standardized testing in Florida's public schools, and established a statewide grading system using the Florida Comprehensive Assessment Test (FCAT) test. He was a strong supporter of school vouchers, which ran into constitutional problems with the Florida Supreme Court, and was a supporter of charter schools.

The court in the voucher case ruled that the state's Opportunity Scholarship Program in place at the time was unconstitutional. The program allowed students in failing schools - those graded F by the state twice in a four-year span - to choose a higher performing public school or a participating private school. The program was ruled unconstitutional in January 2006 because it used public tax money to support education in private schools.

Lower courts had ruled against the voucher program because it violated constitutional provisions requiring separation of church and state. The Supreme Court, however, ignored that argument and found that vouchers violate a state constitutional provision that voters enacted in 1998, for a "uniform, efficient, safe, secure and high quality system of free public schools."

The ruling brought into question the constitutionality of two other Florida voucher programs, one for disabled students and the other for financially disadvantaged families.240In an interview published by the Heritage Foundation in July 2008, Bush continued to press his education agenda. He states, "We can build a world class education system through bigger and bolder reform – higher standards, more school choice, pay for performance, harnessing technology, and stronger accountability. If we give into complacency, we will cede our role as a global powerhouse."[241]

An article summing up the Jeb Bush legacy contained the following observations:

> "Most governors have been committed to the public sector. They grew up knowing and supporting government," said Dominic Calabro, president of Florida TaxWatch, a private watchdog of government spending. "He grew up with a disdain and believed in limited government."[242]

Bush's "passion for reform" called for dismantling government policies and practices that did not reflect his principles strongly enough, and the enactment of those that did. Those who preferred a more activist, progressive role for government grounded in application of democratic decision-making, and who did not buy into the premise that tax cuts and weakened governments are always best were ignored in the heat of Bush's "passion for reform." Indeed, "While seeking reelection in 2002, Bush defined 'real leadership' as making tough choices. For those who disagreed with him, he said, 'You know where I stand.'" His leadership style was characterized as "… shoot-first, take-no-advice method of governing."[243]

Bush's approach to governing, as a general observation, may be characterized best as "principle-driven" and ideologically-based. His views and decision-making style at times mirrored those of a religious fundamentalist. When he took up the cause to prolong the life of Terri Schiavo, a brain-damaged woman who became the centerpiece of a national right-to-die battle, Bush's religious views entered the public arena. His view of the role of government, preferences for supply side economics, principle-based leadership style, and intrusion of religious views into social policy paint a picture of a governor who was more ideologue than reformer in the traditional sense.

It is easy for political moderates and liberals to dismiss such positions entirely, or to relegate them to the realm of electoral posturing. There is much evidence that appeal to fundamentalists was part of a national political strategy engineered and implemented from George W. Bush's White House.[244] While this may be an accurate understanding, it does not preclude the possibility that Jeb Bush was a true believer in the public policy causes he championed, including those that were grounded in religious beliefs.

Those critics who dismiss him as acting purely out of political motivations become either ensnared by the force they oppose or fooled by it. There is much about modern government that demands reform and much about modern society that is unsettling. Jeb Bush governed as a man who held strong convictions.

Karen Armstrong, a scholar who has studied conservative fundamentalist positions closely, concludes arch-social conservatives can serve the purpose of exposing the "darker side of the modern experiment."[245] Often their positions are very popular among large numbers of people upset with aspects of modern society.

Downsides of the Bush Ideological Approach

Jeb Bush was a popular and activist governor of a people in search for direction and in need of vision. But there are major downsides to governing in this way. An ideological approach to governance -- especially one that links public policy to religiosity -- poses a danger to democracy when either side of opposing arguments becomes so entrenched in its respective position that the best of the republican and religious traditions informing the theory of democracy is lost, including the values of toleration and reconciliation. The underlying issues of concern to people are obscured when this happens, and the opportunity for thoughtful dialogue and productive public policy is forfeited.

Polarization is the result: a "with us or against us," "my way or the highway" mentality sets in; and, to use the language of religion, self-righteous and judgmental behavior and its fruits, unhealthy conflict, scape-goating, fanaticism, and formation of warring camps, characterize the political culture. Democracy is also threatened when questions of civil liberty are subsumed by the passionate drive to legislate morality, which is justified by personalized interpretation of theological doctrine.

Since Jeb Bush left office in 2006, the various post-mortems on his administration found in the popular press and in discussions elsewhere are consistent with these observations. While Bush was an activist and popular governor, those attributes do not equate to sustainable leadership. Activism rooted in strong personal convictions and popularity is not enough to produce the quality of leadership sustainability demands. Required is an alignment through the practice of democracy of public needs, aspirations and values with initiatives that foster sustainable outcomes and reflect the features of sustainability.

Politics and governance are full of philosophical contradictions and ambiguities that play out differently over time and place. This is especially true in Florida, whose political culture has evolved and changed so rapidly with enormous population growth. Diversity and uncertainly aptly describe the state's fractured politics.

In an attempt to bring order to the chaos, Bush took a "one best way" ideological approach to governing. He may have succeeded in calming the fears of people who were yearning for certitude and right paths in an uncertain and fast changing world, but his ideology precluded him from using governance pragmatically to advance the state in the direction of a new vision grounded in sustainability. Imposition of his religious beliefs into public policy---for example his attempts to prolong the life of Terry Schiavo and his insistence that public funds be used for religious education---proved to be costly distractions that caused unhealthy political conflict and constitutional problems. These efforts did not advance the state toward its sustainability vision.

Jeb Bush's approach was flawed in two important ways from the standpoint of sustainable governance. First, it misunderstood Florida's special circumstances as a place where provision of basic public services and infrastructure has fallen well behind population growth demands and where well-funded state and local government are needed to address increasingly complex urban problems. Bush's philosophy of government and economics was applied without distinction to all levels of government and at all times. He acted as if his particular beliefs had attained a special status as literal, inerrant and absolute truth closed to checks, balances, and questioning. This broad brush application of these principles in the abstract failed to account for concrete situations where use of different but equally valid governance principles would have been more appropriate.

Secondly, his approach ignored the reasons why those who advance fundamentalist ideologies don't serve democracies well: they become blinded by the "sunshine of their own brilliance", dismissing (and often seeking to punish) those that have different points of view rather than listening and incorporating their ideas into the governance process in a spirit of consensus and mutual respect. Society cannot adapt to challenges and achieve sustainability when this happens.

Armstrong observes that fundamentalists are "highly critical of democracy and secularism."[246] This is because they seek legitimacy and authority from their conceptions of Divine will, and, we might add, economic and political principles associated with them. Democratic decision-making influenced by large numbers of people who do not share arch conservative ideological zeal is experienced by fundamentalists as compromise of principle.

The notion that wisdom is discerned best when principles of leadership are forged and applied to concrete circumstances in collaboration with those being led seems to have been lost on Jeb Bush. His legacy forever will be tainted in the memories of people who otherwise admired his quality by this failure to understand that sustainable public leadership is a two way street.

Jeb Bush did not see that democracy demands inclusive give and take in selecting and applying governance principles and crafting public policy. This is required in a democracy because, as the American nation's founders well understood, no mortal human being acting alone regardless of exalted position, intelligence, spiritual fidelity, or pedigree can be trusted to discern right paths through the complexities of governance.

The best governance decisions require many voices speaking from different perspectives. This has nothing to do with being nice to people by going to the trouble to listen to them. It has everything to do with making quality decisions that can be sustained through time. Pulitzer Prize winning author Ernest Becker provides guiding insight:

...(D)emocracy needs adults more than anything, especially adults who bring something new to the perception of the world, cut through accustomed categories, and break down rigidities. We need open, free, and adaptable people precisely because we need unique perceptions of the real, new insights into it so as to *disclose more of it*. In a democracy the citizens are the artists who open up new reals. The genius of the theoreticians of democracy is that they understood this, that we must have as many different individuals as possible so as to have as varied a view of reality as possible, for only in this way can we get rich approximations of it. Twisted perspectives then get corrected easily because each person serves as part of a corrective on the other.[247]

The American Revolution, the most significant display of the "passion for reform" of governance systems in human history, resulted in a Constitution based on principles that Jeb Bush did not apply: a strong reliance on democratic decision-making grounded in the rule of law through a sharing of powers, and checks and balances; and a separation of politics and religion, church and state.

Bush's open hostility to the judiciary and his bullying of legislators and others when they disagreed with him demonstrate that he did not appreciate the first principle. His mixture of politics and religion---church and state---shows that he did not understand history's lesson implicit in the latter principle: when the two are combined by mortal humans who believe they have discerned God's will, there is a high degree of likelihood that the result will be damaging and unsustainable.

Among the nation's founders, Jefferson and Madison understood the necessity for separation, and what was at stake. The American Revolution was fought to end the "Divine Right of Kings" who were presumed to know God's will in all matters of church and state. Sovereignty passed to the people who are called to discern pragmatic and necessary right paths for secular society through the aegis of democracy and the rule of law, unburdening the churches from government interference in the free exercise of religion.

Freedom of religion and liberty of conscience were viewed as critical to developing a society guided by the wisdom of democracy as determined by a free people with equal opportunities and rights to prosper individually and collectively. Imposition of religious views using the powers of government destroys these opportunities and violates these rights. The leadership and governance behavior of Jeb Bush---and his brother the former President---show that they did not understand (or if they understood, did not agree with) Jefferson's and Madison's motivations and rationale.[248]

The Bush Legacy: Paralyzing Contradictions

There is a resulting sad irony to Jeb Bush's legacy, the fruits of his labor: he left state government at the end of his eight years in office with the leadership behaviors he taught left behind for other major public leaders to imitate. The directions of the state's budget, tax, and growth management, health care for the medically-indigent, and other principal policies remain largely unchanged. These behaviors and policies now require a measure of reform greater and more urgent than when he first assumed the governorship at his 1998 inaugural.

There is an even deeper irony. As noted earlier, the state of Florida's total budget nearly doubled during Bush's eight years in office, from approximately $38 billion to $74 billion.[249] The state under Bush's leadership took advantage of a strong growth economy, easily identified necessary expenditure needs, and spent the money. The governor's ideological preferences for less government spending and reduced taxes were inconsistent with the facts of his administration.

The demands of contemporary state leaders for limited government and tax cuts (beyond revenue reductions due to the state of the economy) following in Bush's foot steps, amount to a similar duplicity, especially since the cuts proposed were made on the backs of local -- not state -- government and schools. Local governments and schools during the robust economic times Bush enjoyed did exactly what state government did. They found that pent up demand for infrastructure and services, rising costs, and population growth justified expenditure of new revenue.

These contradictions and deficiencies notwithstanding, Bush's experiments with out-sourcing, public-private partnerships, and commitment to raising standards, measuring performance, and demanding accountability in education and other areas of public policy are consistent with the general precepts of the government to governance shift. But his undemocratic and authoritarian brand of leadership, ideological preferences for marginalizing the role of government, and imposition of religious views into the public arena stain his legacy as an agent of sustainable governance.

The experience of the Bush administration teaches that broad ideologies should not be applied to specific circumstances where their underlying assumptions do not hold true. This is one reason why ideological governance does not work well in democracies that seek after sustainability. Ideologies with their fixed principles and rigid assumptions are not adaptable to changing and diverse circumstances.

The State of Florida and its local agencies and schools do not fit Bush's belief that, taken together, they constitute a government that has grown "significantly beyond...core responsibilities [and] will eventually grow beyond our ability to pay for it"; or that state buildings in Tallahassee should be made "silent monuments to the time when government played a role larger than it deserved or could adequately fill."

A review of Florida's social and economic indictor rankings among the fifty states found in Chapter IV belies Bush's assumptions, causing his ideological principles to collapse when applied to Florida. Facing the state's harsh realities leads to the inescapable conclusion that blind adherence to arch conservative ideology applied to the unique circumstances of Florida does not serve its ambitious new vision. Ideological rigidity and an inability to adapt, like authoritarian and undemocratic leadership styles, are not compatible with the requirements of sustainability.

Bush is right that too often the ponderous bureaucracy of "government still works like it did in the 1950's" and needs to change to suit the demands of Florida's new vision as a global economic competitor. But he did not advance the search for sustainable governance much further than did Lawton Chiles. The state government Bush left behind, like that of his predecessor, is characterized by unsustainable policies and practices, and a wide gap between the rhetoric of reform and the realities the state faces. There remains a paralyzing contradiction between ideological preferences for tax cuts, spending caps, and treating government as "the enemy" and a genuine need for the activist role of government and the well-funded public investments required by the state's new vision.

In the end, Bush governed in a way that undermined his own vision by failing to reconcile this contradiction. He simply could not have it both ways. A more open and less authoritarian and principle-driven leadership style and approach to governance could have led his administration in a more sustainable direction, and would have better served the state. He confused personal popularity in public opinion polls with genuine alignment between his initiatives and public needs, aspirations and values.

The unsustainable governance practices Bush left in place and taught others to mimic continue to rule the day as Florida draws closer and closer to what former Florida Governor and United States Senator Bob Graham calls a "tipping point." The fate of the state's emerging new vision hangs in the balance.[250]

Conclusion

Contemporary calls for a "shift from government to governance" are made against the backdrop of this summary of Florida's experience with governmental reforms. Governmental arrangements serving the old vision paralleled the business arrangements of the former natural resource based, manufacturing American economy and its Florida embodiment: manufacture of mass tourist attractions and sprawling, rapid population-driven construction.

Contemporary calls to change the "business of government" likewise are rooted in the necessity for congruence between economic and political practices, but suited to the new vision of a sustainable society. This will demand a broadened definition of self-interests, major policy reforms and new governance arrangements.

Radical changes in the approach to governance are demanded, from a reliance on ideology to devising innovative ways of practicing democracy. The government to governance shift when viewed in this light has more traction and holds the potential to go much further in actually changing the business of government than traditional governmental reform attempts were able to do. But Toffler's insight reflected in the epigraph to this chapter must be turned on its head: imagination, experiment, and a willingness to contemplate fundamental must rule the day.

The next chapter examines the dynamics of this shift to the "business of *governance*", and focuses on case examples demonstrating that it already is underway.

I have ever deemed it more honorable and more profitable, too, to set a good example than to follow a bad one.
—Thomas Jefferson

Chapter VIII

THE RE-SHIFTING:
FROM BUREAUCRATIC GOVERNMENT TO SUSTAINABLE GOVERNANCE

Introducing the Shift from Government to Governance

Jeb Bush and others who share his approach to governing likely are supportive of the major features of the "government to governance" shift. Bush in some ways helped lay the groundwork for it. As he observes in his Heritage Foundation interview, the shift may be understood as being partially attributable to private sector and market-driven imperatives, unlike the traditional reform motivations with their exclusive emphasis on efficiency and cost savings.

The much-heralded restructuring of American businesses itself is grounded in the need for global competitiveness and the emergence of "new vision" knowledge-based, technology driven enterprises. The government to governance shift implies that approaches to public policy and administration should be restructured in similar fashion.

The new shift is also broader in scope than the traditional attempts at governmental reforms. This time the roles and relationships among the private, non-profit and public sectors are being called into play in dramatic, transformative fashion. No longer will government's role be segmented from the other sectors and marginalized. The new vision will demand among the sectors a concerted and collaborative approach to solving complex public problems, delivering services, and building public infrastructure and amenities consistent with the needs, aspirations and values being served. There must be a higher quality of interaction, coordination, and congruence among the sectors than ever before if the promise of the new vision is to be fulfilled.

The goals and objectives of sustainability are implicit in the shift. An emphasis on sustainability and away from an obsession with short-term investor profit and damaging patterns of production and material consumption is involved.

The following graphic shows how the shift from government to governance will affect public sector organization and management approaches.[251]

Dimension	Government	Governance
Organizing Principle:	*Systems Theory*	*Network Theory*
Metaphor:	*Assembly Line*	*Internet*
Structure:	*Vertical*	*Horizontal*
Major Actor:	*Government*	*Various Sector Combinations*
Power, Authority, Decision-making:	*Centralized Command and Control*	*Decentralized and Dispersed*
Democratic Process:	*Representative*	*Participatory*
Focus:	*Managing People and Programs*	*Managing Service Delivery Networks*
Policies:	*Centralized/Uniform*	*Decentralized/Diverse*
Accountability:	*Process/Outputs/ Efficiency*	*Outcomes, Results, Impacts*
Policy/Management Skills:	*Internal Focus on Traditional Management of People and Programs*	*External Focus on Collaboration, Negotiation, Network Management*

There is opportunity to change from *government* as bureaucratic service provider to *customers or clients* to *governance* as a community-based and democratic process central to achievement of a sustainable prosperity serving *citizens*. But such change will not be easy. It demands a reframing of the very purpose and role of government.

More than a quarter century ago, a group of scholars led by Robert Bellah wrote a book that became a national bestseller, entitled *Habits of the Heart: Individualism and Commitment in American Life*. The authors could well have been thinking with prescience about Florida when they wrote:

> We cannot simply write off "big government" as the enemy. Reducing its powers where appropriate and decentralizing authority, both political and economic, can be pursued as far as practical. But the effective power of citizens in their associations and movements will only be guaranteed in the long run if we succeed in transforming the spirit of centralized administration itself. We need to discuss the positive purposes and ends of government, the kind of government appropriate for the citizens we would like to be. [This requires] bringing a sense of citizenship into the operation of government itself...[252]

This is precisely what the government to governance shift and the new leadership framework called for in this book seek to accomplish, not by conceptualizing those being served as "consumers", "customers" or "clients", but as engaged citizens joined together in the search for sustainability. An important role of government becomes exercise of its responsibilities and powers in ways that facilitate the transformation to a citizen-led search for sustainability, grounded in democracy. Performance of this public leadership role is entailed in "bringing a sense of citizenship into the operation of government itself".

The spirit of bureaucratic centralized administration, with its unhealthy production and consumption mentalities, separation from founding principles and its decaying values, must give way to a renewed spirit of civitas and servant hood issuing from all sectors of society. This is the classic spirit of the visionary, committed and creative citizen, the entrepreneur, and the patriot that has lifted up

Americans in the past. Sustainable governance depends on its re-emergence.

Case Examples of the Shift in Progress: Visioning and Strategic Planning

It is instructive to witness through real case examples evidence of the governance to government shift taking place in Florida. The many visioning and strategic planning efforts undertaken in Florida during recent years are viewed best as attempts to "bring a sense of citizenship into the operation of government itself" in line with the government to governance shift and Bellah's insights.

Arrington-Marlowe's visioning and strategic planning work for the City of Orlando during 2007 serves as a case example. A vision for the City, a mission for city government, and a strategic plan complete with specific initiatives were undertaken. Attempts were made to link broad goals and strategies to the Central Florida regional visioning effort sponsored by the regional planning council and the MyRegion process.

Interviews and focus groups with scores of civic and business leaders were conducted, and available public opinion data were analyzed. The City's Mayor, Buddy Dyer, was heavily engaged in the process. City Commissioners also were engaged. Top and mid-level professional staff members were organized around "strategic focus areas," and helped to develop the substance of the vision, mission and plan.

We tested whether Orlando was experiencing a government to governance shift. We listened carefully in the interviews and focus groups with elected, business and civic leaders for expressions of points-of-view indicating attributes of the shift, either as empirical observations about the way things are or normative expressions about how things ought to be. We also tested the various strategic focus area task teams after in depth descriptions of the government to governance shift. The responses were highly affirming.

We examined the specific strategic initiatives contained in the plan. We were struck by how many of them aligned with features of the shift, especially the large number of initiatives calling for external focus on collaboration, negotiation, and public management networks, which we will examine further below.

Lawrence W. Arrington and Herbert A. Marlowe, Jr.

We noted that the City of Orlando and Orange County Government were engaged in several high-profile initiatives in collaboration with private and non-profit groups. These included three major new venues that will serve the Central Florida region from Orlando: a new performing arts center, a new events center for the Orlando Magic professional basketball team, and major renovations to the Citrus Bowl. Inter-sector groups have been formed to tackle a variety of social problems facing Orlando, including homelessness, affordable housing, and crime.

These observations indicate that the "government to governance shift" is much more than an intellectual construct. It is occurring in the real world in a non-partisan manner. These Orlando initiatives coupled with the previously referenced MyRegion and 2050 Future Vision experiences suggest that the new leadership framework is taking shape at the regional and local levels in Florida. The framework is developing in bits and pieces as leaders struggle to align public policies, programs and projects with the needs, aspirations and values of the citizenry. Sustainability themes are at the core of these efforts.

We are aware of several other success stories in other regions of Florida -- notably the Tampa-St. Petersburg area -- that serve as case examples of the government to governance shift and emergence of a new leadership framework. As part of a strategic planning effort for Pinellas County in 2005-06, Arrington-Marlowe conducted focus groups and analyzed a public opinion survey designed to garner information about public needs, aspirations and values. The information was used to develop projects approved by public referendum in late 2006 for an extension of the highly-successful "Penny for Pinellas." This initiative involved continuation of the levy of a one-cent local option sales tax. Sustainability themes were evident in the Pinellas experience, including environmental conservation and restoration, developing walk-able and bike-able transportation alternatives, housing, jobs and human services, and parks, recreation and culture.

These case examples and similar experiences at the regional and local levels elsewhere in Florida demonstrate that solid visioning and planning, effective citizen engagement, and intergovernmental and inter-sector cooperation can lead to successfully aligned leadership around sustainability themes -- even when tax increases are involved.

Absent a tepid amendment to the Growth Management Act in 2006 requiring community visioning as part of the cumbersome evaluation and appraisal comprehensive plan update process, state government has provided no proactive leadership to undertake and support visioning or strategic planning processes. Some observers have speculated that legislative leaders are so focused on short term political expediencies that spending the time and energy on long-term visioning and strategic planning is not a part of the state's mode of governing. Furthermore, Florida is so large and diverse that creating a statewide vision is impractical if sponsored by state political leaders.

> Part of the problem is the way Tallahassee works. Safely drawn legislative districts, the influence of political contributions and term limits have produced a shortsighted Legislature incapable of embracing ideas that require short-term pain for long-term gain. Another part of the problem is Florida itself. In 1990, Lawton Chiles won the governor's race as he talked about creating a community instead of a crowd. That has proven to be impossible in a diverse state with 18-million residents, nine television markets and two time zones. Two-thirds of the state's residents were born somewhere else, the population is aging and the cultural differences between Miami and Marianna often seem insurmountable. Building consensus on a long-term vision that requires shared sacrifice is a lost art.[253]

This perspective affirms why the authors believe that regional and local governance systems involving public, non-profit, and private sectors offer the best opportunity for crafting future vision planning attempts. This viewpoint also helps explain why sustainable governance with better quality civic engagement is more likely to occur at the regional and local levels than at the state level. The influence of well-funded and powerful special interest groups concentrated at the state level would be dispersed, diluted and placed on a more level playing field with other, less well-funded and less powerful interest groups as public policy is forged at the regional and local levels. Inter sector collaboration at the regional and local levels would be less influenced by the lobbying culture at the state level, and given a better chance to live up to its promise as an effective way to develop and implement public policy.

The Century Commission has studied the question of state involvement in visioning processes. Its consultant, Dr. Tim Chapin, has recommended that the state support and, perhaps, coordinate regional visioning. In his report, entitled *Engaging the Future through a State-Coordinated Regional Visioning Initiative,* Dr. Chapin examines visioning processes. He draws many useful conclusions.

While regional visioning processes vary in design, they present an opportunity to envision a desired future and to set forth initiatives designed to achieve it. These processes require sufficient funding and political commitment, and can take many months—if not years---of coordinated effort. The best processes are multi-sector in both sponsorship and execution; and are both process and outcome oriented. Inter-sector collaboration helps build relationships that last through time. This approach also builds political support for initiatives when it comes time to implement them.[254]

Chapin found that there is potentially value in pursuing a state coordinated effort because many growth-related problems simply cannot be addressed sufficiently by local governments acting alone; but his main focus is on regional processes because they provide "an avenue for embedding regional-thinking and multi-jurisdictional solutions in an environment often characterized by parochial attitudes and behaviors." A regional ethic can result from these processes, as can inter-sector collaborations, coordinated initiatives and investments. Regional approaches also present opportunities to address transportation and conservation issues collaboratively. This is considered essential to developing sustainable approaches to growth problems.

Chapin concludes with the following observation about Florida's growth management framework, and the need to improve it by emphasizing region visioning processes:[255]

> Between 1970 and 2000, many states bought into the concept that comprehensive planning was a valuable endeavor, as it provides a future-oriented planning and policy framework to guide land use

decisions and infrastructure investments... However, in Florida comprehensive planning was designed primarily as a technical process in which a local government was to demonstrate how it would accommodate its population growth and provide urban services at or above a minimum level of service. Regional visioning offers a tremendous opportunity to reestablish planning as a normative process, whereby a desired future state is envisioned and policies and programs are designed to work towards that vision. A regional vision can provide longer-term, big picture guidance to government actions, something that comprehensive plans have struggled to do given their relatively near-term time frames (10-20 years) and onerous administrative processes (hearings, amendments, EARs).[256]

We will leave it to the Century Commission to determine what role, if any; state government should play in undertaking a state-coordinated visioning process. Some stakeholders at the regional and local levels will be highly suspicious of state involvement, especially if the processes are seen as a top-down mandate. State government as this book amply demonstrates does not enjoy a strong reputation for effective transformative leadership on growth management, tax and budget policy, or governance issues generally. Furthermore, the normal tensions between state and local governments have been exacerbated in recent times by the property tax reform debate.

We suggest three guiding principles for consideration by the Century Commission and others who contemplate the state's role in visioning processes. First, from the Hippocratic Oath: do no harm. Secondly, from the popular book, Reinventing Government by Osborne and Gaebler, the state should consider "steering and not rowing." And, relatedly, from Catholic social thought: operationalize the "principle of subsidiarity," by which it is the role of the superior level of authority to support and encourage, but not dictate to or attempt to do the work for lower levels of authority. The government to governance shift requires re-forging roles and relationships among levels and types of governmental institutions in ways that replace tension and unhealthy conflict (which ultimately is unsustainable) with more compatible defining principles and practices.

Lawrence W. Arrington and Herbert A. Marlowe, Jr.

De-Centralization of Power, Authority and Decision-making

Empowering regional and local areas with more decision-making authority is a feature of the government to governance shift. The evolution of Florida's state-local relations runs parallel to the urbanization of Florida. More local, home rule authority was granted to cities and counties as the state grew and changed during the 20th Century.[257]

Florida counties and cities by virtue of the 1968 Constitutional Revision and subsequent legislation enjoyed a large measure of home rule. The grant of local home rule recognized that as Florida's local areas urbanized, governing from the state level with a "one size fits all" approach became both unwise and impossible. Part of the reasoning for the grant of home rule powers was that the state government had plenty of statewide problems to address, and should not spend its time consumed with questions best resolved by local governments.[258]

Home rule powers are limited by requirements that local legislation cannot be inconsistent with state law, so there is no realistic possibility that strong home rule will result in fractured chaos. Moreover, the power to tax is reserved exclusively to the state government. The property tax is guaranteed to local governments as a local source of revenue by the Constitution, and is limited to ten mills for municipal purposes and the equivalent for general county purposes. As the contemporary fight over property taxes reflects, the state government may condition local government property tax policies. Florida local governments do not enjoy fiscal home rule.

The combination of increasing state mandates to local governments and state government's micro-management of property tax policy represents a counter-trend away from local home rule. This is contrary to the requirements of the government to governance shift; and has been the source of much intergovernmental tension and unhealthy conflict at a time when more, rather than less, harmony among levels of government is needed.

Understanding of Florida's public education policy framework and administrative systems is beyond the expertise of the authors, whose knowledge and direct, hands-on experience is with local government and non-profit providers of public services. But we cannot resist noting that there is much evidence that the state's public education system is performing in unsustainable ways. In fact, it became increasing clear during 2009 that Florida's education system is in full-blown crisis.

As we saw earlier in this chapter, education reforms initiated at the primary and secondary school levels during the administration of former Governor Jeb Bush sparked much controversy and produced mediocre results. Bush failed to address root causes of systemic problems, emphasizing instead an ideologically-based "econo-think" and social conservative approach. The bottom line is that since Bush left office thousands of teachers have been laid off, many public schools have shuttered their doors, and many promising programs have been eliminated.

A Bush era restructuring of the higher education system governance arrangements produced similar outcomes. As noted earlier, the state's universities and community colleges are over-crowded, under-funded, and increasingly are losing quality faculty and students to other states.

Florida's dismal standing among the states on key indicators of public education performance was reported in Chapter IV, and is certainly linked to Florida's antiquated tax structure; and its tourism and population growth economy. But the crisis also has to do with the way the system is structured and managed and can be traced to the consequences of centralized, rules-driven, and bureaucratic governance arrangements and practices.

A case can be made that the entire structure and means of educating students throughout Florida's public education system are rooted in industrial-era manufacturing arrangements and practices. A wholesale break up and re-conceptualization of this bureaucratic system is indicated with innovation, experimentation with new approaches, and creativity unfettered by one-size fits all rules and regulations as guiding principles. Meaningful education "reform" cannot be done without additional revenue generated from more stable and productive sources.

The government to governance shift contemplates decentralized and diverse approaches to governance, as opposed to centralized, command and control from the state level. Local governments, public school districts, community colleges, and the state's regional institutions of higher education are especially vulnerable to the negative consequences of micro-management from centralized bureaucracies at the state level.

Lawrence W. Arrington and Herbert A. Marlowe, Jr.

Diverse approaches to public policy development and implementation are better able to achieve alignment with regional and localized needs, aspirations, and values. This approach mirrors Florida's diversity, recognizing that different parts of the state have developed at different paces, have unique public problems, and aspire to a variety of distinctive future visions. Demographics are widely divergent in various parts of Florida, and manifest populations that are highly diverse culturally, economically, and socially.

Home rule strengthens representative government. Stronger home rule powers will advance sustainable governance because the authority to act locally heightens the opportunity for attainment of distinctive sustainability goals and objectives where they count most: at home.

Accordingly, an issue we encourage the Century Commission to tackle involves promotion of more harmonious governance systems through enactment of more regional and local funding options. As the research for this book demonstrates, there is little hope that the Florida legislature will agree to new sources of revenue in the current political environment. However, if the Century Commission is going to be as forward thinking as we hope, the issue of funding ought to be addressed in tandem with regional visioning and other new leadership framework initiatives for the long-term.

The Legislature and the powerful interests that influence it have a very strong grip on fiscal policy, which restricts freedom and creativity in local decision-making. Sustainability is about both of these. The local option sales and gas tax authorizations are the closest policy movement by the state in the direction of fiscal home rule. While these options have been useful to local governments and schools when local support for new taxes materializes, there are other local option sources that should be extended at both the regional and local levels. This is not the place to go into a detailed analysis of potential options, but it is appropriate here to advocate for them as Florida undertakes the government to governance shift, and hopefully begins to transition to a new leadership framework to support a new vision for the future.

If the state is truly interested in steering policy direction in the future in a progressive way, it may consider an incentive-based approach to fiscal home rule. New revenue options would be granted to regions and localities that meet established state sustainability objectives and otherwise demonstrate leadership that is aligned with the needs, aspirations and values of citizens. Absent major reforms of local revenue arrangements, we agree with the assessment of scholar David Brunori and apply his insights to public schools as well as local governments. He writes:

> Without reform to ensure stable tax revenue, local governments could be weakened to the point of irrelevance. That stable tax revenue must be within the political and legal control of local government institutions. Without such a revenue source, local governments will be incapable of efficiently and effectively providing services. More important, local governments will continue to cede financial and political control to the states.[259]

This is not the path to sustainable governance.

More local funding options will have to come from either new state law or through Constitutional amendment. Local public agencies will have to prove their case by mustering strong political support. Credible plans well-aligned with the public's sense of priorities, needs, hopes, and values will have to be developed. Local agencies must demonstrate the capacity to develop and to administer these initiatives in effective ways. A new framework for developing and demonstrating this capacity is needed.

Local reforms of the formal structure of cities, counties, and school districts through charters, new laws, or Constitutional change are unlikely, if the past is any guide to the future. But there is much that can be done within existing authority and established formal structures. Inter-local agreements among agencies, new ways of relating to non-profit and private sector providers of services and creation of new governance organizations at the regional and local levels are possibilities.

This understanding envisions a more "organic" approach to meeting the state's governance challenges through a variety of different structures and solutions to problems. "Reform" occurs largely from the bottom-up within broad guidelines and authorities established by the state. This allows self-forming and customized adaptations to challenges, and unleashes creativity, experimentation, and opportunity for innovation. Successful models can be "benchmarked" and emulated by other regions and localities and crafted to distinctive circumstances. The oppressive and authoritarian spirit of centralized "command and control" through "top-down" mandates and bureaucratic administration is quenched.

Public leaders assume a key role in convening inter-sector stakeholders, setting agendas for strategic choices, and building coalitions of support. Public agencies provide financial assistance and incentives for public initiatives undertaken by non-profits and the private sector; and deliver selected services directly when most appropriate. Public agencies help manage and hold accountable inter-sector networked and collaborative arrangements tasked with finding sustainable solutions to complex problems.

This describes governmental (including public education) reform and "home rule", 21st Century style. This approach reflects the essence of what we have labeled the "new leadership framework." It is the pathway to sustainable governance; and it is grounded in the talents and energies of civil society working through public institutions as practicality and necessity demand. It holds the promise of reconciliation of opposing views about the proper role of government. Not only does it have the potential to transform the spirit of centralized and bureaucratic institutional controls, it also carries the best hope for bringing the era of ideology to an end.

The balance of this chapter will examine some of these possibilities, and present case examples of success. What many of these examples show is that citizen support, including additional revenues, is made possible when the local citizenry is brought into the planning process and when public initiatives are funded consistent with their preferred community vision. They also show that the best ideas and talent for adapting to the challenges local communities face resides primarily in civil society. The private and non-profit sectors and engaged citizens can unleash the creativity and innovation needed to adapt in sustainable ways when engaged and energized intelligently and when granted the right incentives. Those in positions of public leadership have to understand this insight, buy-in to this governance strategy, and have the knowledge and political will to act on it.

We are aware of many case examples of various attempts to shift from government to governance. Some have met with success, some with mixed results; and some with failure.

One general lesson is clear: patience will be demanded by leaders and followers alike. Transformative change takes time and much intellectual and moral effort. Innovation carries risks and uncertainty. There will be failures and abuses of new prerogatives. But the shift can be a time of exhilarating change and an opportunity to rediscover the genius of democracy and to renew the search for sustainability.

Public Management Networks and Public-Private Partnerships: Breaking Down the Silos

It is useful to study cases where public leaders have demonstrated a capacity to forge excellent working relationships, innovate and move positively toward sustainability goals. The most successful attempts sort out both intergovernmental roles and relationships and those among the sectors resulting in productive *inter-governance relations*. A community and team spirit develops among leaders who understand that sustainable governance requires political maturity and a willingness to work with others. The City of Orlando and Pinellas County experiences cited earlier stand as examples; and there are many others.

Sometimes these lessons are learned after years of expensive litigation and much intergovernmental conflict. Cities and counties in the Tampa-St. Petersburg area with the cooperative involvement of the state of Florida united to tackle one of the State's most vexing problems, water supply, following many years of open hostility and protracted legal maneuvering. Tampa Bay Water (TBW) exemplifies an emerging government to governance approach demanding high quality inter-governance relationships, the public management network.

TBW brought online one of the largest desalinization plant in the world, over-coming complex technical and financial challenges that surely would have caused political collapse had the network been managed with less skillful commitment and perseverance by executive director Jerry Maxwell and the elected leaders with whom he worked. Notable leaders included St. Petersburg Mayor Rick Baker, who went on to serve as Chairman of the Century Commission for a Sustainable Florida, and Pinellas County Commissioner Susan Latvala, who emerged as a statewide local government leader through her service as President of the Florida Association of Counties. Maxwell in 2007 brought the plant to activation, declared victory, and deservedly retired.

The local governments held together through many frustrating fits and starts; and, with the help of a network of private sector technical specialists and state and federal agencies, succeeded in developing a world-class sustainable water supply. No one governmental entity or any single level of government, could have accomplished this feat alone. Nor could the public sector have succeeded without private sector management talent and technology. The results and impact of the Tampa Bay Water experience speak for themselves in spite of all the problems and challenges involved in crossing the sustainability goal line.

The TBW experience demonstrates that public management networks simultaneously can promote collaboration among the sectors; achieve a degree of political stability between disparate government agencies and between state and local governments; harmonize the branches of government by ending litigation; and address a complex urban problem. Technical challenges continue to confront TBW, but the bottom line is that its structure and network of relationships are standing up to them.

Public management networks, if depicted on a graphic, would look more like planets orbiting around a sun (with space craft flying among them!) than a bureaucratic organization chart with its boxes and vertical lines of authority. These networks metaphorically are more akin to the Internet than an assembly line, which is why they look and act so different from traditional vertically-integrated means of organizing government bureaucracies. They are horizontal, multi-dimensional, often combine public, private and non-profit sectors in a collaborative effort, de-centralized, dispersed, and are managed by highly participatory styles blended with high levels of accountability for results.

Rather than concentrating on process, outputs and efficiencies, public management networks have an external focus on outcomes, results, and impacts. The skills required to manage and work within networks are very different from the usual training and qualifications of public administrators. Networks require an external focus on collaboration and negotiation, rather than an internal emphasis on management of people and programs.[260]

Public management networks break down the silos of stand alone government agencies, and the barriers between the public, non-profit, and private sectors. They mirror the organization of business arrangements in the emerging global economy. They are more likely to help achieve sustainability goals and objectives than traditional approaches to organization and management because they unleash levels of creative energy and talent bureaucracies do not. Some networks also involve public-private partnerships, featuring a marriage of private investment and management with public sector oversight and accountability in the delivery of a public service.

Public management networks and public-private partnerships at their theoretical best have people representing different stakeholder interests and multiple backgrounds and experiences working together to solve a complex problem in a reasonably well-organized, open and free manner. The best networks and partnerships employ high levels of quality citizen engagement, and rely on private sector management expertise and technology. This approach to problem-solving is consistent with the virtues of democratic decision-making; and is suited to the search for sustainability.

Public management networks property conceived and managed are pathways to sustainable governance; and will be examined in depth in Part II of our work.

When Arrington-Marlowe completed the Pinellas County Government Strategic Plan in 2006, we were impressed by the number of public management networks described in the plan. Pinellas officials did not label these strategic initiatives designed to attack the county's most urgent problems as "public management networks", but that is precisely what they were.

Like most public leaders, Pinellas officials found themselves in the world of networks. Tampa Bay Water was a prime example and proving ground. Their strategic plan envisioned new approaches to solving problems by creating more networks to attack issues ranging from homelessness, affordable housing and health and human services to economic development. The strategic plan acknowledged this involvement, and called for development of the skills and approaches needed to manage existing networks and establish new ones. As mentioned, we had a similar experience with the City of Orlando strategic plan in 2007.

Networks and public-private partnerships can be used to address some of Florida's most pressing problems in ways that are consistent with the features of sustainable governance examined in Chapter I, and in ways that advance the so-called "Green Economy" noted in Chapter V. What follows are two additional case examples illustrating the use of public management networks and partnerships. The first involves energy and environmental policy. The second illustrates the use of a public management network model called for in strategic planning for a new approach to addressing substance abuse and mental health problems in the criminal justice system.

Waste to Green Energy: The City of Sanford-MaxWest Biosolids Management Partnership[261]

Disposal of human biosolids (also known as "sludge," the end product of the waste water treatment process) is an expensive and environmentally-sensitive job. Tougher regulations are demanding more costly levels of treatment. The traditional disposal practices are land spreading, composting or burying biosolids in land fills.

Land spreading has come under close scrutiny by regulatory agencies because of concerns about ground and surface water pollution. Using landfills for sludge and composting take up valuable space, and are expensive. These methods release methane, a dangerous green house gas which is 23 times more harmful to the atmosphere than carbon dioxide, according to the Global Strategy Institute. The environmental and direct dollar costs of hauling sludge in trucks, which is demanded by these traditional disposal methods, are escalating. The old ways of managing biosolids are unsustainable.

The good news is that sludge contains valuable energy. This noxious waste with the right technology can be processed on-site to produce thermal energy, which, in turn, can be used to replace expensive natural gas used in the waste water treatment process. Green electricity also can be produced for use by the waste water treatment plant or for sale on the grid of the local power company.

Appropriate technology also can be deployed to convert methane produced in the treatment process (or, depending on location, at a land fill) to usable green energy. Thermal energy also can be used to heat some waste water digesters. This increases their production capacity, prolongs their useful life, and avoids major costs for new digester capacity, which run in the millions of dollars.

The City of Sanford located off of Interstate 4 between Daytona Beach and Orlando made national news during 2008-09 when it signed a contract with a private company, Houston-based MaxWest Environmental Systems, Inc. (maxwestenergy.com). The company specializes in waste to renewable energy conversion of biosolids and other carbon-based wastes using a proven technology known as gasification.

Here are some examples of the national attention the Sanford-MaxWest Partnership received:

- *Forbes.com* quoted Sanford Mayor Linda Kuhn, "We are thrilled to incorporate the MaxWest gasification solution at our South Wastewater Reclamation Center. Not only is the MaxWest system cost-effective and efficient, it enables Sanford to be a leader in green disposal technologies. Our hope is that the rest of the country will look to us and follow."
- The April 2008 issue of *Fortune Magazine* reported that Sanford is the first municipality in North America to introduce this innovate biosolids disposal practice. *Fortune* notes that Sanford will save $9 million dollars in natural gas costs during the 20 year life of its contract.
- *MSNBC* noted, "Billed as a "poop-to-power" operation, MaxWest Environmental Systems Inc. will convert the City of Sanford's waste stream "sludge" into methane, carbon dioxide and hydrogen through high-temperature gasification. The city will then use those gases as a source of energy instead of buying natural gas."
- *Florida Trend Magazine* in an article about the MaxWest System published in its July 2008 edition, noted, "In many

municipalities, sludge that's produced during wastewater treatment is trucked to landfills or to remote farmland, where it's spread over the soil to dry. But sludge carries phosphorus and nitrogen, which can pollute groundwater, and methane gas, identified as a contributor to global warming."

The Sanford system was brought online in May, 2009.

The approach Sanford is using has all the marks of an initiative that promotes sustainability. The partnership is visionary and future conscious. It reduces and fixes costs for biosolids disposal, creates green energy, and advances environmental protection and economic development. It is flexible and adaptable because the system is scalable to the amount of sludge processed; meaning the capacity of the gasification system can be increased as the community grows, and green electrical energy can be produced when sludge volumes increase over time. It is collaborative and networked through a public-private business model.

Other nearby municipalities may also use the MaxWest facility, increasing the amount of energy produced while solving their disposal problems. The system also will dispose of yard and wood wastes, which carry expensive disposal costs and have energy value. The entire system can be monitored and managed remotely through SCADA-based technology over the Internet.

This public-private partnership is based on an innovative and entrepreneurial business model that relies on private sector technical, finance and management expertise. The system is developed and managed by a multi-disciplinary team of public and private sector talent comprising a strategic alliance of engineering, finance, manufacturing, energy project development and public administration expertise.

The company will build, own and operate the system on a pay for performance basis. The processing fees paid to the company will come from existing waste water utility operating costs, which will be reduced from present and projected levels. Sanford has no finance costs associated with bond issues, and will require no rate increases to fund the payments for the waste to renewable energy technology. If enough energy is produced long-term, Sanford will share in revenues generated from the sale of green electricity to the grid.

The expertise needed to develop and implement this model is spread out through strategic alliances and contract relationships from Sanford to Houston, Texas to British Columbia, Canada, with equity financing from a global renewable energy fund based in London. This is a vastly different project development, finance, organization and management approach than the traditional governmental bureaucratic model using public employees to administer a public program funded with traditional public sector financing.

This case example exemplifies the "government to governance shift"; the business arrangements of the emerging "Green Economy"; and, with its environmental, social, and economic benefits, is understood best as a pathway to sustainable governance.

Strategic Planning for Sustainable Criminal-Social Justice

Florida is rife with the criminal and human problems of violators of laws governing domestic abuse, substance abuse and child welfare. Often mental health problems co-occur with illegal substance abuse and other criminal acts. Jails and prisons are full of people with these human problems, some of them homeless.

Recidivism rates for these offenders are high, as are the costs of incarceration. The following case example illustrates how the branches and agencies of state and local government involved with the administration of criminal justice are using strategic planning to implement new ways to address social justice in concert with non-profit and private providers of human services.

Re-examining the role of the courts in this regard is significant because collaboration places the judiciary in the non-traditional role of overseeing administration of social as well as criminal justice when judges are called upon to oversee the provision of treatment services to offenders and victims. This role is troublesome when the offenders involved have substance abuse addictions, mental health problems or are homeless; and are arrested for technically unrelated crimes. Judicially-sanctioned treatment in these cases requires that the courts come to terms with their proper role, recognizing that without judicial intervention in the treatment process, the criminal behaviors and incessant recidivism likely will continue.

As pointed out in Chapter IV, Florida's jails and prisons incarcerate more than ten times the number being treated in state forensic mental health facilities, at a cost fifteen times greater than treatment in the community.[262] An article published in February 2008 sets forth the grim statistics:

> Based on recent trends, Florida can expect the number of prison inmates with mental illnesses — now about 16,000 — to nearly double in the next nine years, to more 32,000, with an average annual increase of roughly 1,700. To keep up with such demand, the state would need to open at least one new prison every year. Florida currently spends a quarter of a billion dollars annually to treat roughly 1,700 people under forensic commitment; most of them are receiving services to restore competency so they can stand trial on criminal charges and, in many cases, be sentenced to serve time in state prison. Without a change to the existing system, the state faces potential forensic expenditures of a half-billion dollars annually by the year 2015.[263]

These statistics do not capture problems at the local level, where often over-crowded jails and county corrections facilities are struggling to cope of inmates with mental illness and co-occurring disorders.

In January 2008, the Palm Beach County Criminal Justice Council (CJC) and the Citrus County Public Safety Coordinating Council each were awarded planning grants by the Florida Department of Children and Families, under the auspices of the Criminal Justice, Mental Health and Substance Reinvestment Program. The purpose of each of these planning grants is to develop a strategic plan that will reduce the inappropriate use of the county jail by the mentally ill, substance abusers, and persons with co-occurring disorders (formerly known as "dually diagnosed" populations).

The authors in combination served on the consulting teams that were tasked in both counties with preparing the strategic plans. The teams worked with multi-stakeholder groups representing the judiciary, county administration, law enforcement, and the substance abuse and mental health providers. In each case, the teams developed an environmental scan to identify the key issues (strengths, weaknesses, opportunities, and major challenges) that were addressed in the plans.

The information gathered presented a staggering picture of a complex, multi-dimensional set of problems that demanded a fresh approach to developing sustainable solutions. One behavioral health care provider in Palm Beach County estimated that 45-50% of their patients (both involved and uninvolved in the criminal justice system) have co-occurring disorders. The percentage of the inmate population at the county jail with co-occurring disorders is closer to 70%.

The nature of drug use is complex ("poly-drug" dependency). Another service provider interviewed noted that many of the clients it serves who have been involved in the criminal justice system also have complex health care issues, such as HIV or Diabetes. Many mentally ill, substance abusers, and those with co-occurring problems are homeless in both counties, although exact numbers are unknown.[264]

A draft summary of the interviews conducted in Palm Beach County contained the following insights:

> Several involved stakeholders within the 15th Circuit (Palm Beach County) are highly committed to the idea of creating a Mental Health Diversion Court (as a pilot project) for Palm Beach County, based on their beliefs that such a court would benefit mentally ill individuals appearing before the Court, and would definitely result in a much more appropriate use of the County jail and criminal justice resources in Palm Beach County.
>
> Other stakeholders, who share these overall goals, are concerned that a Mental Health Court would create issues of individual liberty and would inappropriately involve the court in the supervision of mental health treatment. This is an example of an issue in which substantive discussion if warranted and careful design if required to develop approaches that would satisfy the concerns of all parties.[265]

The strategic plans in both counties used a model developed for improving criminal-social justice approaches. The Sequential Intercept Model provides a framework for tracking the flow of people with serious mental illness through stages of their interaction with the criminal justice system. The model "envisions a series of points of interception at which an intervention can be made to prevent individuals from entering or penetrating deeper into the criminal justice system. Ideally, most people will be intercepted at early points, with decreasing numbers at each subsequent point."[266]

The strategic plan analysis identified "weak links" in the overall system, and proscribed specific strategic initiatives designed to correct them. Consensus was sought among the stakeholders on the priorities for implementation among the strategic initiatives.

These efforts illustrate the tools of sustainable governance at work in addressing some of Florida's most complex and expensive public problems. The planning and implementation approaches mirror the descriptions of a public management network comprised of multi-stakeholder groups working together to solve multi-dimensional, interconnected problems. The features of sustainable governance are written all over both efforts. Systemic improvements likely will be made mostly within the constraints of existing resources, given the condition of state and local government budgets.

Summary and Conclusion

Paradigms do not change easily. But that is exactly what is demanded of those engaged in public leadership who are living through the government to governance shift. The literature of public administration is full of papers, articles and books about this shift, public management networks and other new leadership framework approaches. Some of these are noted in the footnotes and bibliography of this book, and we commend them to the reader.

Our observation is that some elected officials and practitioners "roll their eyes" when the subject of a shift from government to governance is discussed. But others become intellectually engaged and thirst for more knowledge about how to adjust to the rising use of new management approaches and arrangements. While much of the academic literature is practically helpful, the real learning will come by doing and "walking the talk."

Like sustainability, the concepts embedded in the government to governance shift are ambiguous, complex, and will take time to sort out. Their use will be advanced if public administration practitioners, their elected leaders and engaged citizens develop the necessary skills, knowledge and approaches as part of crafting a new leadership framework. It is to that task that we turn in Part II, our web-based digital offering.

It is likely that the American Recovery and Reinvestment Act will spur local capacity building for new strategic management approaches consistent with the government to governance shift. As the grants picture became clearer near the deadline for publication of this book, we noted that several opportunities for strategic planning, citizen engagement, public management networks, regional collaboration and other capacity building tools were either required or strongly encouraged by the grants.

Arrington-Marlowe, LLC completed a vision and strategic plan for the City of Oviedo during the summer 2009. This plan created a vision for a sustainable Oviedo, and included an initiative to consider use of a "Green Zone" or "Green Impact Overlay" approach to creating sustainability within an existing community redevelopment area (CRA). This area of the City contains a proposed new town center, includes an older residential area, and also encompasses the "old" downtown, a cross roads along which historic buildings beg renovation and redevelopment.

Interestingly, for years Oviedo's old downtown has been known as a home for chickens which freely range throughout the area. Oviedo, once a remote "old vision" agricultural outpost, is now an "edge City" blended with the Orlando metropolitan area. Its residents want to preserve the heritage of the chickens and the old downtown as part of an effort to transition to a sustainable community.

The Oviedo Strategic Plan is organized around the concepts of sustainability. We believe it serves as an excellent example of a best practice for community visions and plans, and, with its call for the use of a "Green Impact Overlay," points to the innovative use of tools that correlate with the government to governance shift. Use of these tools of sustainable governance position the City for attracting ARRA funds and resources from other sources.

The analyses in this chapter, including the case examples, indicate that the shift to sustainable governance approaches in taking place mostly at the regional and local levels and sometimes with state and federal oversight, encouragement and resources. Each of the case examples reflects a *visionary and future conscious approach* to governance.

The broad visioning and strategic planning tools used in Pinellas County government, Naples, the City of Orlando, and Oviedo serve as examples of local governments developing specific governance strategies designed to realize community visions. The MyRegion effort represents a similar approach on a broad, regional basis.

The case examples show that public leaders are *perceiving and advancing their self-interests, rightly.* Tackling the criminal-social justice issues in Palm Beach and Citrus Counties, for example, demonstrates that local leaders understand that the fates of individuals and the communities in which they live are closely interconnected. If public problems like mental illness and substance abuse go unaddressed, the community's costs to the victims of associated crime, law enforcement, the judicial system, and incarceration join the human tragedies of potentially productive lives wasted.

Each of the case examples reflects the importance of developing sustainable governance approaches that are *aligned with citizens' needs, aspirations, and values; and that involve high levels of quality participation garnered in transparent ways that build trust.*

The MyRegion process with its emphasis on values survey research and other contemporary tools of public engagement serves a model for others to emulate. Pinellas' success with the local option sales tax referenda programs grounded in solid survey and focus group information shows that alignment is possible when care is taken to achieve it, even when tax increases are involved.

The best of the case examples are *reality based.* A cold, hard look at the facts involved in each problem area is absolutely necessary to developing sustainable solutions.

The Palm Beach example is based on sometimes alarming data and insights that require courage to face. Tampa Bay Water had to face the hard core facts about the future of water supply, which if gone unaddressed could have resulted in environmental, economic, social, and governance disasters throughout the region.

Every one of these case examples reflects understanding that the *public problems involved are complex, multi-dimensional, and interconnected*. The emphasis on compact urban development in the MyRegion effort, for example, is grounded in the concept of sustainability, and reflects awareness that urban problems must address economic, social, natural resource and governance components in tandem.

The Palm Beach and Citrus examples show that leaders are aware that the problems of substance abuse, mental health, homelessness, and crime combine to create a toxic mix that produces unsustainable outcomes for whole communities across economic, social, and governance dimensions.

The best of the examples reflect awareness that *creativity, adaptability, and commonsense* are required of sustainable solutions. They also reflect an emphasis on *results* -- not process --and are grounded in *measurement of performance*. The City of Sanford-MaxWest renewable energy initiative, for example, is designed around all these features.

Finally, every one of the case examples demonstrates the importance of *collaborative and networked solutions*. All of them involve multiple stakeholders working together across the public, private, and often non-profit sectors; and most of them will require on-going and adaptable visions, strategic plans, and public management networks.

Taken together these case examples and many others across contemporary Florida teach that the shift from government to governance is an out-growth of the on-going effort throughout the state's history to fashion approaches to governance based on practicality and necessity. These examples are all grounded in the principles and practices of democracy and are devoid of narrow minded and ill-conceived ideological approaches and agendas.

They evince leadership styles grounded in the time-worn understanding that the best results are achieved when engaged stakeholders and citizens participate in crafting solutions aligned with their own needs, aspirations, and values.

In the best examples, the egregious influences of lobbyists and campaign finance are missing. Private and non-profit interests are being perceived broadly and are productively engaged with the public sector in helping to craft solutions.

These examples show that the search for sustainable governance is advancing in Florida, slowly but surely. Public leaders -- sometimes in response to perceived crisis, sometime not -- are experimenting with new approaches and governance arrangements with courage and foresight. No doubt, mistakes will be made as this process unfolds; but much is being learned. These cases exemplify the essence of innovation, and the most promising pathways to a sustainable Florida.

What will follow in digital and web based formats is examination of a "leadership framework" that contains understandings, core competencies, tools, and techniques that can be customized for application in a variety of settings. We have developed the description of this framework with much help from the work of others, and from our own practical consulting and professional experiences "in the trenches" at the regional and local levels.[267]

"... The challenge right now is for us to listen to what's happening globally and to be able to track the emergent forms of spirit...the forms of love and the forms of hope that people are finding on the ground in the midst of these changes...the spirituality that's coming. And it's coming fast." Serene Jones, Theologian, on Bill Moyers Journal, July 3, 2009

CONCLUSION: A TIME FOR REMEMBRANCE AND RECONCILIATION

An Open Letter to the Citizens of Florida and America:

Dear Fellow Citizens:

We are reminded in concluding this book of the epigraph at the beginning of Chapter II, a pronouncement by poet Matthew Arnold, written in 1855, that society is:
Wandering between two worlds, one dead,
The other powerless to be born.[268]
The authors of the book *Habits of the Heart*, from which we have drawn much rich insight, made the same closing observation through Arnold's poetry more than a quarter century ago when their national bestseller was published.

Floridians with all Americans have the capacity to determine whether the present uncertain period will be one of reconciliation of seemingly opposite choices about the mission and role of government; or a period when public institutions become so marginalized and weak that they have virtually no positive role in determining the future direction of the nation and state, leaving our fate to the vagaries of the free enterprise system.

The status quo governance arrangements, tax and budget policies, and growth management approaches have brought Florida state and local governments, public schools and institutions of higher learning -- where this book's emphasis has been -- to a position that has damaged the state's political economy and will rob it of its future promise unless the present course is reversed.

We hope the ideas in this book help point the way toward synthesis of the present polarized views about the proper mission and role of Florida state and local governments; and, in so doing, helps chart the future direction of the American nation as well. As we will show later in this letter, what Americans do and fail to do matters very much to the rest of the world.

The rich meaning of the concept of sustainability possesses the power to transcend the age-old dichotomy between individual pursuits via free enterprise; and collective action through publicly-constituted institutions and the rule of law. Governments must be limited to preserve the liberty needed to preserve freedom and to unleash the entrepreneurial spirit, but this does not mean that they have to be brought to ruin. Private enterprise can benefit from public actions that leverage private market pursuits aligned with public values and interests. Benefits extend to society in general and to the natural environment.

The responsibility for striking the right balance between individual and collective interests ultimately rests with the sovereign people. While some citizens, especially those who benefit directly and substantially from the status quo, are not likely to change fixed ideological positions easily, others who have taken such stances at either end of the political spectrum may well be ready to change to a more balanced position. Crisis has a way of inspiring people to search their souls, and to reevaluate and rise above their normal political positions and civic behaviors.

This gives rise to the notion of "sustainable citizenship." Governance, as contrasted with "government", is grounded in the practice of civic duty in ways that reflect the richness of sustainability. Recognition of the interdependence between the well-being of the individual and the well-being of the community is central to sustainable citizenship; and, ultimately, to sustainable governance. As this interconnection is recognized and put into practice, self-interest is rightly understood, and both individuals and communities thrive together.

Government through the process of governance is called upon to do what is practical and necessary in the concrete circumstances of time and place. We have shown that this approach to governance is in the best of the American tradition, and that use of ideology as a guide has led to much hardship for all of us.

Sustainability requires a civil society comprised of citizens self-organizing through time, growing in vibrancy and power, fully adapting to the collective challenges faced, empowering our public institutions when necessary for the common good, restraining them when not. This image embraces the meaning of sustainable governance and citizenship. This is the definition of a sustainable society, the place sought when the American experiment with democracy began, and the place where we can only hope the search will end.

This is the way Alec Tocqueville observed democracy working in early America. While he did not give his formulation the label a "sustainable society", he might well have done so had the rich theory of sustainability been available to him when he wrote his classic book *Democracy in America* in 1835.

If Tocqueville could return to travel around today's Florida and observe us citizens interacting to solve public problems, he likely would conclude that we have forgotten how to practice democracy with the masterful artistry, passionate commitment, and civility he saw in the experience of the young American nation.

The Florida case study demonstrates that our state and our nation is off course, misaligned with public needs, aspirations and values, and plagued with a rancid political culture, unsustainable public policies, and unworkable governance arrangements. The claims of the traditional components of sustainability -- economic, social, and natural resource -- are at war with each other, with no balance among them.

What Florida and America need at this juncture is a new leadership framework which demands citizenship grounded in a sense of community identity and duty to help discover the common good. The framework also demands the highest quality commitment to excellence in devising new ways of governing so that sustainable solutions to the complex problems we face can be found.

It is up to public leaders to give us that chance, not through the sponsorship of government, but through approaches to governance that draw from all sectors and interested and engaged citizens like us working together. This is the ground on which collective action through public institutions helps build livable and sustainable communities; and where the dignity, freedom, and value of individual people are protected and advanced.

Of all the forces and trends the case study of Florida reveals, among the most vexing and potentially lethal to sustainability is the rising gap between rich and poor. Problems of poverty and income inequity persist in Florida, as reported in Chapter IV. Just 12 states have a more unequal distribution of income. Access to high-quality jobs remains a problem in Florida, which ranks 29th among the states by this measure. Florida's abysmal standing among the states in support for education foreshadows long-term problems with income inequity, declining wages, and opportunity for good jobs.

Just 56 percent of our students entering ninth grade today graduate in four years; only five states do worse than us by this measure. Just under half of high school graduates in Florida pursue higher education, placing the state 43rd in ranking. Florida ranks 38th among the states in expenditures per pupil in public elementary and secondary schools, and 34th in appropriations for higher education.[269] Meanwhile, Florida has become a much more expensive place to live than it was only a few years ago. These trends and statistics point to a "ticking time bomb."

The most vulnerable among us are victims of Florida's obsession with creation of wealth through attracting ever-increasing numbers of visitors and new residents with promises of living a paradise lifestyle. The problem is exacerbated by the highly limited role public institutions have played in Florida history, a role confined to providing infrastructure and services needed to fuel growth and little else.

The chances for a quality education and a good job are diminishing, especially for our most disadvantaged fellow citizens. The Florida economy does not produce high paying jobs; and our commitment to funding education reflects that fact.

The opportunities afforded by social mobility and a strong middle class are nowhere to be found in many parts of Florida; and growing masses of people -- many of them new immigrants seeking a better life -- are disillusioned and angered by their prospects as hard, cold reality takes hold.

Public programs to support the disadvantaged and others in need are not a priority for our elected leaders at the state level. In the language of sustainability, the economic component has received the lion's share of public resources and political support, with an imbalanced and diminished emphasis on the state's social ecology. The rising tide brought about by Florida's version of economic prosperity has not floated all boats. Many of fellow citizens are starting to sink.

Not only are our young people being robbed of opportunity, also problematic is the growing number of residents who cannot afford decent housing and health care, many of them elderly, who in their most advanced years, will need high levels of care and support. Florida is not prepared for these future consequences.

The irony of Florida's traditional pursuit of pleasure and profit is that the quality of life for all residents -- rich and poor and in between -- is de-valued by neglect of the state's social ecology. The plight of those whose life is not pleasurable and who reap no profit from the economy affects us all. Rising crimes rates, neighborhoods in decline, and hordes of homeless people, many with drug abuse and mental health disorders, impoverish the quality of life of all of us citizens.

The human losses of young people with little opportunity for a bright future, middle aged people who cannot find decent jobs, and old people who must live out their days in poverty and disease place unspeakable burdens on the conscience of any civilized person. Our shame, if nothing else, should cause each of us to pause, search our souls, and turn to a new and more sustainable direction.

How can we possibly expect to build "livable and sustainable" communities under such conditions, knowing that key social indicators clearly will result in today's irony turning into tomorrow's tragedy? Any new vision for Florida's future must account for the well-being of the disadvantaged among us as a matter of highest importance.

It has been said often that democracy depends on a strong middle class enjoying freedom and equal opportunity to pursue the good life. There is a reason why people who understand political theory and history reach this conclusion: with no middle class offering opportunities for masses of people, social unrest rises as social conditions deteriorate. Concepts like "quality civic engagement", "sustainable citizenship," and "cultivation of self-interests, rightly understood" have little chance of taking on real world meaning. Society adapts itself to declining conditions by assuming a fighting position that leads to lawlessness, and, if conditions do not improve, open rebellion. The opportunity for self-governance grounded in the principles and practices of democracy declines as this process unfolds, and with it goes sustainability.

This is the breeding ground for reactionary and authoritarian governance as politics becomes a slug fest between rich and poor; strong and weak, those holding power and those without it. In such conditions all the components of sustainability -- economic, social, and natural resource -- go into a state of decline. Governance based on democracy and the rule of law weakens.

Priorities turn to making public investments in building up the capacity to arrest and incarcerate those who commit crimes against the social order, and an obsession, grounded in fear, with arch-conservative economic and social issues.

All of this shifts our focus and resources away from investments in the social, economic, and natural resource components of sustainability. History teaches that this dismal description generally occurs as the conditions precedent to many social and political disruptions. These are not theoretical abstractions that apply to someone else. They apply to us.

As our analysis of the thought of religious writer Karen Armstrong shows, deteriorating social conditions in contemporary times spark fear in the hearts of many of our fellow citizens, who come to crave certainty and security and seek to find them in the seemingly safe harbor of religious fundamentalism. A nasty edge to politics results as fundamentalists seek to use public institutions to perfect society through their interpretations of religious doctrine, or to destroy those institutions that do not demonstrate loyalty to the fundamentalist cause.

Attempts to breach the separation of church and state and a lack of respect for the rule of secular law cause much chaos; and sometimes violence. Civil liberties, the bulwark against tyranny, are threatened, and so is the search for truth through academic and other forms of freedom. A self-reinforcing cycle of recrimination develops between the "righteous" and the "unbelieving," and all hopes for a sustainable society are dashed. This is our world, our nation and our state.

Fundamentalists would do well to remember that grand social visions throughout American history have had religious grounding. So it may be with the vision for a sustainable society. Sustainability, as we examined in Chapter I, while certainly not a religion, nevertheless possesses moral force.

The definition of a sustainable society we have presented it is not unlike the Pauline conception of the Body of Christ, for example. The body's members are interdependent, each having special gifts to contribute to the company of believers, and receive their moral power and direction from the head, who is Christ. The dignity and worth of each individual is respected and nourished. The body's purpose is to be a creative force on earth that glorifies the Creator.[270] Israel in the ancient Judaic tradition under the guidance of the Creator is viewed in much the same way.

Moreover, sustainability's insistence on balance among its components -- especially its concerns for the social and natural ecologies -- is entirely consistent with religious teachings about treatment of the poor and the dispossessed[271]; and the teachings about human stewardship of the natural order.[272] As the epigraph for the introductory chapter indicates, sustainability seeks to give meaning to an interpretation of the Golden Rule: Do onto future generations as you would have them do onto you.

Our friend, colleague, and fellow citizen Randy Reid, the County Manager of Alachua County, Florida, penned an article for *Public Management Magazine,* a publication of the International City Management Association whose Sustainability Committee he chairs. Randy demonstrates that all of the world's great religious traditions offer a version of the Golden Rule, where sustainability has its grounding. He writes,

> If we could admit professionally…that love of people and place are both a human and a professional response and solution to community ills, it might mean everything in terms of embracing sustainability. Many managers possess a strong spiritual sense that our profession of managing communities and organizations can be best understood in the concept of stewardship…(T)his brings an uplifting moral and life affirming 'gift' and 'commitment' that we bring to our communities through our acts of public service. In this sense, we do righteous

work. The spiritual aspect of this sustainable stewardship is important because unbridled greed and competition for depleted resources has historically led to conflict or violence.[273]

We will leave exploration of this correlation with religious doctrines to the theologians, but the point here is that there is no inconsistency between strong religious belief and the concept of sustainability. The theory of sustainability has enormous powers of synthesis and reconciliation, as we have seen in the case of different philosophies about the role of government in society. If fundamentalists would open up to this possibility, perhaps there would be more common ground found than they think with those who advocate in favor of a sustainable society.

The reverse is also true. The recent interest by the religious right on environmental issues, including climate change, holds much promise; and hopefully is a harbinger of things to come. Non-religious proponents of sustainability should remain open to the legitimacy of the faith experience, and remember that ancient religious teachings have been around a lot longer than complex adaptive systems theory, have withstood the test of time, and hold their own unique powers of reconciliation.

It is entirely possible given what we have learned about *complex problems* that, as is the case with differing political philosophies, each side of religious arguments is right in some respects and wrong in others, all at the same time. Working through these polarized positions rationally, we may discover surprising commonality in service to the common good and individual freedom and liberty for all and each of us.

Meanwhile, anyone who believes that history's lessons about political, social, and religious turmoil and disruption cannot happen in our Bellwether state of Florida and in our America doesn't understand the tenets of complex adaptive systems theory, the dynamics of sustainability, world history or the local news.

A case can be made that during the past decade or so Florida has drifted in an unstable and unsustainable direction. Go ask for verification a law enforcement officer who spends nights working in one of Florida's tough neighborhoods or ask one of the "regulars" arrested over and over again or that offender's victims. Ask a medical doctor working at a women's health clinic; or pay close attention to the public spending practices of the State of Florida and the rhetoric of some our recent elected leaders.

You may add to the list of people to ask the recently laid off worker who is burdened with loss of a home due to increasing property insurance, rising costs of electricity, inequitable real estate taxes, and foreclosure. When loss of employer-based health insurance enters the picture, personal and financial disaster is waiting to happen.

De-humanization caused by job loss and economic stress is ugly. Its fruits -- frustration, hopelessness, fear, and growing anger --abound all around us. So do many misguided attempts at leadership from people who are apologists for the status quo, in denial or otherwise clueless about what has gone wrong, and what may be done about it.

There is no greater example of this dynamic on a national basis than the crisis in health care. The incredible debt associated with Obama's great gamble will be recovered only if the American economy is stimulated to produce public and private capital long-term, capital that can retire the nation's debt and be reinvested in the nation's overall prosperity.

The recovery will not occur unless health care costs are made affordable for individual citizens, American businesses and for public funding of health care entitlement programs. This is because the trajectory of the costs of health care will block the redirection and regeneration of the present unsustainable feedback loop. This is the cycle that is causing the economy, the quality of life and the natural environment to spiral downward toward further deterioration.

A rising panic about health care stands in tandem with growing concerns about the natural environment, which have been nascent in American society for many years. If these torrents of discontent converge and spill over to capture streams of other economic and social causes, a full-blown sustainability social movement likely will develop. This may be precisely what is needed to cause the nation to turn in a more sustainable direction. The question is how much blood and treasure will be spent before transformative change takes place.

Even a cursory study of history summons up remembrance that Americans are known for rising up and fighting hard when confronted with forces standing in the way of the search for sustainability. This is because the goals and objectives of sustainability are at the core of the American Dream. The Dream, in turn, is grounded in Winthrop's covenant to be as a "City Upon a Hill" and other visions that have inspired Americans throughout history, as discussed in the introductory chapter.

Americans do not fool around with challenges that threaten to break this covenant. We will take to the streets, go to war, do whatever it takes to meet such threats and defeat them without hesitation. It is much better to use the aegis of democracy, diplomacy and established Constitutional means of seeking justice. This is because seeking justice outside the established institutions of democracy and law always carries the risk that things will get out of hand, that mistakes will be made, and that innocent people will get hurt.

One fork in the road leads to fear, anger, polarization, unhealthy conflict, and open rebellion. The other brings the nation to justice, reconciliation, peace and renewal through the civil practice of democracy and the rule of law. This latter direction is along the road less traveled in recent American history. It must now be rediscovered and taken.

The ultimate direction chosen depends on whether those in positions of public trust -- and those who influence them -- come to view their responsibilities and their fundamental interests in more comprehensive terms. They must see that imbalanced and short-sighted fixation with the economic component of sustainability leads to systemic collapse.

The powerful also must come to know that ideology grounded in what Toffler labeled "econo-think" frustrates democracy and runs counter to the requirements of sustainability. Some contemporary observers are giving this tendency in American culture other names, like "super-capitalism" or "turbo-capitalism." By whatever name is given, this drive for economic profit at all costs diminishes America in the eyes of the world. We are losing our friends and emboldening our foes as a consequence.

In like fashion, those who promote government-centered solutions forget that in America, it is civil society in free enterprise that should hold and exercise power and responsibility, using government only as a practical and necessary means to an end. The path to reconciliation will recognize the points of view of those on both the right and the left of the political spectrum, and blend them in ways that suit the best of America's political tradition.

Moreover, those holding political power must redefine their understanding of what is "politically feasible." They must recognize that the source of their power and the object of their responsibility as public servants lay not with special interests who fund their campaigns, but with the American people. Failure to recognize this risks much organized protest, disunity, civil disobedience, and far worse.

The choice of which path to follow at the crossroads resides in the awareness and the conscience of each one of us. What each citizen does with this deeply personal decision is best determined in the still of the night, on our knees, and in consultation with the very ground of our being.

Our forbearers in American history were in this position many times before us. Now, it is our turn to help define what it means to be Americans in search of the nation's true vision and destiny. It is our time to seal the covenant and to make an oath to it; and to turn away from those who insist on making asinine pledges to starve our public institutions of revenue because they believe that "government is the enemy." It is time once again to separate the truly patriotic from the self-centered and the mean-spirited who take their pleasure and retain their power and influence by dividing us.

Government in America is not the enemy. It is of us, for us, and by us. A case can be made that we have been our own worst enemy long enough; and that the time has arrived when we must take back our government in honor of all those who died defending the freedoms it affords, and on behalf of all those who will enjoy the opportunities of freedom for generations to come.

All of this "gloom and doom" and gut-wrenching fighting for the soul of America is to suggest that the search for sustainable governance carries with it an awesome responsibility to contemporary citizens, and especially to future generations, our own kids and grand kids and theirs.

The time has come to act as a mature and civilized society and world leader. As we suggested earlier, the old categories of political thought -- liberal, conservative, Republican, Democrat, Red, Blue -- none of these apply when it comes time to act in unison as Americans.

It is time for the search to be renewed in earnest, and to find the right ways to give birth to the new world Matthew Arnold wrote poetry about. Arnold wrote his poetry not long after Tocqueville authored *Democracy in America*. Tocqueville caught a glimpse of Arnold's vision of "new world" at one fleeting moment in time.

One reading of American history is that the birth of the "new world" was breached forever long ago as the nation was torn by civil war, experienced the industrial revolution and became a vast empire bent on conquest and self-aggrandizement. Much of our Florida, which became a state in 1845, would languish as a mosquito-infested backwater until the fruits of the nation's industrial pursuits provided markets for a playground of pleasure and profit. The exception is the state's northern and north central regions (of which both authors are multi-generational natives) which were settled in the 1800's by those pursuing the Jeffersonian-Jacksonian vision of an agrarian society. The balance of the state's development after World War II, as we saw in Chapters I and II, would perfect its vision to become a world class tourist destination and retirement haven.

Another view of history suggests that the hope of the new world has never faded, and the direction of American history demonstrates that its birth pangs have been going on since John Winthrop and his colonists first set foot on American soil in 1630 with their vision of a City Upon a Hill. Winthrop proclaimed these words in making the sacred covenant with the Creator, repeated in an expanded version here:

> For we must consider that we shall be as a city upon a hill. The eyes of all people are upon us. So that if we shall deal falsely with our God in this work we have undertaken, and so cause Him to withdraw His present help from us, we shall be made a story and a by-word through the world. We shall open the mouths of enemies to speak evil of the ways of God, and all professors for God's sake. We shall shame the faces of many of God's worthy servants, and cause their prayers to be turned into curses upon us till we be consumed out of the good land whither we are going.
>
> And to shut this discourse with that exhortation of Moses, that faithful servant of the Lord, in his last farewell to Israel,

(Deuteronomy 30). "Beloved, there is now set before us life and death, good and evil," in that we are commanded this day to love the Lord our God, and to love one another, to walk in his ways and to keep his Commandments and his ordinance and his laws, and the articles of our Covenant with Him, that we may live and be multiplied, and that the Lord our God may bless us in the land whither we go to possess it. But if our hearts shall turn away, so that we will not obey, but shall be seduced, and worship other Gods, our pleasure and profits, and serve them; it is propounded unto us this day, we shall surely perish out of the good land whither we pass over this vast sea to possess it.

> Therefore let us choose life,
> that we and our seed may live,
> by obeying His voice and cleaving to Him,
> for He is our life and our prosperity.[274]

We subscribe to the view that Winthrop's hope is still alive, but we must warn that now is the time to push hard because the birth of that precious gift Americans have always longed for is in trouble, as Florida's contemporary experience clearly shows. Citizens of Florida should not want to vindicate Martin Luther's metaphor about human progress, and become the drunk who falls off the horse, losing sight of the purpose of our journey as consciousness turns to stupor.

The renewed effort must begin with and be steered by those who aspire to public leadership positions in civil society. A public leader's job is to scan the environment in which leadership takes place to understand the realities carried by the forces and trends shaping society. A search for empirical facts devoid of ideological shallow-mindedness, personal theological interpretations, and pandering to our fears and frustrations must be undertaken by the public leader. Communicating these facts to those being led is critical to developing an understanding of our needs, aspirations, and values. The whole purpose of "civic dialogue" is to communicate about the factual realities being faced so higher levels of awareness of them can be reached, and responses to them can be made with confidence and broad support.

There is no room for "spin", manipulative "sound bites" or other such attempts to deceive people or avoid reality because it is unpleasant, may not inure to one's short-term interests, and may cause controversy. The best public leaders know that people can deal with reality ultimately, and respect those who present it to them. Misinformation, dishonesty and a lack of transparency throw people off and thwart the species of leadership sustainability demands. Even subtle deceptions mislead; truth never does.

There are bright spots in this otherwise gloomy picture. Floridians have learned first hand that we can pull together and work for the common good of society when natural disaster strikes, and there is no ambiguity about the reality of the crisis being faced. People volunteer to help others. Public agencies drop their siloed and turf-protecting approaches long enough to work together. Non-profit organizations and private businesses rise to the occasion with donations of goods and services. Some news media even contribute by reporting real news rather than sensational drivel. Self-interests for a time are rightly understood as neighbor helps neighbor with sandbags or food. Then, when the disaster passes, things go back to normal.

We face governance, economic, environmental and social disasters caused by our own behaviors, as well as those provided by nature. If crisis is required for real progress to be made toward a sustainable society, America's and Florida's present unsustainable course certainly constitutes one. We should take heart that we and our fellow citizens have the capacity to adapt and respond as Americans who care about their place and example in the world and each other.

Another bright spot is that recent opinion research demonstrates that we share much commonality in our values, needs, and aspirations for the future vision of the state. One interpretation of this data is that Floridians crave sustainability and are vitally concerned about the well-being of future generations. We suspect this sentiment is widely-held by Americans generally, and by citizens around the world.

Our experience with undergraduate and graduate students as we tested the key ideas of this book taught us that they "get it." They crave authenticity, and place high value on practices that promote sustainable ways of living. Sadly but understandably, many of these students have no intention of seeking employment by governments. They perceive public institutions as corrupted, marginalized and incapable. Their parents' generation is responsible for this perception because by example many have rendered it so through neglect of the requirements of citizenship in a democracy. In spite of this, young people have the spirit and the desire to revitalize and reform public service so that some day---and we hope soon---employment by public agencies will be respected and fulfilling once again.

The challenge to public leaders is to communicate the truth of the present crisis, and help us craft sustainable responses that align with our values, needs, and aspirations. If the "tipping point" has been reached, as our elder statesman Bob Graham suggests, the time for action is now.

The analytical model we have used in this book has proven its enormous explanatory value, and its power to help us develop sustainable solutions to public problems. The Florida case study helps expose the perilous nature of unsustainable public policy and governance arrangements, and the hope -- however dim today -- that tomorrow society can achieve progress toward sustainability. The theoretical understanding of sustainability from social science, especially the use of complex adaptive systems theory, has proven its value.

The leadership competencies, principles, tools, and techniques we have agreed to offer in digital and web based formats hold much potential if used as part of a new leadership framework. Together, the analytical model, the Florida case study and the leadership framework will help us build the capacity to analyze, evaluate and respond to governance performance from the perspective of sustainability. These metrics will help determine whether public leadership and public policy are moving us toward the goals and objectives of sustainability: towards meeting "the needs of the present generation without compromising the ability of future generations to meet their needs;" and away from unhealthy production and consumption patterns, environmental degradation and social deterioration.

As authors, we hope this book serves as our contribution to a sustainable society by helping our interested fellow citizens learn to master the art of "sustainability thinking" and advance the art of "sustainability action."

Finally, some of the best potential public leaders among us have been sitting on the sidelines for too long. Entering the public arena in today's political environment is not easy. The level of conflict is high; the hours are long, and the personal sacrifice of time away from private pursuits and family can be difficult.

Some very good leaders who chose to move into the political arena itself have lost official positions or campaigns because they spoke the truth to us. These are our role models and real heroes. They teach us -- even in their defeat -- that in the end there is no greater reward and no more important legacy we can leave than to be known as a true public leader who fought the good fight.

Now is the time for those among us with talent and energy to step up and, in remembrance of the sacrifice of those who preceded us, likewise be willing to sacrifice and risk defeat in order to achieve genuine victory for our fellow citizens and especially for those who will follow. This is the path to a sustainable society, and to greatness as a citizen-leader, as a true Patriot and as a civilization.

A Personal Story

We share a personal story in closing. We were blessed to have working with us in the writing of this book a research assistant and editor who is an international student and summa cum laude political science graduate of Florida's oldest private institution of higher learning, Stetson University. Her name is Alesia Sedziaka, and she is presently a graduate student in International Studies at the University of Arizona.

Alesia is from Belarus, a small country next to Russia in the former Soviet Union. She speaks five languages and plays classical violin and guitar, a testimony to the discipline and training she received as a child growing up in her hometown, Minsk. She can sing, too.

She is a gentle and kind person with a fierce determination to succeed in life. When she was an undergraduate, she won over the hearts of the Stetson and DeLand community. We are confident she is doing the same in Tucson.

During a dinner party for Alesia and her boyfriend at Arrington's home during the Christmas season 2008, we were engaged in conversation about sustainability as a global movement. Someone commented that it is very well that there are so many brilliant young people from nations other than America who are answering the call for a sustainable society.

Alesia listened carefully, and replied that, yes; it is good, but that America must realize that unless it leads the world, sustainability will never materialize on our planet, regardless of how many people from other nations might hope to live on a sustainable planet earth.

Alesia's message should be clear to all of us. She has seen through her family's history and in her own young experience the suffering that is caused by wars, authoritarian dictatorships, terror, Holocaust, and environmental disasters like Chernobyl.

She also has experienced the promise of the American dream, and is seizing her day with excellence, passion, and commitment to building a better world.

She has been away from her family for several years, studying, working, traveling and playing her music. After her exemplary performance at Stetson, several of America's best graduate schools accepted her. The people at the University of Arizona were smart enough to see what she has to offer, and granted her a full scholarship, which is very difficult to earn in today's economy.

She had a grueling first year in Arizona working hard as a student and as a graduate assistant, getting used to a whole new place with new people and a very strange climate. We are happy to report that during both semesters she made straight "A's."

Perhaps the highlight of her year was beholding the Grand Canyon. You should see the photos she and her boyfriend took and sent back to Florida and to Belarus. Her proud mother probably has displayed them all over Minsk by now.

She has struggled during her amazing American journey through the pain of being homesick, adjusting to a totally new culture, putting up with demanding professors and, yes, cranky authors. She has never complained, never blinked once because she knows the opportunity and promise that is hers through the gift of her life. She knows how fortunate she is to be in the land of the free and the home of the brave, for she represents both of these ways of describing America.

Alesia's personal quest personifies the birth pangs of that 'new world waiting to be born' that poet Mathew Arnold wrote about so many years ago. As she prepares herself to go out into the world and make her mark, as strong as she is, she needs help -- yours and ours.

Alesia's hopes for the future and those of her generation throughout the world and of their children depend on American citizens stepping up and providing leadership. We must be inspired by the Alesia Sedziaka's of the world, and not let them down. (She inspired us to hunker down and against all odds actually finish this book!).

Let's show this next generation -- wherever in the world they may be or may go -- what it means to be an American as we continue our search for sustainable governance. As the rock star Bruce Springsteen has written, it is time now to "Come on up for the Rising."

There you will find the hopes and dreams of millions of people like Alesia Sedziaka -- born and unborn -- waiting for American leadership.

Springsteen's song is about the emergency responders on 9-11 who sacrificed their lives so others could live. That same spirit of sacrifice for the benefit of the present and future of the world is now demanded of all Americans. Florida, the Bellwether State and the land of 'pleasure and profit,' has a major atoning role to play.

Alesia represents both our purpose and our role model. She embodies the "emergent forms of spirit" Serena Jones references in the epigraph at the beginning of this concluding chapter. Alesia's presence and performance here teach us -- consistent with the American vision and the covenant that seals it -- that our national purpose is affirmed as the hopes of freedom and opportunity for all people are realized through the pursuit of happiness in reaching human potential.

The remembrance by future generations of our time must be that we lived the pledge, as did our forbearers, to preserve, protect, and defend these gifts with our lives, our fortunes, and our sacred honor.

Lawrence W. Arrington and Herbert A. Marlowe, Jr.
Stetson Carriage House
DeLand, Florida
Your Fellow Citizens

ENDNOTES

[1] Lewis, C. S., The World's Last Night and Other Essays (A Harvest Book, 1952) 93.
[2] A complete list of relevant projects can be viewed at our website <http://www.arringtonmarlowe.com/>.
[3] This definition is used by the U.S. Environmental Protection Agency. It is derived from an earlier, widely disseminated definition by The Brundtland Commission in its report "Our Common Future", published as Annex to document A/42/427, General Assembly, World Commission on Environment and Development, Development and International Co-operation: Environment (New York: United Nations, 1987).
[4] Odom, H.T., Environment, Power and Society (New York: Wiley-Interscience, 1971).
[5] Bateson, G., Steps to an Ecology of Mind (New York: Ballantine, 1972).
[6] McHarg, I., Design with Nature (New York: Doubleday, 1971).
[7] Lazlo, E., Introduction to Systems Philosophy (New York: Gordon & Breach, 1972).
[8] Daly, H.E., and Cobb, J.B., For the Common Good (Boston: Beacon Press, 1989).
[9] Ekins, P., ed., The Living Economy (London: Routledge, 1986).
[10] Hawken, P., The Ecology of Commerce (New York: HarperBusiness, 1993).
[11] Van der Ryn, S. and Cowan, S., Ecological Design (Washington, D.C.: Islznd Press, 1996).
[12] Morehouse, W., ed., Building Sustainable Communities (New York: Intermediate Technology Development Group, 1989).
[13] Perlman, J., "Mega-Cities: Innovations for Sustainable Cities of the 21st Century," in Aberly, D., ed., Futures by Design: The Practice of Ecological Planning (Philadelphia: New Society Publishers, 1994).
[14] Mollison, B., "Permaculture," in Aberly.
[15] Rapport, D., "What Is Clinical Ecology?" In Costanza, R. et. al., ed., Ecosystem Health (Washington, D.C.: Island Press, 1992).
[16] Stephen S. Mulkey, ed., "Towards a Sustainable Florida," The Century Commission for a Sustainable Florida, 1 Sep. 2006: 1-102, 15 Jan. 2008 <http://www.centurycommission.org/current_projects.asp>: 3.
[17] Stephen S. Mulkey, ed., "Towards a Sustainable Florida," The Century Commission for a Sustainable Florida, 1 Sep. 2006: 1-102, 15 Jan. 2008 <http://www.centurycommission.org/current_projects.asp>: 3.
[18] See Mark Roseland and Sean Connelly, Toward Sustainable Communities: Resources for Citizens and Their Governments, rev. ed. (Gabriola Island, BC: New Society Publishers, 2005); James Weaver, Michael Rock, and Kenneth Kusterer, Achieving Broad-Based Sustainable Development: Governance, Environment, and Growth with Equity (West Hartford, Conn.: Kumarian Press, 1997); Tim O'Riordan and Heather Voisey, eds., Sustainable Development in Western Europe: Coming to Terms with Agenda 21 (London, Portland, OR: Frank Cass, 1997); Konrad Ginther,

Erik Denters, and P.J.I.M. de Waart, Sustainable Development and Good Governance (Norwell, MA: Kluwer Academic Publishers, 1995); Martin W. Holdgate, From Care to Action: Making a Sustainable World (Washington, D.C.: Taylor and Francis, 1996).

[19] United Nations, Department of Social and Economic Affairs: Division for Sustainable Development, "Agenda 21, the Rio Declaration on Environment and Development, and the Statement of Principles for the Sustainable Management of Forests," Rio de Janeiro, Brazil, 3 to 14 June 1992 <http://www.un.org/esa/sustdev/documents/agenda21/index.htm>.

[20] The City Council of the City of Eugene, Resolution No. 4618, The City of Eugene, 28 Feb. 2000, 4 Aug. 2008 <http://www.eugene-or.gov>.

[21] See <www.tjpdc.org>.

[22] Robert A. Dahl, Polyarchy (New Haven, Conn.: Yale University Press, 1971) 279.

[23] John W. Gardner, On Leadership (New York: The Free Press, 1993) 121.

[24] Mulkey 3.

[25] Mark Roseland and Sean Connelly, Toward Sustainable Communities: Resources for Citizens and Their Governments, rev. ed. (Gabriola Island, BC: New Society Publishers, 2005) 27.

[26] Alvin Toffler, Power Shift: Knowledge, Wealth, and Violence at the Edge of the 21st Century (New York: Bantam Books, 1991) 238.

[27] John P. Diggins, The Lost Soul of American Politics: Virtue, Self-Interests and the Foundations of Liberalism (University of Chicago Press, 1984) 10.

[28] John P. Diggins 10.

[29] Alfred A. Knopf et al., The Good Society (New York, 1991) 282.

[30] Robert N. Bellah et al., Habits of the Heart: Individualism and Commitment in American Life (New York: Harper & Row, Publishers, 1986) 168.

[31] Alexis de Tocqueville, Democracy in America, trans. George Lawrence, ed. J.P. Mayer (New York: Doubleday, Anchor Books, 1969) 287.

[32] James MacGregor Burns, Leadership (New York: Harper & Row, Publishers, 1978) 431.

[33] Martin W. Holdgate, From Care to Action: Making a Sustainable World (Washington, D.C.: Taylor and Francis, 1996) 130.

[34] U.S. Census Bureau, <http://www.census.gov/>.

[35] VISIT FLORIDA Research, 15 Jan. 2008 <http://media.visitflorida.org/about/research/>.

[36] Mulkey 3.

[37] See The Council for a Sustainable Florida, <http://www.sustainableflorida.org/>; The Florida Chamber Foundation, <http://www.flchamber.com/mx/hm.asp?id=newcornerstone>; 1000 Friends of Florida, <http://www.1000friendsofflorida.org/Publications/main.asp>; The Century Commission for a Sustainable Florida, <http://www.centurycommission.org/current_projects.asp>; MyRegion.org, <http://www.myregion.org/>.

[38] Ron Cunningham, "Slothful Servant," Gainesville Sun 13 Sep. 2008.

[39] Lawrence W. Arrington, "Local Government Reform in the Emerging Mega State: The Florida Charter County Movement," Masters Degree Thesis, Stetson University, 1989, 19.
[40] Gregg M. Turner, A Journey Into Florida Railroad History (Gainesville: University Press of Florida, 2008).
[41] Charles R. Adrian and Charles Press, Governing Urban America, 3rd ed. (New York: McGraw-Hill, 1968) 72.
[42] Lance Banning, The Jeffersonian Persuasion: Evolution of a Party Ideology (Ithaca, New York: Cornell University Press, 1978) 79-90.
[43] Stanley M. Elkins and Eric L. McKitrick, The Age of Federalism: The Early American Republic, 1788-1800 (New York: Oxford University Press, 1995) 15; Wallace Hettle, The Peculiar Democracy: Southern Democrats in Peace and Civil War (Athens, Georgia: University Press of Georgia, 2001) 15.
[44] Banning 105-15.
[45] Philip Hamburger, Separation of Church and State (Cambridge, Massachusetts: Harvard University Press, 2002).
[46] Robert Allen Rutland, The Birth of the Bill of Rights, 1776-1791 (Chapel Hill, North Carolina: University of North Carolina Press, 1955).
[47] Arrington 13-38.
[48] It is not clear whether Tocqueville traveled to Florida as he made his famous trip in the 1830's. Florida was ceded from Spain in 1821 and became a Territory a year later. If he did enter Florida, he likely skirted the northern section as he traveled the Deep South. (Arrington 14).
[49] See Eagleton Institute of Politics Electronic Government Project at <http://www.eagleton.rutgers.edu/e-gov/e-politicalarchive-Progressive.htm>.
[50] "Florida: From Backwater to Boom State," PBS-WEDU, narr. Ed Asner, writ. Gary Mormino, dir. Janine Farver, WEDU, 18, Oct. 2007.
[51] Laura Layden, "Florida Chamber Report: State Economy Is Hardly Over and Out," Naples Daily News: naplesnews.com 4 Dec. 2007, 17 Jan. 2008 <http://www.naplesnews.com/news/2007/dec/04/>.
[52] For the year ending July 1. Sam Roberts, "Fastest-Growing States Show Slower Expansion," The New York Times 27 Dec. 2007, Jan. 17 2008 <http://www.nytimes.com/2007/12/27/us/27census.html>.
[53] U.S. Census Bureau, State Population Estimates <http://www.census.gov/>.
[54] Timothy Chapin and Heather Khan, "Assessing Florida Citizen Attitudes towards Growth, Growth Management, and Quality of Life Issues: Final Report," The Century Commission for a Sustainable Florida, 6 Sep. 2006: 1-19, 17 Jan. 2008 <http://www.centurycommission.org/current_projects.asp>: i.
[55] Leadership Florida, The Second Annual Leadership Florida Sunshine State Survey, 2007, 11 Feb. 2008 <http://www.leadershipflorida.org/mx/hm.asp?id=pub_survey07>.
[56] Ben Warner, "Sustainable Florida: Progress Toward a Shared Vision," The Century Commission for a Sustainable Florida, 31 Aug. 2007: 1-81, 17 Jan. 2008 <http://www.centurycommission.org/current_projects.asp>: 9.

[57] Alvin Toffler, Future Shock (New York: Bantam Books, 1970) 230.
[58] David Halberstam, The Reckoning (New York: Morrow and Co., 1986).
[59] Paul Krugman, "The Madoff Economy," New York Times 19 Dec. 2008.
[60] Simon Johnson, "The Quiet Coup," *The Atlantic*, May 2009, http://www.theatlantic.com/doc/200905/imf-advice.
[61] David Brooks, "The Great Unwinding" New York Times, 11 Jun. 2009.
[61] Thomas L. Friedman, "China to the Rescue? Not!" New York Times 21 Dec. 2008.
[62] Thomas L. Friedman, "China to the Rescue? Not!" New York Times 21 Dec. 2008.
[63] Thomas L. Friedman 21 Dec. 2008.
[64] Barack Obama, speech, George Mason University, Washington, D.C., 8 Jan. 2009.
[65] Doris Kearns Goodwin, Team of Rivals (New York: Simon and Schuster, 2005) 90-91.
[66] Lewis Gould, Grand Old Party: A History of the Republicans (New York: Random House, 2007) 14.
[67] Fareed Zakaria, The Post-American World (New York: W.W. Norton, 2008) 251.
[68] Mary Carroll, rev. of Grand Old Party: A History of the Republicans, by Lewis Gould, American Library Association, 2003 <http://www.amazon.com/Grand-Old-Party-History-Republicans>.
[69] Publishers Weekly, rev. of Grand Old Party: A History of the Republicans, by Lewis Gould, Reed Business Information Inc., 2003.
<http://www.amazon.com/Grand-Old-Party-History-Republicans>.
[70] Paul Krugman, "Bigger than Bush," New York Times 2 Jan. 2009.
[71] Sidney M. Milkis and Jerome M. Meleur, The Great Society and the High Tide of Liberalism (Massachusetts: U. of Massachusetts Press, 2005) 251.
[72] President Bush supported the extension in spite of the objections from the Party's arch-conservative wing. Ultimately, the Act was extended for another 25 years (Charles Babington, "GOP Rebellion Stops Voting Rights Act, Complaints Include Bilingual Ballots and Scope of Justice Dept. Role in South," Washington Post 22 June 2006).
[73] Jason L. Riley, Let Them In. The Case for Open Borders (Penguin Books, 2008).
[74] Robert B. Reich, Supercapitalism: the Transformation of Business, Democracy, and Everyday Life, (NewYork, New York: Vintage Books,2008).
[75] Robert B. Reich, Supercapitalism: the Transformation of Business, Democracy, and Everyday Life, (NewYork, New York: Vintage Books,2008).
[76] David Frum, "Why Rush is Wrong. The Party of Buckley and Reagan Is Now Bereft and Dominated by the Politics of Limbaugh. A Conservative's Lament," Newsweek 7 Mar. 2009 <http://www.newsweek.com/id/188279>.
[77] David Brooks, "The Long Voyage Home," The New York Times 5 May 2009 <http://www.nytimes.com/2009/05/05/opinion>.
[78] David Brooks, "The Long Voyage Home."
[79] Mary McCrory, "Dirty Bomb Politics," Washington Post 20 June 2002.
[80] Alex Leary and Steve Bousquet, "Florida Lawmakers Feel Bite of No New Taxes Pledge," Times/Herald Tallahassee Bureau 6 Apr. 2009.

[81] "Mason-Dixon Poll," Florida Alliance for Concerned Taxpayers, 8 Apr. 2009 <http://www.flaact.com/news09_04_08_2.html>.
[82] Tim Padgett, "Undoing Jeb Bush in Florida," Time Magazine 3 May 2007 <http://www.time.com/time/magazine>.
[83] Theodore Roosevelt, Address, New York, 12 Oct. 1915.
[84] "New Cornerstone Revisited: A Look at Our State in Transition," Florida Chamber of Commerce Foundation, 1 Nov. 2007, 17 Jan. 2008 <http://www.flchamber.com/mx/hm.asp?id=newcornerstone>: 3-7.
[85] Laura Layden, "Florida Chamber Report: State Economy Is Hardly Over and Out," Naples Daily News: naplesnews.com 4 Dec. 2007, 17 Jan. 2008 <http://www.naplesnews.com/news/2007/dec/04/>.
[86] Michael Grunwald, "Is Florida the Sunset State?" The Time Magazine 10 July 2008 <http://www.time.com/time/magazine>.
[87] Jim Saunders, Daytona Beach News Journal 24 April 2009.
[88] "Florida League of Conservation Voters Education Fund State of the Florida Environment Education Page," <http://www.flcv.com>.
[89] See "Smart Growth for Florida's Future: The Florida Sustainable Communities Act," 1000 Friends of Florida, Mar. 2009 <http://www.1000friendsofflorida.com>.
[90] "More Vision, Less Denial," The St. Petersburg Times, editorial, 24 Feb. 2008, 24 Feb. 2008 <http://www.sptimes.com>.
[91] Conor Dougherty, "Is Florida Over?" The Wall Street Journal 29 Sep. 2007, 17 Jan. 2008 <http://online.wsj.com/public/article/>.
[92] Michael Grunwald, "Is Florida the Sunset State?"
[93] Contact The Florida Chamber Foundation, <http://www.flchamber.com/>, for a copy of The Cornerstone Report 2005.
[94] "Tax Reform Runs Aground," The St. Petersburg Times, editorial, 14 Feb. 2008, 14 Feb. 2008 <http://www.sptimes.com/2008/02/14/Opinion/>.
[95] Here are examples of exemptions from the state's 6 percent sales tax and services excluded from taxation (expressed in millions of dollars). Exemptions from the sales tax: $71.3 Electricity for manufacturing; $63.5 Charter fishing boats; $55.3 Boiler fuels used by industries; $42.3 Bottled water; $41.3 Newspaper and magazine inserts; $33.8 Farm equipment; $27.9 Ostrich and livestock feed; $24.7 Free advertising publications; $5.0 Boats temporarily docked in Florida; $0.9 High school and college stadium skyboxes; Services **excluded from taxation:** $658.8 Lawyers; $511.1 Architects and engineers; $168.5 Radio-TV broadcasters; $272.0 Accountants; $87.3 Barber and beauty shops; $64.6 Dry cleaners; $52.8 Data processors; $30.9 Health clubs and golf courses; $22.4 Taxis and limousines; $19.5 Athletic and theatrical agents (From 2007 Florida Tax Handbook).
96 Leadership Florida, "The Second Annual Leadership Florida Sunshine State Survey," 2007, 11 Feb. 2008 <http://www.leadershipflorida.org/mx/hm.asp?id=pub_survey07>.
[97] The Tallahassee Democrat: Tallahassee.com, editorial, 1 Nov. 2007, Jan. 21 2008 <http://tallahassee.com/>.
[98] Contact The Florida Chamber Foundation, <http://www.flchamber.com/>, for a copy of The Cornerstone Report 2005.

[99] United States, The Senate Fiscal Policy and Calendar Committee, The House Policy & Budget Council, and The Legislative Office of Economic and Demographic Research, "State of Florida Long-Range Financial Outlook. Fiscal Year 2008-09 through 2010-11. Fall 2007 Report," The Florida Senate, 2007: 1-95, 17 Jan. 2008 <http://www.flsenate.gov/data/publications/2006/ Senate/reports/>: 10-11; 16.
[100] United States, The Senate Fiscal Policy and Calendar Committee et al. 26-27.
[101] Steve Bousquet, "Budget Takes another Hit," The St. Petersburg Times 9 Jan. 2008, 21 Jan. 2008 <http://www.sptimes.com/2008/01/09/>.
[102] Marc Caputo and Steve Bousquet, "Florida's Budget Hole: $2.3-billion," Times/Herald Tallahassee Bureau 10 Dec. 2008.
[103] Marc Caputo and Steve Bousquet, "Florida's Budget Hole: $2.3-billion."
[104] Mary Ellen Klas, "GOP Lawmakers Utter Heresy: Taxes," Times/Herald Tallahassee Bureau 17 Jan. 2009.
[105] Marc Caputo, "Crist Restores Millions in Cutbacks," Times/Herald Tallahassee Bureau 28 Jan. 2009.
[106] Steve Bousquet et al., "$66.5B Budget, by Nickels and Dimes," Times/Herald Tallahassee Bureau 8 May 2009.
[107] "New Cornerstone Revisited: A Look at Our State in Transition," Florida Chamber of Commerce Foundation, 1 Nov. 2007, 17 Jan. 2008 <http://www.flchamber.com/mx/hm.asp?id=newcornerstone>.
[108] Hank Fishkind, "Analysis of County Spending Patterns 1999-2006: Where Did the Money Go?" The Florida Association of Counties, 7 Mar. 2007: 1-54, 22 Jan. 2008 <http://www.fl-counties.com/proptax/_doc/fishkind_study.pdf>: 1.
[109] The Office of the Majority Whip Representative Ellyn Bogdanoff, "The Florida Budget for Fiscal Year 2007-2008," Whip's Policy Brief 3 May 2007: 6.
[110] Steve Bousquet, "Short Term Budget: The Crunch is in the Here and Now, This Time,"
The St. Petersburg Times 24 Feb. 2008, 24 Feb. 2008 <http://www.sptimes.com>.
[111] Data from The Office of the Majority Whip Representative 6.
[112] Leadership Florida, "The Second Annual Leadership Florida Sunshine State Survey," 2007, 11 Feb. 2008
<http://www.leadershipflorida.org/mx/hm.asp?id=pub_survey07>.
[113] Aaron Deslatte, "Florida's Property-Tax Amendment: Questions and Answers," OrlandoSentinel.com 20 Jan. 2008, 26 Feb. 2008 <http://www.orlandosentinel.com>.
[114] Jim Ash, "Tax Plan Passes: the People Have Spoken," The Tallahassee Democrat: Tallahassee.com 30 Jan. 2008, 30 Jan. 2008 <http://tallahassee.com/>.
[115] Alex Leary, "Florida Businesses Wish for More Tax Relief," The St. Petersburg Times 26 Dec. 2007, 23 Jan. 2008 <http://www.sptimes.com/2007/12/26/>.
[116] Leary <http://www.sptimes.com/2007/12/26/>.
[117] Steve Bousquet, "Budget Takes Another Hit," The St. Petersburg Times 9 Jan. 2008, 21 Jan. 2008 <http://www.sptimes.com/2008/01/09/>.
[118] "'Best' Isn't Good Enough," editorial, HeraldTribune.com 2 Nov. 2007, 23 Jan. 2008 <http://www.heraldtribune.com/article/>.

[119] The St. Petersburg Times, editorial, 31 Oct. 2007, 25 Jan. 2008 <http://www.sptimes.com>.
[120] Alex Leary, "Rubio Pushes 'Other' Tax Cut," The St. Petersburg Times 20 Dec. 2007, 25 Jan. 2008 <http://www.sptimes.com>.
[121] Alex Leary, "Rep. Rubio Veers Off with Another Tax Cut Plan," The St. Petersburg Times 21 Nov. 2007, 23 Jan. 2008 <http://www.sptimes.com>.
[122] Alex Leary and Jennifer Liberto, "Session Set, but with Less Harmony," The St. Petersburg Times 2 Mar. 2008, 2 Mar. 2008 <http://www.sptimes.com>.
[123] Mary Ann Lindley, "Rubio's glory is fading with his retro rhetoric," The Tallahassee Democrat: Tallahassee.com 13 Jan. 2008, 23 Jan. 2008 <http://tallahassee.com/>.
[124] Lindley <http://tallahassee.com/>.
[125] "Do No Harm. Huge Economic, Political Challenges Face Florida," editorial, The Tallahassee Democrat: Tallahassee.com 2 Mar. 2008, 2 Mar. 2008 <http://tallahassee.com/>.
[126] Nicholas Johnson, "Budget Cuts or Tax Increases at the State Level: Which is Preferable during an Economic Downturn?" Center on Budget and Policy Priorities 8 Jan. 2008, 28 Jan. 2008 <http://www.cbpp.org/1-8-08sfp.htm>.

Stiglitz and Orzag's analysis is worth quoting at length:

[E]conomic analysis suggests that tax increases would not in general be more harmful to the economy than spending reductions. Indeed, in the short run (which is the period of concern during a downturn), the adverse impact of a tax increase on the economy may, if anything, be smaller than the adverse impact of a spending reduction, because some of the tax increase would result in reduced saving rather than reduced consumption. For example, if taxes increase by $1, consumption may fall by 90 cents and saving may fall by 10 cents. Since a tax increase does not reduce consumption on a dollar-for-dollar basis, its negative impact on the economy is attenuated in the short run. Some types of spending reductions, however, would reduce demand in the economy on a dollar-for-dollar basis and therefore would be more harmful to the economy than a tax increase…

Basic economy theory suggests that direct spending reductions will generate more adverse consequences for the economy in the short run than either a tax increase or a transfer program reduction. The reason is that some of any tax increase or transfer payment reduction would reduce saving rather than consumption, lessening its impact on the economy in the short run, whereas the full amount of government spending on goods and services would directly reduce consumption…

The more that the tax increases or transfer reductions are focused on those with lower propensities to consume (that is, on those who spend less and save more of each additional dollar of income), the less damage is done to the weakened economy. Since higher-income families tend to have lower propensities to consume than lower-income families, the least damaging approach in the short run involves tax increases concentrated on higher-income families. Reductions in transfer payments to lower-income families would generally be more harmful to the economy than increases in taxes on higher-income families, since lower-income families are more likely to spend any additional income than higher-income families. Indeed, since the recipients of transfer payments typically spend virtually their entire income, the negative impact of reductions in transfer payments is likely to be nearly as great as a reduction in direct government spending on goods and services.

For states interested in the impact only on their own economy rather than the national economy, the arguments made above are even stronger. In particular, the government spending that would be reduced if direct spending programs are cut is often concentrated among local businesses.... By contrast, the spending by individuals and businesses that would be affected by tax increases often is less concentrated among local producers — since part of the decline in purchases that would occur if taxes were raised would be a decline in the purchase of goods produced out of state. Thus, more of the reduction in purchases that results from tax increases than from government budget cuts falls on out-of-state goods (relative to in-state goods), lessening the adverse impact of a tax increase on the state economy. Reductions in direct government spending consequently could have a larger adverse impact on a state's economy than tax increases, which have a stronger adverse impact on out-of-state goods and services.

The conclusion is that, if anything, tax increases on higher-income families are the least damaging mechanism for closing state fiscal deficits in the short run. Reductions in government spending on goods and services, or reductions in transfer payments to lower-income families, are likely to be more damaging to the economy in the short run than tax increases focused on higher-income families. In any case, in terms of how counter-productive they are, there is no automatic preference for spending reductions rather than tax increases. [emphases added] (From Peter Orzag and Joseph Stiglitz, "Budget Cuts vs. Tax Increases at the State Level: Is One More Counter-Productive than the Other during a Recession?" Center on Budget and Policy Priorities, Revised 6 November 2001, 28 Jan. 2008 <http://www.cbpp.org/10-30-01sfp.htm> as quoted in Johnson <http://www.cbpp.org/1-8-08sfp.htm>).

[127] Johnson <http://www.cbpp.org/1-8-08sfp.htm>.
[128] Catherine Dolinski, "Florida Budget Deficit Sharpens Debate On Taxes," The Tampa Tribune 22 Sep. 2008.
[129] David Brooks, "Middle-Class Capitalists," The New York Times 11 Jan. 2008, 23 Jan. 2008 <http://www.nytimes.com/2008/01/11/>.

[130] Louis Uchitelle, "Economists Warm to Government Spending but Debate Its Form," The New York Times 7 Jan. 2009.
[131] "Area Home Sales, Prices Sink," Daytona-Beach News-Journal Online 31 Dec. 2007, 25 Jan. 2008 <http://www.news-journalonline.com/NewsJournalOnline/>.
[132] "Housing Boom Bust," MiamiHerald.com 23 Dec. 2007, 25 Jan. 2008 <http://www.miamiherald.com>.
[133] Peter S. Goodman, "This Is the Sound of a Bubble Bursting," The New York Times 23 Dec. 2007, 24 Jan. 2008 <http://www.nytimes.com/2007/12/23/>.
[134] Damien Cave, "In Florida, Despair and Foreclosures," The New York Times 8 Feb. 2009.

[135] Caputo and Bousquet, "Florida's Budget Hole:$2.3-billion."
[136] Steve Huettel, "Florida Leads Nation in Job Losses," St. Petersburg Times 20 Dec. 2008.
[137] Jeff Harrington, "For Many, Finding a New Job Is Their Job," St. Petersburg Times 21 May 2009.
[138] Marc Caputo, "Property Tax Gap Could Cost Florida Schools. School Property Taxes Are Forecast to Lose $1 Billion Next Year, Casting Doubt on the Governor's Budget Proposal," Times/Herald Tallahassee Bureau 6 Mar. 2009 <http://www.miamiherald.com/569/story/935289.html>.
[139] "Florida and Metro Forecast," Institute for Economic Competitiveness. College of Business Administration. University of Central Florida, Mar. 2009 <http://www.bus.ucf.edu/hitec/Forecasts.htm>.
[140] Mary Ann Lindley, "Rubio's glory is fading with his retro rhetoric," The Tallahassee Democrat: Tallahassee.com 13 Jan. 2008, 23 Jan. 2008 <http://tallahassee.com/>.
[141] "The Sad Truth on Universities," The St. Petersburg Times, editorial, 21 Feb. 2008, 21 Feb. 2008 <http://www.sptimes.com>.
[142] "The Sad Truth on Universities" <http://www.sptimes.com>.
[143] "The Sad Truth on Universities" <http://www.sptimes.com>.
[144] "University Lifeline," editorial, The Times 24 Nov. 2008 <http://www.tampabay.com/opinion/editorials>.
[145] John Stuart Mill, On Liberty (West Valley City, UT: Boomer Books, 2007) xi-xii.
[146] Linda Trimble, "School Officials Seek Fund Solutions," Daytona Beach News Journal 20 Dec. 2008.
[147] Shaila Dewan and Kevin Sack, "A Safety-Net Hospital Falls into Financial Crisis," The New York Times Jan. 8 2008, 24 Jan. 2008 <http://www.nytimes.com/2008/01/08/>.
[148] Risa Polansky, "Jackson Faces Major Financial Hurdles, Operation Threatened," Miami Today 26 June 2008, 5 Aug. 2008 <http://miamitodaynews.com>.
[149] The Kaiser Family Foundation, The Kaiser Commission on Medicaid and the Uninsured, 24 Jan. 2008 <http://www.kff.org/about/kcmu.cfm>.
[150] U.S. Census Bureau, "Current Population Survey," 24 Jan. 2008 <http://www.census.gov/hhes/www/hlthins/cps.html>.
[151] Caputo and Bousquet, "Florida's Budget Hole:$2.3-billion."
[152] Florida Partners in Crisis, <http://www.flpic.org/>. Florida Partners in Crisis is a grass roots statewide organization that promotes state and community collaboration across the mental health, substance abuse and criminal justice systems to reduce contact of people with mental illnesses and substance use disorders with the justice system and support their recovery. Its board of directors and membership includes judges, law enforcement, health and human services providers and other interested and engaged people.
[153] Mike Thomas, "As Rendezvous with Harsh Reality Nears, Crist May Consider Senate Bid," The Orlando Sentinel 8 Feb. 2009.
[154] Interviews with Sam Bell, Tallahassee, FL, 24 July 2008 and January 2009.

[155] Mark Schlueb, "Dyer Straits: Orlando to Lay off 100-plus Emergency Workers," The Orlando Sentinel 13 May 2009 <http://www.OrlandoSentinel.com>.
[156] Kate Santich, "Orlando-area Homeless Count Increases 17 Percent," The Orlando Sentinel Writer 13 May 2009 <http://www. OrlandoSentinel.com>.
[157] The Constitution of the State of Florida, Article XI, Section 6.
[158] A full services tax in 2008 would produce an estimated $23.4-billion, an amount almost as much as the $23.5-billion generated by the state's 6 percent tax. Comparison of these figures reflects the transition to a service-based economy. (Steve Bousquet, "Panel to Vote on Sales Tax Change," The St. Petersburg Times 25 Feb. 2008, 25 Feb. 2008 <http://www.sptimes.com>).
[159] Steve Bousquet, "Sales Taxes Stir a Fight," The St. Petersburg Times 16 Dec. 2007, 24 Jan. 2008 <http://www.sptimes.com>.
[160] Bousquet "Sales Taxes Stir a Fight," <http://www.sptimes.com>.
[161] "Tax Reform Runs Aground," The St. Petersburg Times, editorial, 14 Feb. 2008, 14 Feb. 2008 <http://www.sptimes.com/2008/02/14/Opinion/>.
[162] Steve Bousquet, "Tax Swap Plan Moves up. Services Tax Won't Make It to the Voters, but Other Changes Could," The St. Petersburg Times 26 Feb. 2008, 26 Feb. 2008 <http://www.sptimes.com>.
[163] Bousquet "Tax Swap Plan Moves up. Services Tax Won't Make It to the Voters, but Other Changes Could," <http://www.sptimes.com>.
[164] Alex Leary and Steve Bousquet, "Florida Tax Plan Would Slash Property Tax, Boost Sales Tax" St. Petersburg Times 18 Mar. 2008.
[165] Bousquet "Sales Taxes Stir a Fight," <http://www.sptimes.com>.
[166] Alex Leary and Ron Matus, "Tax Cut, Voucher Plans Tossed," St. Petersburg Times 4 Sep. 2008.
[167] Editorial, Daytona Beach News Journal 17 Aug. 2008.
[168] Steve Bousquet, "25 Most Influential Floridians," The St. Petersburg Times 13 Jan. 2008, 25 Jan. 2008 <http://www.sptimes.com>.
[169] "Tax Reform Runs Aground" <http://www.sptimes.com/2008/02/14/Opinion/>.
[170] Editorial, St. Petersburg Times 5 Sep. 2008.
[171] Mary Ellen Klas, "High Court Axes 3 Key Amendments," Miami Herald 4 Sep. 2008.
[172] Alex Leary and Ron Matus, "Tax Cut, Voucher Plans Tossed."
[173] Klas, "High Court Axes 3 Key Amendments."
[174] Mary Ellen Klas, "Bense 'Very Disappointed' in Ruling; Others Thrilled," The Miami Herald Blog, 3 Sep. 2008 <http://miamiherald.typepad.com/nakedpolitics/2008/09/bense-very-disa.html>.
[175] Martin Dyckman, "Let Voters Have a Say on State Income Tax," St. Petersburg Times 11 Sep. 2008.
[176] Josh Hafenbrack, "Sun Sentinel Florida Legislature to Re-examine Property Tax Relief Again. State High Court Struck Down Earlier Initiative," Tallahassee Bureau 5 Sep. 2008.
[177] Mulkey 5.

[178] Lester R. Brown, Plan B 2.0: Rescuing a Planet Under Stress and a Civilization in Trouble, updated and expanded (New York, London: Earth Policy Institute, W.W. Norton & Company, 2006) 228-29.
[179] Van Jones, The Green Collar Economy (New York: HarperCollins Publishers, 2008) 180.
[180] Thomas L. Friedman, "Georgia on My Mind," The New York Times 7 Sep. 2008.
[181] Michelle Wyman, "President Obama and Local Governments: A Partnership With Potential," ICLEI e-News 12 Nov. 2008 <http://www.iclei.org>.
[182] Cloe Waterfield, "City of Naples, Florida Greenhouse Gas Emissions Report, Inventory Year 2006," June 2008.
[183] "Obama speech: Full text. Prepared Text of Barack Obama's speech at George Mason University near Washington on January 8," The Financial Times 8 Jan. 2009 <http://www.ft.com/cms>.
[184] Paul Steinhauser, "Poll: America's Honeymoon with Obama Continues," CNNPolitics.com 24 Dec. 2008 <http://www.cnn.com/2008/POLITICS/12/24/obama.approval>.
[185] Frank Newport, "As Inauguration Nears, Americans Still Confident in Obama. Sixty-five Percent Confident in Obama's Ability to Be a Good President," Gallup Poll, 7 Jan. 2009 <http://www.gallup.com/poll>.
[186] Barack Obama, "The Action Americans Need," The Washington Post 5 Feb. 2009.
[187] "Republican Disapproval Up, But Obama Strong In Florida, Quinnipiac University Poll Finds," Quinnipiac University Polling Institute, 16 Apr. 2009 <http://www.quinnipiac.edu>.
[188] Edmund L. Andrews "Doubts About Obama's Economic Recovery Plan Rise Along With Unemployment," New York Times, July 9, 2009.
[189] Paul Krugman "The Town Hall Mob," New York Times, August 7, 2009.
[190] Adam Smith, "Protesters in Ybor City Drown Out Health Care Summit on Obama Proposal," St. Petersburg Times, August 7, 2009.
[191] "More Vision, Less Denial," The St. Petersburg Times, Editorial, 24 Feb. 2008, 24 Feb. 2008 <http://www.sptimes.com>.
[192] "Budget Plans Lack Vision," St. Petersburg Times, Editorial, 8 Jan. 2009.
[193] T. Wayne Bailey, Professor of Political Science, Stetson University, personal interview, 8 Aug. 2008.
[194] Neil Skene, "Growth Management Act II," Florida Trend 1 Aug. 2007 <http://www.floridatrend.com>.
[195] Tim Chapin, "Engaging the Future through a State-Coordinated Regional Visioning Initiative," Department of Urban & Regional Planning, Florida State University, 13 Nov. 2007.
[196] "A Time for Leadership: Management and Florida 2060," 1000 Friends of Florida, Aug. 2006 <http://www.1000friendsofflorida.org>.
[197] Dr. Stephen S. Mulkey, "Towards a Sustainable Florida: A Review of Environmental, Social and Economic Concepts for Sustainable Development in Florida," 2006: 4.

[198] "A Time for Leadership: Management and Florida 2060."
[199] Charles E. Connerly, Timothy Stewart Chapin, and Harrison T. Higgins, eds., Growth Management in Florida. Planning for Paradise (Aldershot: Ashgate Press, 2007).
[200] Parker Neils, "Pain in Paradise: Florida's Failed Fix All," Research in Review Spring 2008 <http://www.rinr.fsu.edu>.
[201] Neils, "Pain in Paradise: Florida's Failed Fix All."
[202] Neils, "Pain in Paradise: Florida's Failed Fix All."
[203] "2005 Legislative Wrap Up Report" 1000 Friends of Florida, 2005 <http://www.1000friendsofflorida.org>.
[204] See <http://1000 friendsofflorida.org>.
[205] David Brooks "The Great Unwinding," New York Times, June 11, 2009.
[206] "About Smart Growth," Smart Growth Online, <http://www.smartgrowth.org/about/default.asp>.
[207] "Smart Growth for Florida's Future: The Florida Sustainable Communities Act."
[208] Neils, "Pain in Paradise: Florida's Failed Fix All."
[209] Neils, "Pain in Paradise: Florida's Failed Fix All."
[210] James Miller, "Volusia Environmental Map Heads to State Officials for Review," Daytona Beach News Journal Online 8 Aug. 2008 <http://www.news-journalonline.com/index.htm>.
[211] Volusia Forever, <http://volusiaforever-echo.com/forever>.
[212] Neils, "Pain in Paradise: Florida's Failed Fix All."
[213] Clay Henderson, personal interview, 9 Aug. 2008.
[214] Neils, "Pain in Paradise: Florida's Failed Fix All."
[215] Timothy Chapin and Heather Khan, "Assessing Florida Citizen Attitudes Towards Growth, Growth Management, Quality of Life Issues: Report," Report Prepared for the Century Commission for a Sustainable Florida, Department of Urban & Regional Planning Florida State University, 6 Sep. 2006 <http://www.centurycommission.org/current_projects.asp>.
[216] "Where in the World Are We? 2009 Progress Report for the Central Florida Region," <http://www.myregion.org>.
[217] Chapin, "Engaging the Future through a State-Coordinated Regional Visioning Initiative."
[218] Chapin and Khan, "Assessing Florida Citizen Attitudes Towards Growth, Growth Management, and Quality of Life Issues:Final Report."
[219] "Central Florida Growth Vision: Mid-Project Report," Sep. 2006 <http://www.myregion.org>.
[220] "Central Florida Growth Vision: Mid-Project Report."
[221] "Century Commission Citizen Values Update: St. Petersburg/Tampa Bay Area Values Pilot Study Interim Report," Century Commission for a Sustainable Florida, May 2007 <http://www.centurycommission.org>.
[222] Mulkey, "Towards a Sustainable Florida: A Review of Environmental, Social and Economic Concepts for Sustainable Development in Florida."

[223] "Smart Growth for Florida's Future: The Florida Sustainable Communities Act."
[224] Note to Reader: The authors borrowed the phrase "government to governance" from Dr. Lawrence Martin, Professor of Public Administration at the University of Central Florida, who assisted Arrington-Marlowe with the City of Orlando strategic plan.
[225] John Rawls, A Theory of Justice, rev. ed. (Belknap Press of Harvard University Press, 1999). See also <http://www.cesj.org/thirdway/economicjustice-defined.htm>.
[226] Alvin Toffler, Power Shift (New York: Bantam Books, 1991) 238.
[227] Toffler 253.
[228] Go to http://www.pbs.org/moyers/journal/transcripts/index.html. This link provides a transcript of Bill Moyers' interview dated June 12, 2009 with Robert Reich, author of Supercapitalism: the Transformation of Business, Democracy, and Everyday Life, (NewYork, New York: Vintage Books,2008).
[229] Mark Roseland and Sean Connelly, Toward Sustainable Communities: Resources for Citizens and Their Governments, rev. ed. (Gabriola Island, BC: New Society Publishers, 2005).
[230] David Leonhardt, "The Big Fix," New York Times Magazine 1 Feb. 2009.
[231] Allison J. DeFoor, personal interview, 31 July 2008.
[232] Howard Troxler, "Less Crime is Better Than More Prisons" St. Petersburg Times 15 July 2009.
[233] Zakaria, The Post-American World.
[234] Go to http://www.bayareacouncil.org/takeaction_ccc.php.
[235] Lawrence W. Arrington, Local Government Reform in the Emerging Mega State: The Florida Charter County Movement, Masters Degree Thesis, Stetson University, 1989.
[236] David Osborne and Ted Gaebler, Reinventing Government (Reading, MA: Addison-Wesley Publishing Company, Inc., 1992).
[237] David Osborne and Peter Plastrik, Banishing Bureaucracy: the Five Strategies for Reinventing Government (New York: Addison-Wesley Publishing Company, Inc., 1997).
[238] Author Lawrence Arrington in a private conversation with Lt. Governor Buddy McKay in the 1997-98 timeframe confirmed the veracity of the latter part of this conclusion. McKay told Arrington that employee unions and reluctant legislative leaders stymied many reform ideas.
[239] Jeb Bush, inaugural address, Jan. 2003. Contact Office of the Secretary of State, FL.
[240] Ron Matus and Steve Bousquet, "Court Throws out Vouchers," St. Petersburg Times 6 Jan. 2006.
[241] Dan Lips, "Education Notebook: Jeb Bush Discusses Florida's Education Reforms," interview with Jeb Bush, The Heritage Foundation, 22 July 2008 <http://www.heritage.org/Research/Education/ednotes99.cfm>.
[242] Kleindienst 7 Jan. 2007.
[243] Kleindienst 7 Jan. 2007.

[244] Garry Wills, Head and Heart: American Christianities (New York: Penguin Press, 2007) 495-96.
[245] Karen Armstrong, The Battle for God (New York: Ballantine Books, 2001) 166.
[246] Armstrong The Battle for God.
[247] Ernest Becker, The Birth and Death of Meaning, 2nd ed. (New York: The Free Press, 1971) 163-64.
[248] Garry Wills, Head and Heart: American Christianities: 173-252.
[249] The Office of the Majority Whip Representative Ellyn Bogdanoff, "The Florida Budget for Fiscal Year 2007-2008," Whip's Policy Brief 3 May 2007: 6.
[250] Michael Grunwald "Is Florida the Sunset State?"
[251] Graphics are the courtesy of Dr. Larry Martin, Professor of Public Administration, University of Central Florida.
[252] Robert N. Bellah et al., Habits of the Heart: Individualism and Commitment in American Life (New York: Harper & Row, Publishers, 1986).
[253] Tim Nickens, "Long-term Planning Same as It Ever Was," The St. Petersburg Times 24 Feb. 2008, 24 Feb. 2008 <http://www.sptimes.com/2008/02/24/Opinion>.
[254] Chapin, "Engaging the Future through a State-Coordinated Regional Visioning Initiative."
[255] The following was quoted earlier in the Growth Management Section of this paper, and is worth repeating here.
[256] Chapin 14-15.
[257] Steven L. Sparkman, "The History and Status of Local Government Powers in Florida," University of Florida Law Review 25 (1973): 286 as quoted in Arrington 29.
[258] Arrington 29.
[259] David Brunori, Local Tax Policy: A Federalist Perspective, 2nd ed. (Washington, D.C.: Urban Institute Press, 2007) Chapter 1, 29 Jan. 2008 <http://www.urban.org/books/localtaxpolicy/intro.cfm>.
[260] Stephen Goldsmith and William D. Eggers, "Government by Network: The New Public Management Imperative," Deloitte Research/Ash Institute at Harvard, 2004: 1-27, 29 Jan. 2008 <http://www.deloitte.com/dtt/article/>; Stephen Goldsmith and William D. Eggers, Governing by Network: The New Shape of the Public Sector (Washington, D.C.: Brookings Institution Press, 2004).
[261] In the interests of full disclosure, both authors have business interests in the company highlighted in this case example, and are investors in it.
[262] Florida Partners in Crisis, <http://www.flpic.org/>. Florida Partners in Crisis is a grass roots statewide organization that promotes state and community collaboration across the mental health, substance abuse and criminal justice systems to reduce contact of people with mental illnesses and substance use disorders with the justice system and support their recovery. Its board of directors and membership includes judges, law enforcement, health and human services providers and other interested and engaged people.

[263] Stephen H. Grimes, "Mental-health Reform Has Human, Fiscal Urgency," The Tallahassee Democrat: Tallahassee.com 25 Feb. 2008, 25 Feb. 2008 <http://tallahassee.com/>.
[264] Draft copy of the Strategic Plan of the Palm Beach County Criminal Justice Council.
[265] Draft copy of the Interview Summary of the Palm Beach County Criminal Justice Council Strategic Plan.
[266] Mark Munetz and Patricia Griffin, "Use of the Sequential Intercept Model as an Approach to Decriminalization of People with Serious Mental Illness," Psychiatric Services 57 (2006).
[267] For access to this Leadership Framework, go to <http://www.arringtonmarlowe.com>.
[268] Matthew Arnold, Stanzas from the Grand Chartreuse (1855).
[269] Contact The Florida Chamber Foundation, <http://www.flchamber.com/>, for a copy of The Cornerstone Report 2005.
[270] See, for example, 1 Corinthians 12:12-14; Ephesians 1:22-23; 1 Corinthians 12:27-28.
[271] See Matthew 25:31-46; Also see Jim Wallis, God's Politics: Why the Right Gets It Wrong and the Left Doesn't Get It (San Francisco: Harper, 2005) 209-70.
[272] See, for example, Genesis 1:28; Colossians 1:16.
[273] Randall Reid, "The Moral Imperative for Sustainable Communities," Public Management Magazine, International City Management Association May 2009.
[274] See the website of the John Winthrop Society for a full copy of the text of this sermon, entitled, "A Model of Christian Charity," <http://www.winthropsociety.org/home.php>.

BIBLIOGRAPHY

Aaby, A. "Computational Complexity and Problem Hierarchy." 2002 <www.cs.wwc.edu/~aabyan/Theory/complexity.html>.
"About Smart Growth." Smart Growth Online, <http://www.smartgrowth.org/about/default.asp>.
Ackoff, R. Redesigning the Future. New York: John Wiley, 1974.
"Area Home Sales, Prices Sink." Daytona-Beach News-Journal Online 31 Dec. 2007. 25 Jan. 2008 <http://www.news-journalonline.com/NewsJournalOnline/>.
Armstrong, Karen. The Battle for God. New York: Ballantine Books, 2001.
Arnold, Matthew. Stanzas from the Grand Chartreuse. 1855
Arrington, Lawrence W. Local Government Reform in the Emerging Mega State: The Florida Charter County Movement. Masters Degree Thesis. Stetson University, 1989.
Ash, Jim. "Group Paints Ominous Property Tax Picture." The Tallahassee Democrat: Tallahassee.com 9 Jan. 2008. 25 Jan. 2008 <http://tallahassee.com/>.
Ash, Jim. "Tax Plan Passes: the People Have Spoken." The Tallahassee Democrat: Tallahassee.com 30 Jan. 2008. 30 Jan. 2008 <http://tallahassee.com/>.

Bailey, T. Wayne. Professor of Political Science, Stetson University. Personal interview. 8 Aug. 2008.

Barabasi, A. Linked. London: Penguin, 2003.

Bateson, G. Steps to an Ecology of Mind. New York: Ballantine, 1972.

Becker, Ernest. The Birth and Death of Meaning. 2nd ed. New York: The Free Press, 1971.

Bell, Sam. Interview. Tallahassee, FL. 24 July 2008.

Bellah, Robert N., et al. Habits of the Heart: Individualism and Commitment in American Life. New York: Harper & Row, Publishers, 1986.

Bennet, A. and Bennet, D. Organizational Survival in the New World. Butterworth-Heinnemann, 2004.

"'Best' Isn't Good Enough." Editorial. HeraldTribune.com 2 Nov. 2007. 23 Jan. 2008 <http://www.heraldtribune.com/article/>.

Blackwell, S. The Meme Machine. Oxford: Oxford University Press, 1999.

Bousquet, Steve, et al. "$66.5B Budget, by Nickels and Dimes." Times/Herald Tallahassee Bureau 8 May 2009.

Bousquet, Steve. "Budget Takes Another Hit." The St. Petersburg Times 9 Jan. 2008. 21 Jan. 2008 <http://www.sptimes.com/2008/01/09/>.

Bousquet, Steve. "25 Most Influential Floridians." The St. Petersburg Times 13 Jan. 2008. 25 Jan. 2008 <http://www.sptimes.com>.

Bousquet, Steve. "Panel to Vote on Sales Tax Change." The St. Petersburg Times 25 Feb. 2008. 25 Feb. 2008 <http://www.sptimes.com>.

Bousquet, Steve. "Sales Taxes Stir a Fight." The St. Petersburg Times 16 Dec. 2007. 24 Jan. 2008 <http://www.sptimes.com>.

Bousquet, Steve. "Short Term Budget: The Crunch is in the Here and Now, This Time." The St. Petersburg Times. 24 Feb. 2008. 24 Feb. 2008 <http://www.sptimes.com>.

Bousquet, Steve. "Tax Swap Plan Moves up. Services Tax Won't Make It to the Voters, but Other Changes Could." The St. Petersburg Times 26 Feb. 2008. 26 Feb. 2008 <http://www.sptimes.com>.

Brin, D. The Transparent Society. Reading, MA: Addison-Wesley, 1998.

Brock, W., Mailer, K., and Perrings, C. "Resilience and Sustainability: the Economic Analysis of Non-Linear Dynamic Systems." In Gunderson, L. and Holling, C., ed. Panachy: Understanding Transformations in Human and Natural Systems. Washington, D.C.: Island Press, 2002.

Brooks, David. "The Long Voyage Home." The New York Times 5 May 2009 <http://www.nytimes.com/2009/05/05/opinion>.

Brooks, David. "Middle-Class Capitalists." The New York Times 11 Jan. 2008. 23 Jan. 2008 <http://www.nytimes.com/2008/01/11/>.

Brown, Lester R. Plan B 2.0: Rescuing a Planet Under Stress and a Civilization in Trouble. Updated and expanded. New York, London: Earth Policy Institute, W.W. Norton & Company, 2006.

Brunori, David. Local Tax Policy: A Federalist Perspective. 2nd ed. Washington, D.C.: Urban Institute Press, 2007.

"Budget Plans Lack Vision." St. Petersburg Times. Editorial. 8 Jan. 2009.
Bugden, R. and Izard, R. "10 Key Questions about a Business Case." IT Brief 13 (2004).
Burns, James MacGregor. Leadership. New York: Harper & Row, Publishers, 1978.
Burton, R. and Obel, B. Strategic Organizational Design: Developing Theory for Application. Norwell, MA: Kluwer Academic Publishers, 1998.
Bush, Jeb. "Improvement Requires Willingness to Change." In "Innovators in Action 2007." Reason Foundation. 2007 <http://reason.org/news/show/1002747.html>.
Bush, Jeb. Inaugural address. Jan. 2003.
Caputo, Marc, and Steve Bousquet. "Florida's Budget Hole: $2.3-billion." Times/Herald Tallahassee Bureau 10 Dec. 2008.
Caputo, Marc. "Crist Restores Millions in Cutbacks." Times/Herald Tallahassee Bureau 28 Jan. 2009.
Caputo, Marc. "Property Tax Gap Could Cost Florida Schools. School Property Taxes Are Forecast to Lose $1 Billion Next Year, Casting Doubt on the Governor's Budget Proposal." Times/Herald Tallahassee Bureau 6 Mar. 2009 <http://www.miamiherald.com/569/story/935289.html>.
Carley, K. and Gasser, L. "Computational Organization Theory." In Gerhard Weiss., ed. Distributed Artificial Intelligence. Cambridge, MA: MIT Press, 1999.
Carpenter, S., Brock, W. and Ludwig, D. "Collapse, Learning and Renewal." In Gunderson, L. and Holling, C., ed. Panachy: Understanding Transformations in Human and Natural Systems. Washington, D.C.: Island Press, 2002.
Cave, Damien. "In Florida, Despair and Foreclosures." The New York Times 8 Feb. 2009.
"Central Florida Growth Vision: Mid-Project Report." Sep. 2006 <http://www.myregion.org>.
"Century Commission Citizen Values Update: St. Petersburg/Tampa Bay Area Values Pilot Study Interim Report." Century Commission for a Sustainable Florida. May 2007 <http://www.centurycommission.org>.
The Century Commission for a Sustainable Florida. <http://www.centurycommission.org/current_projects.asp>.
Chanan, G. Community Involvement: the Roots of Renaissance? Housing Support Unit. Office of the Deputy Prime Minister. London: H.M. Government, 2002.
The City Council of the City of Eugene. Resolution No. 4618. The City of Eugene. 28 Feb. 2000, 4 Aug. 2008 <http://www.eugene-or.gov>.
Chapin, Timothy. "Engaging the Future through a State-Coordinated Regional Visioning Initiative." Department of Urban & Regional Planning, Florida State University, 13 Nov. 2007.
Chapin, Timothy, and Heather Khan, "Assessing Florida Citizen Attitudes Towards Growth, Growth Management, Quality of Life Issues: Report." Report Prepared for the Century Commission for a Sustainable Florida. Department of Urban & Regional Planning Florida State University. 6 Sep. 2006 <http://www.centurycommission.org/current_projects.asp>.

Civic Leadership for Community Transformation. Syracuse, NY: Onandanga Citizens League, 2001.
Connerly, Charles E., Timothy Stewart Chapin, and Harrison T. Higgins, eds. Growth Management in Florida. Planning for Paradise. Aldershot: Ashgate Press, 2007.
The Constitution of the State of Florida. Article XI. Section 6.
Crislip, D. "The New Civic Leadership." In Kellerman, B. and Matusak, L., eds. Cutting Edge: Leadership. College Park, MD: James Macgregor Burns Academy of Leadership, 2000.
Dahl, Robert A. Polyarchy. New Haven, Conn.: Yale University Press, 1971.
Daly, H.E. and Cobb, J.B. For the Common Good. Boston: Beacon Press, 1989.
Dawson, R. Living Networks. New York: Prentice Hall, 2003.
DeFoor, Allison J. Personal interview. 31 July 2008.
Deslatte, Aaron. "Florida's Property-Tax Amendment: Questions and Answers." OrlandoSentinel.com 20 Jan. 2008. 26 Feb. 2008 <http://www.orlandosentinel.com>.
Dewan, Shaila, and Kevin Sack. "A Safety-Net Hospital Falls into Financial Crisis." The New York Times Jan. 8 2008. 24 Jan. 2008 <http://www.nytimes.com/2008/01/08/>.
Diggins, John P. The Lost Soul of American Politics: Virtue, Self-Interests and the Foundations of Liberalism. University of Chicago Press, 1984.
Dolinski, Catherine. "Florida Budget Deficit Sharpens Debate On Taxes." The Tampa Tribune 22 Sep. 2008.
"Do No Harm. Huge Economic, Political Challenges Face Florida." Editorial. The Tallahassee Democrat: Tallahassee.com 2 Mar. 2008. 2 Mar. 2008 <http://tallahassee.com/>.
Dougherty, Conor. "Is Florida Over?" The Wall Street Journal 29 Sep. 2007. 17 Jan. 2008 <http://online.wsj.com/public/article/>.
Duchin, F. and Lange, G. The Future of the Environment. New York: Oxford University Press, 1994.
Dyckman, Martin. "Let Voters Have a Say on State Income Tax." St. Petersburg Times 11 Sep. 2008.
Editorial. Daytona Beach News Journal 17 Aug. 2008.
Editorial. The St. Petersburg Times. 31 Oct. 2007. 25 Jan. 2008 <http://www.sptimes.com>.
Editorial. The St. Petersburg Times 2 Mar. 2008.
Editorial. The St. Petersburg Times 5 Sep. 2008.
Ekins, P., ed. The Living Economy. London: Routledge, 1986.
Eoyang, G. "A Brief Introduction to Complexity in Organizations." Presentation. Chaos Network Conference, 1996.
Fishkind, Hank. "Analysis of County Spending Patterns 1999-2006: Where Did the Money Go?" The Florida Association of Counties. 7 Mar. 2007: 1-54. 22 Jan. 2008 <http://www.fl-counties.com/proptax/_doc/fishkind_study.pdf>.
The Florida Chamber Foundation. <http://www.flchamber.com/mx/hm.asp?id=newcornerstone>.

"Florida in 2060: Not a Pretty Picture?" 1000 Friends of Florida. Dec. 2006. 18 Jan. 2008 <http://www.1000friendsofflorida.org/Publications/main.asp>.
"Florida and Metro Forecast." Institute for Economic Competitiveness. College of Business Administration. University of Central Florida. Mar. 2009 <http://www.bus.ucf.edu/hitec/Forecasts.htm>.
"Florida League of Conservation Voters Education Fund State of the Florida Environment Education Page." <http://www.flcv.com>.
Florida Partners in Crisis. <http://www.flpic.org/>.
Florini, A. "The End of Secrecy." Foreign Policy (1998).
Fosler, R., Alonso, W., Meyer, J. and Kern, R. Demographic Change and the American Future. Pittsburg: University of Pittsburg Press, 1990.
Frazier, S. Psychotrends. New York: Simon and Schuster, 1994.
Friedman, G. and Friedman, M. The Future of War. New York: St. Martin's Press, 1996.
1000 Friends of Florida.
<http://www.1000friendsofflorida.org/Publications/main.asp>.
Friedman, Thomas L. "Georgia on My Mind." The New York Times 7 Sep. 2008.
Frum, David. "Why Rush is Wrong. The Party of Buckley and Reagan Is Now Bereft and Dominated by the Politics of Limbaugh. A Conservative's Lament." Newsweek 7 Mar. 2009 <http://www.newsweek.com/id/188279>.
Frydman, B., Wilson, I. and Wyer, J. The Power of Collaborative Leadership. Woburn, MA: Butterworth-Heineman, 2000.
Funke, J. and Frensch, P. A. "Complex Problem Solving Research in North America and Europe: An Integrative Review." Foreign Psychology 5 (1995).
Gallopin, G. "Planning for Resilience." In Gunderson, L. and Holling, C., ed. Panachy: Understanding Transformations in Human and Natural Systems. Washington, D.C.: Island Press, 2002.
Gardner, John W. On Leadership. New York: The Free Press, 1993.
Gharajedaghi, J. Systems Thinking: Managing Chaos and Complexity. Boston: Butterworth-Heinemann, 1999.
Gharajedaghi, J. Systems Thinking. San Francisco: Barrett Koehler, 1999.
Ginther, Konrad, Erik Denters, and P.J.I.M. de Waart. Sustainable Development and Good Governance. Norwell, MA: Kluwer Academic Publishers, 1995.
"Global Values, Moral Boundaries." Institute for Global Ethics 1996 <www.globalethics.org>.
Goldsmith, Stephen, and William D. Eggers. Governing by Network: The New Shape of the Public Sector. Washington, D.C.: Brookings Institution Press, 2004.
Goldsmith, Stephen, and William D. Eggers. "Government by Network: The New Public Management Imperative." Deloitte Research/Ash Institute at Harvard. 2004: 1-27. 29 Jan. 2008 <http://www.deloitte.com/dtt/article/>.
Goodman, Peter S. "This Is the Sound of a Bubble Bursting." The New York Times 23 Dec. 2007. 24 Jan. 2008 <http://www.nytimes.com/2007/12/23/>.
Goodman, Peter S. and Floyd Norris. "No Quick Fix to Downturn." The New York Times 13 Jan. 2008. 24 Jan. 2008 <http://www.nytimes.com/2008/01/13/>.

Grimes, Stephen H. "Mental-health Reform Has Human, Fiscal Urgency." The Tallahassee Democrat: Tallahassee.com 25 Feb. 2008. 25 Feb. 2008 <http://tallahassee.com/>.

Grunwald, Michael. "Is Florida the Sunset State?" The Time Magazine 10 July 2008 <http://www.time.com/time/magazine>.

Hafenbrack, Josh. "Sun Sentinel Florida Legislature to Re-examine Property Tax Relief Again. State High Court Struck Down Earlier Initiative." Tallahassee Bureau 5 Sep. 2008.

Harrington, Jeff. "For Many, Finding a New Job Is Their Job." St. Petersburg Times 21 May 2009.

Hatcher, Monica. "Real Estate: Condo Buildings Buckling under Hundreds of Foreclosures." MiamiHerald.com 9 Jan. 2008. 24 Jan. 2008 <http://www.miamiherald.com/>.

Hawken, P. The Ecology of Commerce. New York: HarperBusiness, 1993.

Henderson, Clay. Personal interview. 9 Aug. 2008.

Holdgate, Martin W. From Care to Action: Making a Sustainable World. Washington, D.C.: Taylor and Francis, 1996.

Holland, J. Emergence. New York: Basic Books, 1998.

Holling, C., Gunderson, L., and Ludwig, D. "In quest of a theory of adaptive change." In Gunderson, L. and Holling, C., ed. Panachy: Understanding Transformations in Human and Natural Systems. Washington, D.C.: Island Press, 2002.

"Housing Boom Bust." MiamiHerald.com 23 Dec. 2007. 25 Jan. 2008 <http://www.miamiherald.com/>.

Huettel, Steve. "Florida Leads Nation in Job Losses." St. Petersburg Times 20 Dec. 2008.

Hutchins, E. Cognition in the Wild. Cambridge, MA: MIT Press, 1995.

Johnson, H. Green Plans. Lincoln, NE: University of Nebraska Press, 1995.

Johnson, Nicholas. "Budget Cuts or Tax Increases at the State Level: Which is Preferable during an Economic Downturn?" Center on Budget and Policy Priorities 8 Jan. 2008. 28 Jan. 2008 <http://www.cbpp.org/1-8-08sfp.htm>.

The Kaiser Family Foundation. The Kaiser Commission on Medicaid and the Uninsured. 24 Jan. 2008 <http://www.kff.org/about/kcmu.cfm>.

Kettl, D. The Transformation of Governance. Baltimore: Johns Hopkins Press, 2002.

Kim, W. and Mauborgne, R. Blue Ocean Strategy. Boston: Harvard Business School Press, 2005.

Klas, Mary Ellen. "As Revenue Shrinks, Florida GOP Lawmakers Talk of Taxes." Times/Herald Tallahassee Bureau 18 Jan. 2009.

Klas, Mary Ellen. "Bense 'Very Disappointed' in Ruling; Others Thrilled." The Miami Herald Blog, 3 Sep. 2008 <http://miamiherald.typepad.com/nakedpolitics/2008/09/bense-very-disa.html>.

Klas, Mary Ellen. "GOP Lawmakers Utter Heresy: Taxes." Times/Herald Tallahassee Bureau 17 Jan. 2009.

Klas, Mary Ellen. "High Court Axes 3 Key Amendments." Miami Herald 4 Sep. 2008.

Kleindienst, Linda. "The Jeb Bush Era Ends in Florida. Outgoing Governor Did Things His Way." South Florida Sun-Sentinel 7 Jan. 2007: A04.
Knopf, Alfred A., et al. The Good Society. New York, 1991.
Layden, Laura. "Florida Chamber Report: State Economy Is Hardly Over and Out." Naples Daily News: naplesnews.com 4 Dec. 2007. 17 Jan. 2008 <http://www.naplesnews.com/news/2007/dec/04/>.
Lazlo, E. Introduction to Systems Philosophy. New York: Gordon & Breach, 1972.
Leadership Florida, "The Second Annual Leadership Florida Sunshine State Survey," 2007, 11 Feb. 2008
<http://www.leadershipflorida.org/mx/hm.asp?id=pub_survey07>.
Leary, Alex. "Florida Businesses Wish for More Tax Relief." The St. Petersburg Times 26 Dec. 2007. 23 Jan. 2008 <http://www.sptimes.com/2007/12/26/>.
Leary, Alex. "Rep. Rubio Veers Off with Another Tax Cut Plan." The St. Petersburg Times 21 Nov. 2007. 23 Jan. 2008 <http://www.sptimes.com>.
Leary, Alex, and Ron Matus. "Tax Cut, Voucher Plans Tossed." St. Petersburg Times 4 Sep. 2008.
Leary, Alex. "Rubio Pushes 'Other' Tax Cut." The St. Petersburg Times 20 Dec. 2007. 25 Jan. 2008 <http://www.sptimes.com>.
Leary, Alex and Jennifer Liberto. "Session Set, but with Less Harmony." The St. Petersburg Times 2 Mar. 2008. 2 Mar. 2008 <http://www.sptimes.com>.
Leary, Alex, and Steve Bousquet. "Florida Lawmakers Feel Bite of No New Taxes Pledge." Times/Herald Tallahassee Bureau 6 Apr. 2009.
"2005 Legislative Wrap Up Report." 1000 Friends of Florida. 2005 <http://www.1000friendsofflorida.org>.
Leonhardt, David. "The Big Fix." New York Times Magazine 1 Feb. 2009.
Lindley, Mary Ann. "Rubio's glory is fading with his retro rhetoric." The Tallahassee Democrat: Tallahassee.com 13 Jan. 2008. 23 Jan. 2008 <http://tallahassee.com/>.
Lips, Dan. "Education Notebook: Jeb Bush Discusses Florida's Education Reforms." Interview with Jeb Bush. The Heritage Foundation. 22 July 2008
<http://www.heritage.org/Research/Education/ednotes99.cfm>.
Marlowe, H.A. "Citizen as Customer: A Problematic Model." Working paper.
Marlowe, H.A. "Facilitative Leadership." Working paper.
Marlowe, H. A. "Mutual Accountability." Working paper. 2004.
Marlowe, H. A. "Partnership Thinking." Working paper. 2004.
Marlowe, H.A. "Public Problems and Complexity Theory." Working paper.
Marlowe, H.A. and Arrington, L. "Ten Rules for Consensus Building. IQ Report." ICMA 2004.
"Mason-Dixon Poll." Florida Alliance for Concerned Taxpayers. 8 Apr. 2009 <http://www.flaact.com/news09_04_08_2.html>.
Matus, Ron, and Steve Bousquet. "Court Throws out Vouchers." St. Petersburg Times 6 Jan. 2006.
McClean, B. and Elkin, M. The Smartest Guys in the Room: The Amazing Rise and Scandalous Fall of Enron. New York: Portfolio, 2003.

McDonald, Steve, ed. "2003-2004 Florida Annual Policy Survey Report." Florida State University Survey Research Laboratory. 14 June 2004: 1-15. Jan. 18 2008 <http://www.fsu.edu/~survey/surveys.htm>.
McHarg, I. Design with Nature. New York: Doubleday, 1971.
Mill, John Stuart. On Liberty. West Valley City, UT: Boomer Books, 2007.
Miller, James. "Volusia Environmental Map Heads to State Officials for Review." Daytona Beach News Journal Online 8 Aug. 2008 <http://www.news-journalonline.com/index.htm>.
Mirel, B. Designing for Usefulness for Complex Problem-solving. University of Michigan: School of Information, 2003.
Mitroff, I. Smart Thinking. San Francisco: Berrett-Koehler, 1998.
"A Model of Christian Charity." <http://www.winthropsociety.org/home.php>.
Mohrman, S., Cohen, S. and Mohrman, A. Designing Team-based Organizations. San Francisco: Jossey-Bass, 1995.
Mollison, B. "Permaculture." In Aberly, D., ed. Futures by Design: The Practice of Ecological Planning. Philadelphia: New Society Publishers, 1994.
Morehouse, W., ed. Building Sustainable Communities. New York: Intermediate Technology Development Group, 1989.
"More Vision, Less Denial." The St. Petersburg Times. Editorial. 24 Feb. 2008. 24 Feb. 2008 <http://www.sptimes.com>.
Mulkey, Stephen S., ed. "Towards a Sustainable Florida." The Century Commission for a Sustainable Florida. 1 Sep. 2006: 1-102. 15 Jan. 2008 <http://www.centurycommission.org/current_projects.asp>.
Munetz, Mark, and Patricia Griffin. "Use of the Sequential Intercept Model as an Approach to Decriminalization of People with Serious Mental Illness." Psychiatric Services 57 (2006).
MyRegion.org. <http://www.myregion.org/>.
Neils, Parker."Pain in Paradise: Florida's Failed Fix All." Research in Review Spring 2008 <http://www.rinr.fsu.edu>.
"New Cornerstone Revisited: A Look at Our State in Transition." Florida Chamber of Commerce Foundation. 1 Nov. 2007. 17 Jan. 2008 <http://www.flchamber.com/mx/hm.asp?id=newcornerstone>.
Newport, Frank. "As Inauguration Nears, Americans Still Confident in Obama. Sixty-five Percent Confident in Obama's Ability to Be a Good President." Gallup Poll, 7 Jan. 2009 <http://www.gallup.com/poll>.
Nickens, Tim. "Long-term Planning Same as It Ever Was." The St. Petersburg Times 24 Feb. 2008. 24 Feb. 2008 <http://www.sptimes.com/2008/02/24/Opinion>.
Obama, Barack. "The Action Americans Need." The Washington Post 5 Feb. 2009.
"Obama speech: Full text. Prepared Text of Barack Obama's speech at George Mason University near Washington on January 8." The Financial Times 8 Jan. 2009 <http://www.ft.com/cms>.
Odom, H.T. Environment, Power and Society. New York: Wiley-Interscience, 1971.

The Office of the Majority Whip Representative Ellyn Bogdanoff. "The Florida Budget for Fiscal Year 2007-2008." Whip's Policy Brief 3 May 2007.

Oliver, R. The Coming Biotech Age. New York: McGraw-Hill, 2000.

O'Riordan, Tim, and Heather Voisey, eds., Sustainable Development in Western Europe: Coming to Terms with Agenda 21. London, Portland, OR: Frank Cass, 1997.

"Orlando's Bold Blueprint." Research in Review Spring 2008 <http://www.rinr.fsu.edu/issues/2008spring/cover06_a.asp>.

Orzag, Peter, and Joseph Stiglitz. "Budget Cuts vs. Tax Increases at the State Level: Is One More Counter-Productive than the Other during a Recession?" Center on Budget and Policy Priorities. Revised 6 November 2001, 28 Jan. 2008 <http://www.cbpp.org/10-30-01sfp.htm>.

Osborne, David, and Peter Plastrik. Banishing Bureaucracy: the Five Strategies for Reinventing Government. New York: Addison-Wesley Publishing Company, Inc., 1997.

Osborne, David, and Ted Gaebler. Reinventing Government. Reading, MA: Addison-Wesley Publishing Company, Inc., 1992.

Oyibo, G. Highlights of the Grand Unified Theorem: Formulation of the Unified Field Theory or the Theory of Everything. Nova Science Publications, 2002.

Panacek, L. and Marlowe, H. A. "Organizational Transparency." Presentation to the Child Welfare League of America. Washington, D.C. 2005.

Periott, H. Planning for the Post-industrial City. Washington, D.C.: Planners Press, 1980.

Perlman, J. "Mega-Cities: Innovations for Sustainable Cities of the 21st Century." In Aberly, D., ed. Futures by Design: The Practice of Ecological Planning. Philadelphia: New Society Publishers, 1994.

Pierce, N. and Johnson, C. Boundary Crossers: Community Leadership for a Global Age. Academy of Leadership Press, 1998.

Polansky, Risa. "Jackson Faces Major Financial Hurdles, Operation Threatened." Miami Today 26 June 2008. 5 Aug. 2008 <http://miamitodaynews.com>.

Posen, A. "Six Practical Views of Central Bank Transparency." Institute for International Economics 2002 <www.iie.com>.

Rapport, D. "What Is Clinical Ecology?" In Costanza, R. et. al., ed. Ecosystem Health. Washington, D.C.: Island Press, 1992.

Rawls, John. A Theory of Justice. Rev. ed. (Belknap Press of Harvard University Press, 1999).

Recovery.gov <http://www.recovery.gov>.

Reich, Robert B., Supercapitalism: the Transformation of Business, Democracy, and Everyday Life, New York: Vintage Books, 2008.

Reid, Randall. "The Moral Imperative for Sustainable Communities." Public Management Magazine, International City Management Association May 2009.

"Republican Disapproval Up, But Obama Strong In Florida, Quinnipiac University Poll Finds." Quinnipiac University Polling Institute. 16 Apr. 2009 <http://www.quinnipiac.edu>.

Roberts, Sam. "Fastest-Growing States Show Slower Expansion." The New York Times 27 Dec. 2007. Jan. 17 2008 <http://www.nytimes.com/2007/12/27/us/27census.html>.
Roseland, Mark, and Sean Connelly. Toward Sustainable Communities: Resources for Citizens and Their Governments. Rev. ed. Gabriola Island, BC: New Society Publishers, 2005.
Rubin, H. Collaborative Leadership. Thousand Oaks, CA: Corwin, 2002.
"The Sad Truth on Universities." The St. Petersburg Times. Editorial. 21 Feb. 2008, 21 Feb. 2008 <http://www.sptimes.com>.
Santich, Kate. "Orlando-area Homeless Count Increases 17 Percent." The Orlando Sentinel Writer 13 May 2009 <http://www. OrlandoSentinel.com>.
Saunders, Jim. Daytona Beach News Journal 24 April 2009.
Schlueb, Mark. "Dyer Straits: Orlando to Lay off 100-plus Emergency Workers." The Orlando Sentinel 13 May 2009 <http://www.OrlandoSentinel.com>.
Schmidt, J. "Complex Adaptive Systems." AI Journal (2002).
Schwanninger, M. and Koerner, M. "Managing Complex Projects." 2002 <http://www.ifb.unisg.ch/org/IfB/ifbweb.nsf/SysWebRessources/beitrag37/$FILE/DB 37 Project Management.pdf>.
Schwartz, P. The Art of the Long View. New York: Doubleday, 1991.
"Second Annual Report to the Governor and the Legislature." The Century Commission for a Sustainable Florida 16 Jan. 2008: 1-15. 31 Jan. 2008 <http://www.centurycommission.org/>.
Skene, Neil. "Growth Management Act II." Florida Trend 1 Aug. 2007 <http://www.floridatrend.com>.
"Smart Growth for Florida's Future: The Florida Sustainable Communities Act." 1000 Friends of Florida, Mar. 2009 <http://www.1000friendsofflorida.com>.
Sparkman, Steven L. "The History and Status of Local Government Powers in Florida." University of Florida Law Review 25 (1973): 271-307.
Steinhauer, Jennifer. "Taxes Are Reassessed in Housing Slump." The New York Times 23 Dec. 2007. 24 Jan. 2008 <http://www.nytimes.com/2007/12/23/>.
Steinhauser, Paul. "Poll: America's Honeymoon with Obama Continues." CNNPolitics.com 24 Dec. 2008 <http://www.cnn.com/2008/POLITICS/12/24/obama.approval>.
The Tallahassee Democrat: Tallahassee.com. Editorial. 1 Nov. 2007. Jan. 21 2008 <http://tallahassee.com/>.
"Tax Reform Runs Aground." The St. Petersburg Times. Editorial. 14 Feb. 2008. 14 Feb. 2008 <http://www.sptimes.com/2008/02/14/Opinion/>.
Taylor, M. Confidence Games: Money and Markets in a World without Redemption. The University of Chicago Press, 2004.
Taylor M. "The Four Axes of Civic Leadership." Research paper. Coventry: Local Government Centre, University of Warwick, 1993.
Thomas, Mike. "As Rendezvous with Harsh Reality Nears, Crist May Consider Senate Bid." The Orlando Sentinel 8 Feb. 2009.

"A Time for Leadership: Management and Florida 2060." 1000 Friends of Florida, Aug. 2006 <http://www.1000friendsofflorida.org>.
Tocqueville, Alexis de. Democracy in America. Trans. George Lawrence, ed. J.P. Mayer. New York: Doubleday, Anchor Books, 1969.
Toffler, Alvin. Power Shift: Knowledge, Wealth, and Violence at the Edge of the 21st Century. New York: Bantam Books, 1991.
Trimble, Linda. "School Officials Seek Fund Solutions." Daytona Beach News Journal 20 Dec. 2008.
U.S. Census Bureau. <http://www.census.gov>.
U.S. Census Bureau. "Current Population Survey." 24 Jan. 2008 <http://www.census.gov/hhes/www/hlthins/cps.html>.
United States. The Senate Fiscal Policy and Calendar Committee, The House Policy & Budget Council, and The Legislative Office of Economic and Demographic Research. "State of Florida Long-Range Financial Outlook. Fiscal Year 2008-09 through 2010-11. Fall 2007 Report." The Florida Senate. 2007: 1-95. 17 Jan. 2008 <http://www.flsenate.gov/data/publications/2006/Senate/reports>.
"University Lifeline." editorial, The Times 24 Nov. 2008 <http://www.tampabay.com/opinion/editorials>.
Uchitelle, Louis. "Economists Warm to Government Spending but Debate Its Form." The New York Times 7 Jan. 2009.
Van der Ryn, S. and Cowan, S. Ecological Design. Washington, D.C.: Islznd Press, 1996.
VISIT FLORIDA Research. 15 Jan. 2008 <http://media.visitflorida.org/about/research/>.
Volusia Forever. <http://volusiaforever-echo.com/forever>.
Wallis, Jim. God's Politics: Why the Right Gets It Wrong and the Left Doesn't Get It. San Francisco: Harper, 2005.
Warner, Ben. "Sustainable Florida: Progress Toward a Shared Vision." The Century Commission for a Sustainable Florida. 31 Aug. 2007: 1-81. 17 Jan. 2008 <http://www.centurycommission.org/current_projects.asp>.
Waterfield, Cloe. "City of Naples, Florida Greenhouse Gas Emissions Report, Inventory Year 2006." June 2008.
Weaver, James, Michael Rock, and Kenneth Kusterer. Achieving Broad-Based Sustainable Development: Governance, Environment, and Growth with Equity. West Hartford, Conn.: Kumarian Press, 1997.
"Where in the World Are We? 2009 Progress Report for the Central Florida Region." <http://www.myregion.org>.
Wills, Garry. Head and Heart: American Christianities. New York: Penguin Press, 2007.
Wilson, W.J. When Work Disappears. New York: Random House, 1997.
Woofram, S. A New Kind of Science. Champaign, ILL: Wolfram Media, 2002.
Wyman, Michelle. "President Obama and Local Governments: A Partnership With Potential." ICLEI e-News 12 Nov. 2008 <http://www.iclei.org>.
Zakaria, Fareed. The Post-American World. New York: W.W. Norton, 2008.